History of the Jats

Contribution to the History of Northern India

(Upto the death of Mirza NAJAF KHAN, 1782)

by

KALIKA RANJAN QANUNGO

With a Foreword by

Jadunath Sarkar

Edited and Annotated by

Dr. Vir Singh

Originals

(an imprint of Low Price Publications)

Delhi-110052

First Published 2003
Reprinted 2013

ISBN 10: 81-8454-129-5 (H.B.)
ISBN 13: 978-81-8454-129-8 (H.B.
ISBN 10: 81-8454-130-9 (P.B.)
ISBN 13: 978-81-8454-130-4 (P.B.)

Published by
Originals
(an imprint of Low Price Publications)
A-6, Nimri Commercial Centre,
Ashok Vihar Phase-IV, Delhi-110052
Phones: 011-27302453, Fax: 011-47061936
e-mail: info@Lppindia.com
url: www.Lppindia.com

Printed at
IIP Printers, D-17, Raja Garden, New Delhi
Phone: 25441120

EDITOR'S NOTE

History of the Jats by Prof. K.R. Qanungo was originally published in 1925. This work doubtlessly enjoys the stature of a pioneering work on Jat History. Prof. Qanungo makes an extensive study of the subject. Post-Qanungo works on the subject do not diminish the importance of this work as later writers subscribe to his views on many points and quote him with respect. The Jats are fortunate to have Prof. Qanungo, as their historian, as the Rajputs had Col. Tod, the Marathas Grant-Duff and the Sikhs Cunningham.

With the establishment of Surajmal Memorial Education Society, the book was reprinted in 1982 under the supervision of Dr. P.S. Dabas. While maintaining the improvements in the 1982 edition of the book, the following changes have been incorporated in this edition:

(i) Two and a half page introduction to Prof. Qanungo's other work *Shershah* and some opinions on it have been eliminated, as these were not relevant to the contents of this work.

(ii) Diacritical marks used to denote Hindi, Sanskrit and Persian sounds have been omitted as they have been used sparingly in the original work itself.

(iii) Prof. Qanungo has admitted in his author's note that due to bad handwriting and inadvertence he could not preserve consistency in the spelling of proper names. In this edition we have tried to give correct spelling of proper names and places.

Proper Names:

Anoopgir	:	Anoopgiri	Bishnu Puran	:	Vishnu Puran
Bishun Singh	:	Bishan Singh	Dalil Singh	:	Dalel Singh.
Bijoy Singh	:	Bijay Singh	Tunwar	:	Tanwar
Jawahir Singh	:	Jawahar Singh	Kansh	:	Kans
Mesned	:	Masnad	Newal Singh	:	Nawal Singh
Pramar	:	Parmar	Neelkanth Nagor	:	Neelkanth Nagar
Rohilla	:	Ruhela			

Proper Places:

Ajmir	:	Ajmer	Bainchari	:	Banchari
Badaon	:	Badaun	Benaras	:	Banaras
Biana	:	Bayana	Bikanir	:	Bikaner
Gohud	:	Gohad	Haidrabad	:	Hyderabad
Hariana	:	Haryana	Irak	:	Iraq
Jainagar	:	Jaynagar	Jaisalmir	:	Jaisalmer
Kuhmir	:	Kumher	Kerauli	:	Karauli
Lachmangarh	:	Lachhmangarh	Lachman N.	:	Lachhman Narayan
Okla	:	Okhla	Panjab	:	Punjab
Sakkartal	:	Sukkartal	Sinsani	:	Sinsini

According to the Persian pronounciation the author has added *'h'* consonant where the name ends in vowel *'a.'* Consonant *'h'* is deleted.

Abdullah	:	Abdulla	Burmah	:	Burma
Daulah	:	Daula	Kotah	:	Kota
Kot Kobulah	:	Kot Kobula	Korah	:	Kora
Kanudah	:	Kanuda	Maharajah	:	Maharaja
Mullah	:	Mulla	Narelah	:	Narela
Rajah	:	Raja	Resalah	:	Resala
Subah	:	Suba	Subahdar	:	Subedar

The author has used some old words of Scotish language for readers convenience, the words in use have been given in brackets:

-cess (rate) -sept (clan or *gotra*) -laird (*zamindar*)

(iv) Out of 43 *'Additions & Corrections'* given by the author in the first edition of 1925, 32 have already been made in the 1982 edition. The remaining 11 corrections on pages 115, 123, 170, 182, 193, 194, 199, 210, 217, 221, 222 of the first edition and the following errors, which did not find mention in the corrigendum, have also been corrected:

Page No. of 1925 edition	Errors	Corrections
IV	Struggles	Struggle
V	he has denied himself	he denied himself
2	the stature	their stature
5	this interesting people	these interesting people
21	out landish peoples	out landish people
38	fell in fight	fell in the fight
63	becomes	became
88	latter	letter
112	aspired to play	aspired him to play
115	माराठा	माराठ्या
164	hang upon	hung upon
185	Renell's atlas	Rennell's atlas
196	none were	none was
210	जंग हुर	जंग हुब
220	had order	had orders
221	Agra. The known character	Agra, the known character
226	throughout the whole night	throughout the night
254	depradations	depredations
274	no other alternative	no alternative
276	bief Panipat	bief of Panipat
332	Semitic bood	Semitic Blood
334	Bishnu Puran	Vishnu Puran

As mentioned above 32 errors of the corrigendum and a few others had been corrected in the 1982 edition. On carefully compairing with the first edition I found that 211 printing mistakes had crept in the 1982 edition. It is shocking that a particular publisher has published as his own the 1982 edition of our book word for word, line for line and page for page by photo composing process, *also carrying over not only our corrections and modifications but also all the printing mistakes in that edition verbatim,* without the permission of the rightful publisher of the 1982 edition. Is it not an example of plagiarism prevalent in this great country of ours?

(v) The author has not maintained consistency in writing the names of the chapters and sub-titles as is evident from the variety of headings in the first chapter of 1925 edition. Generally the author has given name of subtitles on the folio. In our edition the title of the book is written on the left side top and the name of the chapter on the right pages instead of subtitles.

(vi) In the first edition the foot-notes were shown by star and dagger etc. marks (viz.,*) on every page. In this edition number of foot-notes are written in ascending order of the whole chapter.

(vii) *The Author mis-takes Bharatpur for Thun Fort of Churaman and at another place for Fatehgarhi of Khemkaran Sogoria. The correct information about Ramgarh (Aligarh), Sukkartal Fort and Neemrana are also supplied in this edition.* Qanungo forgets to mention Ghasira expedition and seven years countless operations during 1688-1695. These and other omissions have been pointed out in our foot-notes, which are given in Roman Numbers. Annotations based on recent studies is the process of research. Thus 32 footnotes describing and clarifying certain facts have been added to update this pioneering work in this edition.

(viii) The Appendix - 'Details of the death of Suraj Mal' was given in the middle of the book after VIII chapter. It has been shifted to the end of the book as Appendix 'D' with other appendies.

(ix) The author has given bibliography of main sources only in his first edition. We have incorporated remaining sources also cited by the author as bibliography B.

Under the dynamic leadership and guidance of Society's President, **Sh. Ram Niwas Mirdha**, former Union Minister, the Society has been organizing Seminars, Conferences and Workshops of National level on various topics relevant to the life and education of the rural people. The *Research and Publication Centre* of the Society has been undertaking the collection, preservation and publication of material on rural heritage. The society has established a rich library on its campus for the use of research scholars. It also provides financial assistance to scholars in different Universities, who wish to pursue research on any aspect of Jat Community. Till now the Society has published ten books and given research scholarships for two students.

We feel immense pleasure and express our gratitude to Shri OM PRAKASH CHAUTALA, Honourable Chief Minister of Haryana, for providing sum of rupees five lacs for the Research centre of the society for various research and allied activities mentioned above. The society looks forward for his constant encouragement in future also.

My special thanks are reserved for Prof. Dilbagh Singh and Dr. S.S. Rana for advancing valuable suggestions in reshaping this historical document on Jats. Sh. S.P. Singh also deserves commendations for providing necessary infrastructure and boosting my moral courage while I was on with this work. My thanks also reserved for the library staff of the *Indian Council of Historical Research* and *Jamia Millia Islamia* for extending much-needed help from time to time. I also thank the publisher, for bringing out the book in time and in a nice form. I honestly hope that this updated work will provide a clean mirror of the Jat History to the readers.

19th September, 2002

Dr. Vir Singh
Director
Research & Publication Centre
Suraj Mal Memorial Education Society

FOREWORD

The Jats are one of the most important races among the Indian population today, as during the Muslim period, and their traditions go back to dim antiquity. A critical study of the past history of such a race on the basis of all the available material cannot fail to be a subject of deep interest and instruction to all Indians. Such a study is presented in this book.

It represents the loving and devoted labour of Professor Kalika R. Qanungo for years together. He denied himself holidays and worked at this history in my library by sacrificing his vacations. All known sources, printed and manuscript, Persian, Marathi, French and English, (besides Sanskrit for the mythical age), have been utilised here, and this History of the Jats represents a synthesis never attempted before, and leaving (so far as I can see) nothing for future workers unless new materials are discovered hereafter. Professor Qanungo has already proved his sound critical powers and true historical spirit in his first book, *Sher Shah,* which at once leaped into the position of the standard work on the subject. In his *History of the Jats,* he has not been content to be a closet student of written records. He has lived and worked among the Jat boys of his former college at Delhi, he has won their love and confidence (as I was pleased to learn when I spent a day there three years ago), and has visited their historic places and tribal gatherings and talked with old Jats whose memories are richly stored with the past. The information he has thus gathered by a personal quest spread over a wide field is concentrated in this book and gives it a unique value.

As will be expected from the high quality of his earlier work, he has here sifted the evidence impartially and reviewed events and characters from the broad point of view of India as a whole, instead of narrowing his vision to a single tribe. This wider outlook, this philosophical detachment from the particular dynasty or community dealt with, is specially necessary in any history of India in the 18th century that deserves to live as a true history. For, the Jats were only one out of the many threads that made up the tangled web of North Indian history during the decline of the Mughal empire. The Jats, Ruhelas, Sikhs, Marathas, Rajputs, Oudh Nawabs, English Company, French adventurers, besides the Delhi Emperors and their semi-independent nobles – all entered into the criss-cross of Indian politics during that one century which saw the rise, maturity and downfall of the Jats as the makers of Indian history; and, therefore, Professor Qanungo has done wisely in studying the contemporary history and interplay of *all* of these Powers, before he felt himself competent to write this account of the Jats alone – though very little of his labour appears on the surface to the reader of the following pages.

Here is a first-rate contribution to the critical study of the Fall of the Mughal Empire. The Jat people may be congratulated on having secured such a historian. Possibly the ignorant among them may grumble that their tribal prejudices have not been flattered; but truth is great and will prevail, and Qanungo has sought truth with singleness of aim and backed by all the resources available to scholarship in his way.

May, 1925 **JADUNATH SARKAR**

AUTHOR'S NOTE

This volume owes its inception to the enthusiasm of my Jat pupils at Delhi for a history of their race which I promised to them four years back. The task proved more formidable than had appeared to me at the outset. The political history of the Jats is inextricably interwoven with the general history of the Mughal Empire in the eighteenth century; and their origin is still a mystery to themselves as well as to scholars. I ventured into the dark and unfamiliar realms of Indian antiquity and ethnology to search for the lost pedigree of the Jat; but I do not pretend to have discovered the right one. I am painfully aware of the many imperfections of this volume. Through my bad hand-writing or inadvertence, I have failed to preserve consistency in the spelling of proper names and allowed several regrettable errors to creep in for which a revised list 'errata' has been found necessary.

I take this opportunity to acknowledge with gratitude the generosity of Chaudhuri Chhajju Ram of Alakhpura, Hissar, who has borne a considerable portion of the expenses of publishing this volume. Sentiment and duty alike impel me to thank my beloved pupils Chaudhuri Sadi Ram, B.A., Pandit Mukhyaram, B.A., and others for their devoted services during our historical tours and investigations. It is hardly necessary for me to reiterate the extent of my obligations to my master, Professor Jadunath Sarkar, without whose constant help and guidance I could have hardly hoped to traverse so confidently this strange and obscure field of Indian history.

Lucknow University,
30th April, 1925

KALIKARANJAN QANUNGO

CONTENTS

CHAPTER I

ORIGIN AND EARLY HISTORY

Country and the people

The Jats are a tribe so widespread and numerous as to be almost a nation by themselves, now numbering about nine million souls. The region mainly occupied by them may be roughly defined as bounded on the north by the lower ranges of the Himalayas, on the west by the Indus, on the south by a line drawn from Hyderabad (Sindh) to Ajmer and thence to Bhopal, and on the east by the Ganges: the Jat country spreads, so to say, in a fan-like form with Sindh as its base. Beyond the Indus there is also a sprinkling of the Jat population in Peshawar, Balochistan and even to the west of the Sulaiman range.[1] This race forms the backbone of the agricultural community in the Punjab, Sindh, Rajputana and the western portion of the Gangetic Doab. Up to the beginning of the thirteenth century the Jats had been a compact people, having community of blood, community of language, and a common religion. But at present about one-third of them are Muslims, one-fifth Sikhs, and the rest are Hindus. The Jat is a Jat after all, whether he be a Hindu, Sikh or Muslim; he tenaciously clings to his tribal name as a proud heritage, and with it the tradition of kinship.

They are indeed a bold peasantry, their country's pride, accustomed to guide the ploughshare and wield the sword with equal readiness and success - second to no other Indian race in industry or courage. In physique, they belong to the same ethnic group as the Rajput and the Khatri, and represent a type, which "approaches most closely to that ascribed to

1. In Karman and Iraq there is a mixed Jat and Gipsy population of about 20,000 souls, and in Makran and Afghanistan about 50,000. See *Asia* by A.H. Keene, ed. Sir Richard Temple, pp. 210, 218.

the traditional Aryan colonists of India. Their stature is mostly tall, complexion fair, eyes dark, hair on face plentiful, head long, nose narrow and prominent but not very long".[2]

In character the Jat resembles the old Anglo Saxon and the ancient Roman, and has indeed more of the characteristics of the Teuton than of the Celt in him. He is tough, slow, unimaginative, and unemotional, lacking brilliance, but possessed of great solidity, dogged perseverance and an eminently practical turn of mind. He is hardly ever convinced by words without concrete facts. Sturdy independence and patient vigorous labour are among his good points, as Ibbetson has noted. Another trait of the Jat character which has been marked by good observers, is his strong individualism. "The Jat is of all the Punjab races the most impatient of the tribal or communal control and the one which asserts the freedom of the individual most strongly. In tracts where, as in Rohtak, the Jat tribes have the field to themselves, and are compelled, in default of rival castes or enemies, to fall back upon each other for somebody to quarrel with, the tribal ties are strong. But as a rule a Jat is a man who does what seems right in his own eyes and sometimes what seems wrong also, and will not be said nay by any man.... He is independent and he is self-willed; but he is reasonable, and peaceably inclined if left alone."[3]

The Jat is still in the tribal stage of social evolution, knowing no caste distniction or kulinism (i.e. social precedence based on birth). All tribesmen are on a dead level of equality, modified only by habitual respect to elders. The Jat invariably marries the widow of his elder brother, and this alone stands in the way of his being recognized as a pure Kshatriya[I]. But it is a custom which obtained in the Vedic[4] age among the pure Aryans of the three higher castes.

"The distinction between the Jats and Rajputs both sprung from a comman stock, is marked by the fact that the

2. Risley's *People of India*, p. 8.
3. Ibbetson, quoted in the *Punjab Glossary*, ii. 366.
I. It is a post-vedic brahminical rigid classification. —Ed.
4. A passage in the *Rig Veda* quoted by Zimmer shows that in some cases, at any rate, the widow married her husband's younger brother. Macdonell's *History of Sanskrit Literature*, p. 126.

former practises and the latter abstains from a usage [karewa] which more than any other is regarded as a crucial test of relative social position."[5] In the government of their villages, they appear much more democratic than the Rajput; they have less reverence for hereditary right and a preference for elected headmen. The clanish feeling is very strong among them. Hereditary feud is carried on as a sacred duty. An old Jat would hardly die in peace until he has unloaded his breast by telling his heirs the good and the evil done unto him and his ancestors by his neighbours and enjoining upon them revenge for injury and return of good services. Family [kunbha] may fight against family; one sept (clan) against another, but when it is a question of tribal honour, or quarrel with a rival caste, every member of the clan, capable of wielding a *lathi* (quarter-staff), will loyally assemble to carry out implicitly the order of the tribal elders, laying aside for the moment their own differences.

The origin of these interesting people is enveloped in the mist of obscurity, which the light of scientific research has yet to dispel. In physical features, language, character, sentiments, ideas of government, and social institutions, the present-day Jat is undeniably a better representative of the ancient Vedic Aryan than any member of the three higher castes of the Hindus, who have certainly lost much of their original character in the course of evolution through many centuries. But the Jat's tribal designation, is supposed to point to a foreign and less exalted origin, viz. Indo-Scythian. The European pioneers of Indian antiquities and ethnology apparently started with the presumption that fine and energetic martial peoples like the Rajput and the Jat must have been comparatively newcomers from the north-west into India who overcame the effete descendants of the Vedic Aryans and pushed them eastward and southward; because within the known historic period from Alexander to Ahmad Shah Durrani the foreign immigrants have invariably imposed their rule upon the children of the soil. Besides this it is a known fact that several foreign horders such as the Sakas, Yuehchis, Kushans and Hunas from Central Asia, the reputed

5. Ibbetson, *Census Report*, 1881, para 446.

home of the Parthian races, entered India successively during the period 100 B.C.- 600 A.D. and were absorbed by Hindu society. If so, where are their modern representatives? The Rajput and the Jat with their war like habits, unorthodox customs and confused traditions about their origin, tempted the ingenuity of the scholars, who at once identified them with the Sakas and Hunas. The fanciful theory of Col. Tod, who suggested kinship among the Indian Jats, the Goths of the Roman Empire, and the Juts of Jut-land, cast a mighty spell upon several generations of scholars. The Jat tribe's name sounded in the scholarly ear like that of the Gaete, Yuti and Yetha of the Oxus region. The philologist for the first time raised his note of protest against this. Dr. Trumpp and Beames[6] very strongly claimed a pure Indo Aryan descent for them both in consideration of their physical type and language, which has been authoritatively pronounced as a pure dialect of Hindi, without the slightest trace of Scythian. But they were silenced by the progressing science, which established the unassailable dictum "Language is not a proof of race."

Next, the anthropologists appeared in the field armed with his scientific apparatus to measure the skulls and noses of the various peoples of India for the purpose of restoring their lost pedigree. This investigation resulted in the sevenfold classification of the races of India by Sir Herbert Risley, who declared the Rajput and the Jat to be the true representatives of the Vedic Aryans. This was the first scientific assault upon the Indo-Scythian theory.[7] But science does not stand still. Since then Risley's theory and

---

6. He remarks:- "The theory of the Aryan origin of the Jats, if it is to be overthrown at all, must have stronger arguments directed against it than any that have yet been adduced. Physical type and language are considerations which are not to be set aside by mere verbal resemblance, especially when the words come to us mingled beyond recognition by Greek and Chinese" [Elliot's *Memoirs of the Races of North-Western Provinces of India*, i. 135-137].
7. Risley says:- "Of the people themselves [Scythians] all traces seem to have vanished and the student who enquires what has become of them finds nothing more tangible than the modern conjecture that they are represented by the Jats and Rajputs. But the grounds

classification have been attacked by many scholars[8] on different grounds.

Whatever may be the difference of opinion as regards the validity of the test of anthropometry, or language, each considered by itself, none can at the present state of our knowledge, disagree with Sir Herbert Risley in his remarks:- "In India where historical evidence can hardly be said to exist, the data ordinarily available are of three kinds-physical characteristics, linguistic characteristics and religious and social usages. Of these the first two are by far the most trustworthy. Most anthropologists indeed, are inclined to adopt without much question, the opinion of late Sir William Fowler who wrote to me some years ago, that physical characters are the best, in fact the only true test of race; language, customs etc. may help, or give indications but they are often misleading."[9] The Jat has been declared by all eminent authorities, to pass successfully the combined test of the physical type and language[10] of a true Aryan.

As regards religious and social usages, all observers generally agree that in these points the Jats do not differ much from other Hindu communities of admittedly Aryan origin. Science may be said to have succeeded fairly well in establishing the Indo-Aryan origin of the Jats, but this cannot meet with much acceptance till they are definitely identified

---

for this opinion is of the flimsiest description and consists mainly of the questionable assumption that the people who are called Jats at the present day must have something to do with the people who were known to Herodotus as the Gatae." [*People of India,* 60-61].

8. Anthropometry is about to share the fate of Philology as a test of race. Prof. Ridgeway says:-"As the physical anthropologists cannot agree upon principles of skull measurement, the historical enquirer must not at present base any argument on this class of evidence." (Quoted in Mr. Chanda's *Indo-Aryan Races,* p.62).
9. Risley's *People of India,* p.6.
10. Grierson notices some Pisaca peculiarities in the Sindhi and Punjabi, spoken by a considerable section of the Jat community. But "these peculiarities are probably not derived from invaders of Pisaca speech, but from the stock language spoken by the invaders akin to the *Homo-Alipnus* of Eastern Turkestan." [R.P. Chanda's *Indo-Aryan Races,* p. 78].

with some Aryan tribe of old mentioned in Sanskrit literature.[II] Accurate sceintific data for such investigation having almost disappeared, scholars have been compelled to proceed in this direction rather in an unscientific way, viz., relying mainly upon the similarity of sounds. The *Mahabharat* contains several chapters, devoted to the description of the different tribes of the Punjab and Sindh–the home of the Jat people within historic times. A people known as the *Jartrikas* is mentioned therein along with the *Madrakas*–both called Bahikas or outlanders. Sir James Campbell and Grierson consider this to be the earliest notice of the Jats in Sanskrit literature.[11] The acrimonious reply of Karna to Shalya, king of Madrakas contains a graphic though distorted picture of the habits and character of these people. "The Madras are always false to their freinds... without affection, always wicked, untruthful, and cruel. That wicked people eat fried barley and fish and in their house father, son, mother, mother-in-law, father-in-law, uncle, daughter, son-in-law, brother, grand-sons, with friends and guests, menial and maidservant, male and female together, drink wine with cow's flesh, and sometimes cry, sometimes laugh and delight in indecent talk and songs... Their women, overcome with wine, dance naked... They are of *fair complexion* and tall stature, *wearing blankets*, eating large quantities of food, shameless and lax in the observance of the laws of purity.

II. Prof. R.K. Dwivedi (Allahabad University) and Prof. Maheshwari Prasad (BHU) have traced some Jat clans in Sanskrit literature in their articles presented in the Seminars held in 1995 and 2001 respectively in New Delhi. Mr. B.S. Dahiya has also given the list of ancient Jat clans in his book, *'Jats–The Ancient Rulers: A Clan Study–Pre-muslim period'*. —Ed.

11. Sir James Campbell holds them to be foreigners who entered India along with the Kush horde (about B.C. 150-100) whose greatest representative was Kanishka [*Bom. Gaz.* Vol. IX, part 1, p. 459]. Grierson considers them as degraded Aryans and not *infidels ab initio.* Baraha Mihir mentions two people, *viz. Jatasuras in the north-east, and Jatadharas in the south* near the Kaveri, whose names may sound like that of the Jats in the scholarly ear of Grierson.

See *Brihat Samhita,* Sans. text ed. by Sudhakar Dwivedi, Vol. X. part 1, pp. 293, 289.

The Bahikas, who *have been expelled* from the region of the Himalayas, the Ganges, the Jamuna, the Saraswati and Kurukshetra should be avoided. The Bahikas are not created by Prajapati, the creator of the orthodox Aryans, they are the offspring of a *Pishach* couple, named Bahi and Heek who dwelt on the bank of the Bipasa (the Beas). There is a town named Sakala and a river named Apagà where a section of the Bahikas, known as the *Jartrikas,* dwell. Their character is very reprehensible. These people, eat contentedly a large quantity of meat and boiled barley, or barley-bread, cow's flesh with garlic and fried barley. Their women drink wine, laugh and dance in public, sing indecent songs in a loud shrill voice like that of a camel or an ass; they become very unrestrained and boisterous specially on festive occasions when they dance and shout, calling one another, "Thou ill-fated one; husband-slayer etc." A bahika who had to sojourn for a time in the Kuru-jangal country sang the following song about the women of his country: "Though a Bahika. I am at present an exile in the Kuru-Jangal country; that *tall and fair-complexioned* wife of mine, *dressed in her fine blanket* certainly remembers me when she retires to rest. Oh! when shall I go back to my country crossing again the Satadru (the sutlej) and the Iravati and see the beautiful females of fair complexion, wearing stout bangles, dressed in blanket and skins, eye-sides coloured with the dye of *Manshila,* forehead, cheek and chin painted with collyrium [tatooing]? When shall we eat under the pleasant shade of the *Shami, Peelu and Karir,* loaves and balls of fried barley powder with waterless churned curd [*kunjik*], and gathering strength, take away the clothes of the wayfarers and beat them?" Among the Madrakas and Shakalas, young and old both drink heavily and sing aloud, "Vainly are they born who do not eat the flesh of boars, cocks, kine, asses, camels and sheep."

The above sketch brings vividly before us a picture of the Land of the Five Rivers and its people in the classic age. Its first impression almost leads one to suppose that these Jartrikas were the ancestors of the modern Jats. But on closer examination this identification of the two peoples proves most illusory. The above extract that the Bahikas were not created by Prajapati, clearly indicates the belief of the dwellers of the Vedic Aryandom that the outer nationalities originated from an ethnic stock or stocks that were quite different from the stock or stocks which they themselves originated.[12] These people were apparently the ancestors of the speakers of what Grierson calls the modern Pisàca languages–the Kashmiris, the Dards, and the kafirs of the Hindukush. The later or outlandish Aryans were broad or medium headed and therefore were least likely to be the ancestors of the longheaded Jat people. The fact that the Bahika women wore fine blankets and skins, perhaps shows that they were immigirants from some colder countries. The tall, fair, debauched and filthy women of kashmir are perhaps the truer representatives of the ancient Bahika females. The Jats observe some, though not all the ten customary ceremonials of the Hindus. The *Upanayana* ceremony does not indeed take place at the usual time, but at the time of marriage. It is the custom for *purohits* to place on them at their marriages the *janeo* or sacred thread, removing it a few days after marriage.[13] The Bahikas married within the same *got [Vamsa]*, which the Jat does not. The Jats observe the same law of succession as that of the other Hindus, and in no case is the sister's son regarded as the lawful heir in preference to their own sons - a custom attributed to the Bahikas. No doubt the orthodox Hindus of Sindh still contemptuously call the Jats of that province *Baheka*[14] or aliens; but it is least likely that the name of one insignificant tribe *Jartrika,* not known for morality, character, power or purity of conduct, should be adopted by many millions of people, inhabiting the large stretch of country from Afghanistan to Malwa. Besides *no Jat tribe remembers any connection with Sakala;* almost all of them believe their ancestors to have been immigrants from the interior of India. This suggested identification based on similarly sounding tribal names alone cannot therefore be accepted as valid.

12. R.P. Chanda's *Indo-Aryan Races,* i. 42.
13. *Hoshiarpur Dist. Gaz.* 1883, p. 56. The Brahmans who have taken to agriculture rarely perform the investiture ceremony separately at the prescribed time. Boys are given *janeo* at the time of marriage, in cases of early marriage.
14. *Asia* by A.H. Keene, p. 296.

Jatharas and the Jats

As the European scholars have ransacked Greek and Latin literatures to establish the Indo-Scythian origin of the Jat, so some educated leaders of Jat society were also engaged in proving their undoubted Kshatriya origin by identifying the Jats with some one of the numerous warrior clans of our classic age. Pandit Giribar Prasad, a Jat Sanskrit scholar of Aligarh, employed a Shastri named Angad Sharma to investigate the origin of the Jats in the light of the orthodox literature. The Shastri, also depending mainly on the similarity of sound, lighted upon the Jatharas, as the hypothetical ancestors of the Jats. He propounded a learned theory in a little Sanskrit pamphlet, *Jatharotpatti*. It is a *catena* of all the ancient texts mentioning the tribe of Jatharas, whose origin is related as follows in the *Padma Puràn*–"When the son of Bhrigu [i.e., Parashuram] exterminated the warrior-class, their daughters, seeing the world empty of the Kshatriya and being desirous of getting sons, laid hold of the Brahmans and carefully cherishing the seed sown in their womb [Jathara] brought forth Kshatriya sons called Jatharas."[15]

Growse remarks that "There is no great intrinsic improbability in the hypothesis that the word *Jàtharas* has been shortened into *Jat*, but if one race is really descended from the other, it is exceedingly strange that the fact should never have been so stated before. This difficulty might be met by replying that the Jats have always been, with very few exceptions, an illiterate class, who were not likely to trouble themselves about recording their mythological pedigrees; while the story of their parentage would not be of sufficient interest to induce outsiders to investigate it. But a more unanswerable objection is found in a passage, which the Shastri himself quotes from the *Brihat Samhita* (xiv. 8). This places the home of the Jatharas in the south-

15. क्षत्राशून्ये पुरालोके भार्गविन यदाऔते।
विलोक्याक्षत्रियां धात्रीं कन्यास्तेषां सहस्रशः ऑ
ब्राह्मणान् जगृहुस्तस्मिन् पुत्रोत्पादन लिप्सया।
जठरे धारितं गर्भं संरक्ष्य विधिवत् पुरा।
पुत्रान् सुषुविरे कन्या जाठरान् क्षत्रावंशआन् ऑ

eastern quarter, whereas it is certain that the Jats have come from the west. Probably the leaders of Jat society would refuse to accept as their progenitors both the Jatharas of the Beswa pandit and Sindhian Zeths of Genl. Cunningham; for the Bharatpur princes affect to consider themselves as of the same race as the Yadavas."[16]

The second Jat attempt at solving the mystery of his origin is found in a small booklet entitled *The Ethnology of the Jats,* written by Chaudhuri Lahiri Singh, a Jat pleader of Meerut, at the request of the Census officials of 1883. This author also derives the word *Jat* from *Jathara;* but he differs from the author of the *Jatharotpatti* by making the Jathras a foreign people deriving their name from the mountain Jathara, mentioned in the *Mahabharat, Vishnu Puran* and *Bhagavat.* The first two mention the country of the Jatharas along with Kalinga, Kashi, and Aparkashi.

However, the Jats cannot be held to be the same people as the ancient Jatharas, because the doubtful testimony of the similarity of sounds breaks down in the face of the significant absence of any tradition whatsoever, connecting the two peoples. This claim is strange enough even to startle the majority of the Jats. One might close his eyes against the absurdity of the case, if the Jatharas had been altogether an extinct people. But they still survive in southern India, without claiming any connection with Jats. These Jatharas belong to a subsection of the Deccani Maratha Brahmans called *Karhadas.*[17]

The alleged Yadava origin of the Jats

The foregoing dissertation has left the Jat, so to say, hanging in the mid-air. We know this much that there is no scientific ground, philological, or ethnological, for rejecting his claim to the Indo-Aryan blood, and that he is neither a Scythian, nor a cross between a Brahman and a Kshatriya widow [Jathar]. He is not a foreign invader either from the plains of Central Asia or the fictitious Jathar mountain, but

16. *Growse's Mathura* (1874), pp. 21-22.
17. Mr. G.B. Jathar has kindly supplied me with this valuable piece of information in a letter, dated 8th August 1924, *Deccan* College, Poona.

a true son of India, who points to Malwa and Rajputana as the home of his ancestors before they migrated to the Punjab and the trans-Indus region. The Jats are difficult to persuade that they are not descended from the ancient Yadavas, though they cannot produce any evidence in support of this claim. Now that all fantastic theories as to their origin have exploded at the touch of science, we cannot with justice refuse to accept the alleged Yadava origin of the Jats, at least tentatively, so long as it is not positively disproved. It is only fair to put this tradition to the test of historical investigation, and see whether there is any rational ground for believing in it.

Al-Beruni, who wrote at the beginning of the eleventh century, thus relates the story of Sri Krishna's birth: "Then there was born a child in the city of Mathura to Vasudeva by the sister of Kansa, at that time ruler of the town. *They were a Jatt family, cattle-owners, low Shudra* people." The Yadus, as we learn from the *Vishnu Puran*, though somewhat above the Jat status of "low Shudra" of the eleventh century, were well-nigh approaching it, being little esteemed by the more orthodox Aryan tribes with monarchical constitution. (Wilson's *Vishnu Puran*, pp.602-603.) There is no greater improbability in deriving Jat, Jat or Jut, - as the tribal name is pronounced in various forms in the different provinces- from the Indian Yadu or Yadava than from the Chinese Yuti or Ye-ta-li-to. If the phonetic difficulty alone stands in the way of recognising the Yadava origin of the Jats, there cannot be any objection in identifying the Jats with the *Jatas* or *Sujatas*, a branch of the great Haihaya Yadavas.[18] "The

18. Of the hundred sons of Kartavirya, the five principal were Sura, Surasena, Vrishana, Madhu and *Jayadhwaja*. From the last sprang up the five great divisions of the Haihaya tribe, the Talajanghas, Vitihotras, Avantyas, Tundikeras, and *Jatas* also called *Sujatas from the prolific number* (Wilson's *Vishnu Puran* pp. 417-418). Wilson seems to entertain a doubt whether the Haihayas are not the Huna and Saka tribes engrafted upon the great genealogical tree of the Aryans by the clever Puranic ethnologists. *The Jats were known by the name of Sus, Abars,* and many other names, as Beames says. We shall meet these contensions in the appendix *"The Yadus."*

Sujatas" says the *Vishnu Puran, "are not commonly specified for their great number."* (Wilson, p.418, foot-note 20). So, we need not wonder if the *Brihat Samhita* or any other later Sanskrit work does not mention the *Jatas* by their particular tribal designation. It may be argued that the Haihayas were a southern people inhabiting the region of the Narmada, and were therefore little likely to be the ancestors of the modern Jats, who are mainly found in Sindh and the Punjab. We may point out that the Jats are not, even to this day, rare in the Narmada Valley, in Bhopal and other places, and that the Haihayas are also mentioned among the *Western Peoples* in the *Brihat Samhita* (Sans. text, chap. 14, p.291). The tribe of Yadu gradually shifted towards the north-west. The Jat clans of Bal, Bhular, Chahal, and Kahlon point out to Malwa, Dharnagar [Dhar], and the Deccan as their original home (Rose's *Punjab Glossary,* ii)

The ancient Yadavas, like the modern Jats, were not a homogeneous tribe but a composite race, rather a confederacy of tribes, consisting of Andakas, Bhojas, Kukkuras, Dasharnas etc. Prolific were the progeny of Yadu; so are the Jats to-day. But it will be too far from the truth to maintain that this multiplication is due to birth alone. The affiliation of one tribe into another was a common phenomenon in the tribal stage of society. The facts that there are conflicting traditions about the origin of the different Jat *gots* and that even the Babbars of Dera Ghazi Khan claim to be Jats, clearly illustrate this. These were apparently an out-landish people affiliated to the Yadu clan. This is supported by a passage in the *Bhagavat Puran* which says that King Sagara, after exterminating the Haihayas, turned his arms against the Saka, Yavana, and *Barbaras* who had fought as the allies of the Haihayas, against his ancestors (Sans. text, Sakanda ix, chap. 8). The *Harivamsa* describes a long standing hereditary feud between the descendants of Puru and Yadu–which was also a struggle between orthodoxy and heterodoxy, a struggle between the pure Indo-Aryans and the out-landish peoples headed by the Yadavas. A similar phenomenon of a tribal feud in which even aliens range themselves under one faction or another has not altogether disappeared in the Rohtak and Delhi districts, where the country-side is divided into two factions—Dahiya and Ahulanas: "*the Gujars and Tagas* of the tract, the Jaglan Jats of *thapa* Naultha, and the Làtmàr Jats of Rohtak joining the Dahiyas, and the Huda Jats of Rohtak . . . joining the Ahulanas. This division runs right through Sonepat and more faintly through Delhi tahsil, and is so firmly rooted in the popular mind that Muhammadans even class themselves with one or the other party. Thus the Muhammadan Gujars of Panch-i-Gujran call themselves Dahiyas, and so do all the neighbouring villages"(*Rose's Punjab Glossary*, ii. 220). Modern history does not contain a more faithful picture of the tribal feuds of the bygone ages.

The race of Yadu suffered a fearful retribution at the hands of Parashuram who had all but exterminated the ungodly and tyrannical warrior-caste. The few fugitives from his terrible battle-axe took shelter in mountains or concealed themselves among the lower classes. Without instruction and without ceremonials they grew up like Shudras. The liberal-minded Rishi Kashyapa reclaimed them and restored them to the rank of Kshatriyas. This was perhaps the first creation of a class of Neo-Kshatriyas, like that of the Agnikulas in the subsequent ages. The Kassab [Kashyap] Gotri Jats with pretensions to Rajput blood may thus owe their kinship with the ancient Yadavas, to the good services of their patron saint.

The Jat community has been, within historic times, the great refuge of the high caste victims of Hindu social tyranny, and the uplifter of the depressed and untouchables to a more respectable status, transforming all recruits to a homogeneous Aryan mould both in physique end sentiment. If the origin of the Jat is to be correctly traced we must ascend the main stream and not the tributaries. To say that the Jat is of foreign origin, because some outlandish tribes were admitted into his community is as absurd to say that the Ganges descends not from the Himalayas but from the Vindhya because the Son brings some waters of the later mountain to swell her stream.

Migration of the People

There is no authentic history of how the Jats migrated

to the north-west, beyond the boundary of India; because even at the dawn of Indian history, they were found in occupation of the country between Kirman and Mansura, and other tracts, bordering on Persia by the early Arab geographers and historians.[19] They were the first Hindu people with whom the Arabs came into contact, and all the Hindus were known to the Arabs by the name *Jat* only. They formed the rear of the far-flung Hindu dominion then beginning to retire to the east of the Indus before the impetuous onset of Islam. This eastward retreat of a section of the Jats has to a great extent lent colour to the theory that they were barbarian invaders of India. It is likely that the Jats, always enterprising and eager for military service, migrated beyond the Indus as mercenaries of the Persian and Maurya Emperors. They suffered a good deal in the subsequent ages for their heresy against orthodox Brahmanism. In Sindh they were reduced from the status of rulers to that of helots by the Brahman usurper Chach. And this defiance of orthodoxy was greatly responsible for the social degradation of the Jats during the Middle Ages.

The Jats and their early history

The various waves of migration from Central Asia in the early centuries of the Christian era partly submerged, and partly swept the Jats and other Indian races back upon the shores of the Indus. The inaccessible desert of Sindh became the new home of the Jats. They had lost their caste, owing to their intercourse with impure races, their unreformed ways of life, and indifference to the rules of caste and Brahmanical teaching. They had become half *Mlechchas*[20] just like the poorer section of the Hindus of Kabul, who are but half Mohammadans in the eyes of the orthodox. It was perhaps for this reason that Yuan Chwang

19. Elliot's *History of India* i, 14, 449, ii. 247.
20. One modern writer remarks:-"These Jats of the Indus Valley have never adopted the institution of caste in its integrity, and are regarded by the rest of Hindus *with a feeling which is embodied* in the expression *Baheka* or aliens (*Asia,* by A.H.Keene, p. 296). This is undoubtedly the same terms as *Baheka* of the *Mahabharat* applied to Jartrikas, Madras, and peoples of Sindhu-Sauvira.

calls the king of Sindh in the seventh century A.D. a Shudra (Beal, *Buddhist Records of the Western World,* ii. 272) and Al-Beruni found the Jats in no higher social grade in the eleventh century. There they settled as agriculturists and lived under their old tribal organization, which, however, was replaced later on by a monarchy.

The author of *Mujmal-ut-Twarikh* records an interesting legend that a joint embassy was sent by the Jats and Meds of Sindh to the Count of King Duryodhana, asking for a ruler to govern them. "The Jats and Meds . . . dwelt in Sindh and on the banks of the river which is Bahar (mouth of the Indus?) . . . . The Meds held the ascendancy over the Jats, and put them to great distress, which compelled them to take refuge on the other side of the river Pahan (Panjnad river?), but being accustomed to the use of boats, they used to cross the river and make attacks on the Meds, who were owners of sheep. It so came to pass that the Jats enfeebled the Meds, killed many of them and plundered their country. The Meds then became subject to the Jats.

"One of the Jat chiefs (seeing the state to which the Meds were reduced) made the people of his tribe understand that there was a time when the Meds attacked the Jats and harassed them, and that the Jats in their turn had done the same with the Meds. He impressed upon their minds the utility of both tribes living in peace, and then advised the Jats and Meds to send a few chiefs to wait on King Dajushan (Duryodhana), son of Dahrat (Dhritarashtra), and beg of him to appoint a king to whose authority both tribes might submit . . . After some discussions they agreed to act upon it, and the Emperor Dajushan nominated his sister Dassal [Dushala], wife of King Jandrat [Jayadratha] a powerful prince to rule over the Jats and Meds. Dassal went and took care of the countries and cities . . . There was no Brahman or wise man in the country. She therefore wrote a long letter to her brother for assistance, who collected 30,000 Brahmans from all Hindustan, and sent them with their goods and dependents to his sister" (Elliot, i, 104).[21]

21. This is no doubt a legend which is not even countenanced by the *Mahabharat.* However, we have a striking twelfth century parallel to it in the history of Bengal. Adisur, the reputed founder of the

Though the story cannot be literally true, it seems to be a vague reminiscence of an immigration into Sindh of a colony of pure Aryans, mostly Brahmans, from the middle country. These were perhaps invited by some enlightened prince who thought of reclaiming his subjects and clansmen from ignorance and heresy. Perhaps the name of the famous city of Brahmanabad points to the place where the Brahman immigrants first settled. They prospered under the patronage of the native princes till they became so powerful that about 10 A.H. Chach, the Brahman father of Dahir, - usurped the throne of his master, King Sahasi Ray II through the influence of the fair but faithless queen Suhandi, who had fallen in love with him. He married the widowed queen formally and reigned vigourously for 40 years, leaving behind him the reputation of a wise and enlightened prince. But he was an implacable foe of the Jats, the bulk of whom were reduced to serfdom. He degraded the Jats and Luhanas and bound over their chiefs. He took hostages from them and confined them in the fort of Brahmanabad.

He obliged them to agree to the following terms: "That they should never wear any swords but sham ones; that they should never wear undergarments of shawl, velvet, or silk; that they should put no saddles on their horses, and should keep their heads and feet uncovered; that when they went out they should take their dogs with them; that they should carry firewood for the kitchen of the chief of Brahmanabad; they were to furnish guides and spies, and were to be faithful when employed in such offices." (*Chach Nama,* Elliot, i. 151). When Muhammad Bin Qasim invaded the territory of Dahir the Jats of the western border joined the invader, while those of the eastern countries fought for Dahir (See *Chach Nama,* Mirza Kalich Beg's translation, pp. 124, 137).

After the completion of the conquest, Muhammad Bin Qasim asked the ex-minister of Dahir who was made wazir by the conqueror, what was the position of the Jats in the

---

Sur dynasty invited five Brahmans from Kanauj to officiate as his priests, who afterwards revived Brahmanism in Bengal and became founders of orthodox Brahman families there.

time of his late master. He replied that "they were not allowed to wear soft clothes, used to wear a black blanket beneath (*lungi?*), and throw a sheet of coarse cloth over their shoulders. . . . They used to take their dogs with them when they went out of doors, so that they might by these means be recognised. . . . It was their business to conduct parties from one tribe to another . . . the caravans used to travel day and night under their guidance. *There is no distinction among them of great and small.* They have the disposition of savages, and *always rebelled against their sovereign.* They plunder on the roads, and within the territory of Debal all join with them in *their highway robberies* (Elliot, i. 187). The change of rulers brought no improvement of their lot; Muhammad Bin Qasim maintained the former rules regarding them. The Jats were in independent possession of the country of Kaikan (supposed to be in south-eastern Afghanistan - Elliot, i. 383), which was conquered from them by the Arab general Amran Bin Musa in the reign of the Khalif Al-Mutasim-bi-llah, -A.D. 833-81, (Elliot, i. 448). During the same reign another expedition was sent against the Jats who had seized upon the roads of Hajar (?). . . and spread terror over the roads and planted posts in all directions towards the desert. They were overcome after a bloody conflict of twenty-five days. Twenty-seven thousand of them were led in captivity to grace the triumph of the victor. It was a custom among these people to blow their horns when marshalled for battle (Elliot, ii. 247).

Other scanty notices of the Jats in Persian histories prior to the reign of Aurangzeb are not of any political importance, but they are eminently illustrative of their national characteristics. They have shown in all periods—whether against Sultan Mahmud of Ghazni, or against Nadir Shah and Ahmad Shah Abdali—the same propensity to fall upon the rear of a retreating army undeterred by the heaviest odds, or the terror-inspiring fame of great conquerors. When encountered they showed the same obstinate and steady courage, unmindful of the carnage on the field or of the miseries that were in store for them after defeat. They seem to have a wonderfully short memory as regards the terrible lessons taught by the merciless sword of their enemies.

The Jats had the audacity to attack the army of Mahmud of Ghazni on his return from Somnath. His seventeenth expedition was undertaken for chastising them. He had to fight a great naval battle in which his genius shone no less splendidly than on land. "He led a large force towards Multan, and when he arrived there he ordered fourteen hundred boats to be built each of which was armed with three firm iron pikes, projecting one from the prow and two from the sides, so that anything which came in contact with them would infallibly be destroyed. In each boat were twenty archers, with bows and arrows, grenades, and naphtha; and in this way he proceeded to attack the Jats, who having intelligence of the armament, sent their families into the islands and prepared themselves for the conflict. They launched, according to some four, and according to others eight thousand boats, manned and armed, ready to engage the Muhammadans. Both fleets met, and a desperate conflict ensued. Every boat of the Jats that approached the Muslim fleet, when it received the shock of the projecting pikes was broken and overturned. Thus most of the Jats were drowned and those who were not so destroyed were put to the sword. The Sultan's army proceeded to the places where their families were concealed and took them all prisoners" (*Tabakat-i-Akbari*, quoted in Elliot, ii. 478).

After the defeat of Prithviraj in 1192 A.D., the Jats of Haryana raised the standard of tribal revolt, and under a capable chief, named Jatwan, besieged the Muslim commander at Hansi. On receiving this news Qutb-ud-din marched twelve *farsakhs*, i.e., about 40 miles during one night. Jatwan raised the siege of Hansi and prepared for an obstinate conflict. "The armies attacked each other" says the author of *Taj-ul-Maasir* "like two hills of steel, and the field of battle [on the borders of the Bager country] became tulip-dyed with the blood of warriors . . . Jatwan had his standards of God-plurality and ensigns of perdition lowered by the hand of power" (Elliot, ii. 218). About 1530, the Jats formed *mandals*[22] round Sunam and Ṣamana with the Bhattis, Minas,

22. Mandal, is not a *stronghold*, as Elliot supposes. It means a confederacy, union of several villages or tribes for a common

and kindred tribes, withheld tribute and plundered the roads. Sultan Muhammad Bin Tughlaq marched against them, destroyed their *mandals*, and they were torn from their old lands, and scattered (*Tarikh-i-Firoz shahi*, Elliot, iii. 245). Timur dwells with considerable satisfaction on his suppression of the Jats, whom he describes as a robust race, demon-like in appearance and as numerous as ants and locusts, a veritable plague to the merchants and wayfarers (*Malfuzat-i-Timuri*, Elliot, iii. 429).

Babur found the Jats living amongst the mountains of Nil-ab and Bhera, where they acknowledged the ascendancy of the Gakkar chiefs (*Memoirs of Babur*, A. S. Beveridge, p. 387). They still retained their old turbulent and predatory habits. He says: "If one go into Hindustan the Jats and Gujars always pour down in countless hordes from hill and plain for loot in bullock and buffalo. These ill-omened people are just senseless oppressors! . . . When we reached Sialkot, they fell in tumult on poor and needy folks who were coming out of the town to our camp, and stripped them bare. I had the silly thieves sought for, and ordered two or three of them cut to pieces." (*Ibid*, p.454).

During the period of confusion intervening between the death of Babur and the accession of Sher Shah to the throne of Delhi, one bold robber chief Fath Khan Jat of Kot Kobulah devastated the whole tract of Lakhi Jungle, and kept in ferment the high roads from Lahor to Panipat. Haibat Khan Niazi, governor of the Punjab on behalf of Sher Shah, crushed him after a severe campaign.[23] The Jats had little scope for their lawless activity under the strong government of the Surs and the Mughals down to the accession of Aurangzeb. They remained quiet till the religious persecution of that Emperor and the misrule of the provincial viceroys goaded them into rebellion.

---

object and mutual assistance. Such organisation, though rare, is not unknown even now in that part of the country, formed either for communal interests or for resisting unjust demands and making their grievances felt.

23. Haibat Khan's operations against Fath Khan Jat. [Author's *Sher Shah*, pp. 308-311.]

CHAPTER II

JAT HISTORY IN AURANGZEB'S REIGN

Hindu reaction and the Rise of the Jat Power

After the enchanted sleep of a century, administered successively by the hypnotic spell of Akbar, the genial indifference of Jahangir, and the mild pattings of Shah Jahan, Hindu India woke to life again in the second half of the seventeenth century, being rudely shaken by the pious activity of the saintly Emperor Aurangzeb. Accustomed to look upon the occupant of the throne of Delhi, though of an alien faith, as the shadow of God on earth, *(दिल्लीश्वरो वा जगदीश्वरो वा)* the awakened Hindus found to their surprise and sorrow that the impartial Ruler of Hindustan had changed into a militant missionary of Islam. He reverted to the old and forgotten ways. *Jaziya* (poll-tax) was reimposed; temple destruction and image-breaking went on briskly under strict imperial supervision; cart-loads of broken idols came in from all quarters, and were buried under the stair-cases of the Jama mosques of Delhi and Agra. Hindus were excluded from public offices, and an ordinance was issued to dismiss all Hindu clerks from the revenue department. Hindu religious fairs were abolished and public celebration of their festivals prohibited. Custom duty was altogether abolished in the case of Muslim traders while that on the Hindus was retained at the old rate. Hindus were tempted out of heathenism by the grant of State subsidies. In short "Every device short of massacre in cold blood was restored to in order to convert heathen subjects."[1] We are not inclined to attribute this, either to Aurangzeb's deliberate wickedness, depravity of

1. Sarkar's *Hist. of Aurangzib*, iii. 290.

heart, or short-sighted policy. This was rather the outcome of the severe and uncompromising pursuit of an idea, neither eccentric nor vicious. His fault lay in his failure: he carried to his grave this unfulfilled dream of an Islamic India.

However, by this open enemity, Aurangzeb unknowingly revived Hindu Nationalism, which the cruel kindness of his predecessors had well-nigh succeeded in killing. From the far-off Maharashtra came the pulsation of a new life which moved northwards stirring the paralysed limb of Hindu society. In the Punjab, persecution turned a humble sect of sentimental devotees into ferocious warriors. The Sikhism of Guru Govind was a veritable counterblast to Islam. Fanaticism was met with fanaticism; Sikhs went out to fight Muslim armies singing, "He is of the *Khalsa* who fights in the Van, *who slays a Khan.*" Aurangzeb's attempt to imprison Jaswant's wives and infant son opened the eyes of the Rajputs. The brave Durgadas led the way and the Rathor blades were unsheathed for the defence of liberty and religion. His countrymen paid a tribute to his memory, saying "Had not Durga been born in the house of Askarn,[2] all would have been circumcised."

In 1669, another sturdy race, the Jats living almost under the very shadow of the imperial capital rose in revolt. This was but one flare of the mighty conflagration, kindled throughout India, by the missionary zeal of the Emperor. The Jat peasants of the Mathura and Agra districts had long been the victims of oppression and misrule. Their religious susceptibilities were shocked by the destruction of the Hindu temples of Mathura, whose lofty spires seemed to mock the edifices of Agra. They saw their fields devastated and their wives and daughters carried off to gratify Muslim lust. One *faujdar* of Mathura, Murshid Quli Khan used to make raids upon the villages to procure beautiful women. Another infamous practice of his was this: at the time of Hindu fairs and festivals, "the Khan, painting his forehead and wearing

---

2. **It is said once a Jat carried off the palm of poetic victory from a *charan* by reciting the following extempore lines:-**
ढमक ढमक ढोल बाजे दे दे ठोर नागराकी।
आसो घर दुग्गा नहीं होती सुन्नयत हो जाती सॉराक़ी॥
Marwar Census Report (vernacular) 1892, vol. iii. p. 56.

a *dhoti* like a Hindu used to walk up and down in the crowd. Whenever he saw a woman whose beauty filled even the Moon with envy, he snatched her away like a wolf, pouncing upon a flock, and placing her in the boat which his men kept ready on the bank (of the Jamuna) he sped to Agra."[3]

Aurangzeb appointed as governor of Mathura, Abdun Nabi, "a religious man" in the sense understood by his master. He entered heartily into the Emperor's policy of "rooting out idolatry, and fell in the fight against the Jats (about 10th May 1666).[III] The victorious rebels, under the leadership of Gokla, the zamindar of Tilpat, looted pargana Sadabad. So serious was the menance that the Mughal Government offered him pardon on the condition of giving up his booty. The rebel refused to come to terms. Aurangzeb sent a very strong army under Radandaz Khan, Hassan Ali Khan and other high officers, and himself marched from Delhi to the affected area. Hassan Ali delivered an attack upon three fortified villages of the Jats and won a very costly victory. The peasants fought long and steadily, displaying that cool obstinate valour which had ever characterised them. When resistance became hopeless, many of them slew their women and rushed upon the Mughals to sell their lives dearly. Gokla mustered 20,000 men and offered fight to the imperial forces at a place 20 miles from Tilpat, charging their lines most gallantly. But courage could hardly make up the deficiency in discipline and equipment. After a very long and bloody contest, they had to give way before the superior discipline and artillery of the Mughals. They fell back upon Tilpat, and there held out for three days. The Mughals lost 4000 men in killing 3000 rebels. Gokla was taken prisoner; his limbs were hacked off one by one on the platform of the police office of Agra. [Sarkar's *Hist. of Aurangzib*, iii. 330-336]. Gokla's blood did not flow in vain; it watered the newly-sprouted seedling of liberty in the heart of the Jats.

3. Sarkar's *History of Aurangzib*, iii. 332.

III. Abdun Nabi was killed on 12th May 1669 (21st Zil Hijja, 1079 A.H.) at village Sahora (about 6 miles from Mathura). G.C. Dwivedi, *The Jats: their role in the Mughal Empire*, p. 28. —Ed.

Rajaram Jat (1686-1688)

Fifteen years after the death of Gokla Jat, a more capable leader appeared among the Jats in the person of Rajaram, son of Bhajja Singh, laird *(zamindar)* of Sinsini.[4] He united his own clan, the Sinsinwar Jats, with the Sogorias under their chief Ramchehra, who owned the castle of Sogor.[5] He gave the disorderly host of tribesmen the appearance of a regular army, embodied in regiments, equipped with firearms, and trained to obey their captains. Small forts (*garhi*) were built at advantageous positions, amidst the almost trackless jungles of the Jat country, and strengthened by mud walls that could defy artillery.[V]

Rajaram soon put an end to the authority of the Mughals in the Agra district, closing the roads to traffic and plundering many villages. Safi Khan, the governor of Agra, became practically besieged in the city, and it was after a very severe fighting that Mir Abul Fazl, the *faujdar* of the place, succeeded in saving Akbar's tomb at Sikandra, from being sacked by Rajaram. The Jats soon showed greater audacity. Near Dholpur they surprised the camp of the renowned Turani warrior Aghar Khan and carried off his carts, horses and woman. The Khan while pursuing the raiders, was killed with his son-in-law, and 80 followers.

Worn out with the unending chase of the Maratha fox in the south, the unhappy Emperor was startled at the yell of the Jat wolves howling for their prey under the very walls of his capital. As early as May, 1686, Aurangzeb had recognised the gravity of the situation by detaching against

4. Sinsini, 16 miles n.w. of Bharatpur.
5. Sogor is spelt as *Sogghair* in the French MS. of Wendel, it lies four miles to the south-east of Bharatpur. Rustam Sogoria and Khemchand[IV] Sogoria were the prominent leaders of their *got*. Suraj Mal captured Bharatpur[IV] from the last named chief. Ramchehra, rather an awkward name, occurs nowhere except in the French MS.

IV. Suraj Mal captured *Fatehgarhi* from Khemkaran Sogoria in 1733 and founded Bharatpur fort at that site in 1743. The name is Khemkaran not Khemchand Sogaria. U N Sharma, *Jaton Ka Navin Itihas*, I, pp. 325 - 330. —Ed.

V. For Raja Ram (1682 - 1688) and Ram Chehra see Wendel's Memoirs (Hindi): *Hindustan Mein Jat Satta*, pp. 89 - 93; U.N. Sharma, *Jaton ka Navin Itihas*, I, p. 123; Ganga Singh, *Bharatpur ka Itihas*, I, pp. 75 - 82; G. C. Dwivedi, *The Jats: their role in the Mughal Empire*, pp. 34 - 48. —Ed.

the Jats a great general, Khan-i-Jahan Kokaltash Zafar Jang. Now the success of Rajaram and the failure of Khan-i-Jahan thoroughly alarmed him, and in December he ordered his son Azam to go there and command the operations in person. But the prince had only reached Burhanpur, when he was recalled to the Emperor's side by the more pressing need of retrieving Mughal prestige before Golkonda (July 1687). The prince's eldest son, Bidar Bakht, a gallant lad of 17, was however sent (in December 1687), to assume the supreme command in the Jat war, while Khan-i-Jahan was to continue as his advisor and chief officer.

But before the prince could arrive, the Jat leader committed more atrocities. Early in 1688, Mir Ibrahim of Hydrabad (newly entitled Mahabat Khan) was marching to his viceroyalty of the Punjab. Near Sikandra he was encamped on the back of the Jamuna, when Rajaram attacked him, but was repulsed after a long and stubborn fight with the loss of 400 men, while the Mughals lost 190 in killed and wounded. Rajaram soon returned to the scene, and profiting by the delay in the coming of Shaista Khan, the new *subedar* of Agra, he plundered Akbar's tomb,[6] taking away its carpets, gold and silver vessels, lamps, etc. and damaging the building. Khan-i-Jahan did nothing to check him.

Bidar Bakht, on his arrival, infused greater vigour into the Mughal operations. At this time an internecine (deadly) war was raging between the Shekhawat and Chauhan clans of Rajputs for lands in the Bagtharia and some other *parganas.* The Chauhans enlisted the support of Rajaram, while the Shekhawats gained the armed help of the Mughal *faujdar* of Mewat. A severe battle was fought between them near the village of Bijal. The Rajputs grappled with one another in deadly animosity, and many were slain on both sides. In the thick of the contest, Rajaram was shot dead by a Mughal musketeer hiding in a tree (4th July 1688).

---

6. Ishwardas, 132b. Manucci (ii. 320) adds "They began their pillage by breaking in the great gates of bronze which it had, robbing the valuable precious stones and plates of gold and silver, and destroying what they were not able to carry away. Dragging out *the bones of Akbar, they threw them angrily into the fire and burnt them."*

Raja Bishan Singh's campaign against the Jats

After the death of Rajaram, the leadership of the Jats was assumed by his old father Bhajja Singh of Sinsini. "Bishan Singh Kachhwah, the new Raja of Amber (Jaipur), was appointed by the Emperor as *faujdar* of Mathura with a special charge to root out the Jats and take Sinsini as his own *jagir* [Ishwardas, 133*a*]. He gave the Emperor a written undertaking to demolish the fort of Sinsini (Ishawar, 139*a*, 135*b*), as he was burning to distinguish himself and win a high *mansab* like his father Ram Singh and grandfather Mirza Raja Jai Singh. Bidar Bakht laid siege to Sinsini. But the compaign in the *jungles* of the Jat country severely taxed the invading army.

The Mughals before Sinsini had to undergo great hardship from scarcity of provisions and water, as the enemy by frequent attacks cut off the grain-convoys and watering parties. Incessant night-attacks kept the siege-camp in perpetual alarm. "The men were prostrated by hunger, and the animals perished in large numbers through weakness." But the besiegers held tenaciously on, and in four months carried their trenches to the gate of the fort, mounted guns on raised platforms, and laid mines. The jungle round the fort was cleared. One mine under the gate was fired, but the Jats having previously detected it and blocked its further side with stones, the charge was driven backwards, destroying many of the artillerymen and supervising officers of the Mughal army. A second mine was then laid and carried under the wall in a month's time. It was successfully fired (*end of January*, 1690), the wall was breached, the Jat defenders lining it were blown up, and the Mughals stormed the fort after three hours of stubborn opposition. The Jats disputed every inch of the ground and were dispersed only after losing 1500 of their men. On the imperial side 200 Mughals fell and 700 Rajputs were slain or wounded. The remnant of the garrison was put to the sword [Ishwardas, 136*b*-137*a*; *M.A.* 334; Hamid-ud-din's *Ahkam*, § 26].

Next year (21st May, 1691) Raja Bishan Singh surprised the other Jat stronghold of Sogar. The Raja hastened there with the imperial army. By chance, as the gate of this little fort was kept open at the time for admitting grain the invaders entered it at the gallop, slaying all who raised their hands and taking 500 of the rebels [Ishwar]. The result of these operations was that the new Jat leaders went into hiding in 'nooks and corners' unknown to the imperialists. The tribesmen returned to the peaceful work of cultivation and the district enjoyed peace for some years.[7] [VI]

Churaman Jat (1695-1721)

Churaman, the younger brother of Raja Ram, assumed the leadership of the Jats after the death of his father Bhajja Singh[VII] of Sinsini. "He had a genius for organization and making clever use of opportunities,"[8] combining in his character the stubborness of a Jat with the cunning and political sagacity of a Maratha. His moral maxim was that of the sixteenth century Muslim theologians like Sayyid Rafiud-din Safavi, who assiduously preached to the faithful that no faith should be kept with the infidel.[9] Churaman served many a Muslim master, but he was never faithful to any for faithfulness sake. He was a hard, practical politician, who could boast of never losing his head under the impulse of any noble sentiment like fidelity, honour or compassion, which had indeed no room in his cold heart: yet this was the man who built up the fortune of the Jats and made the Jat Power an important political factor to be reckoned within the eighteenth century politics of Northern India.

The author of *Imad-us-Saadat* gives the following account of the early career of Churaman. "He began his career as

---

7. This section is partly a summary, and for the most part quotation *verbatim* from Prof. J.N. Sarkar's article, *"The Breaking-up of the Mughal Empire: Jats and Gaurs"* published in the Modern Review, October, 1923.

VI. The author has summarized the account of two operations only given by J.N. Sarkar in the said article. He has not mentioned the numerous operations by the imperialists against the Jat peasants during 1688 - 1695. In Appendix C also, the author gives a very brief account of the Jat Rising in Aurangzeb's reign and mentions only one major operation against Sinsini. For this gap period of 7 years read Qanungo, *The History of Diggi House, Ch. VII &VIII.* —Ed.

VII. Brij Raj and Bhajja Singh were brothers. Churaman was the son of Brij Raj and Raja Ram of Bhajja Singh. Thus, Churaman and Raja Ram were cousins. U.N. Sharma, *Jaton ka Navin Itihas*, I, 342 also 180. —Ed.

8. Prof. J.N.Sarkar's article *"Jats and Gaurs"* — Modern Review, October, 1923.

the leader of a gang of highwaymen, plundering caravans and wayfarers. Within a short time he collected under his command 500 horses and one thousand footmen. Nanda Jat, the father of Bhure Singh, and grandfather of Daya Ram and Bhup Singh, the notorious castellans of Hathras and Mudsan, also joined him with 100 horsemen. As his establishment became too large to be maintained by the plundering of merchant caravans, he began to loot *parganas.* At this time he built a place of refuge in a low marshy and thickly wooded tract about 48 *kos* from Agra, digging a deep moat around it. There he used to deposit his booty, and, by gradual additions, it was turned into a mud fort which afterwards became known as Bharatpur.[VIII] He brought

---

VIII. The author mis-takes Bharatpur for *Thun*. All the account given here is related to Churaman's strong mud-fort *Thun*. Shivdas is a contemporary writer whose work *Shahnama* was written in 1722. Shivdas says that Thun was built in the impenetrable *jungle* of thorny bushes that even the birds found it difficult to pass through it. The sky-high rampart of *Thun* were encircled with a ditch, which was so deep that water burst up from the bottom. Shivdas, *Shah Nama Munawwar Kalam*, 19; *Iqbal Nama* 23; (both Askari trans.), G.C. Dwivedi, *The Jats: their role in the Mughal Empire*, pp. 49 - 50, f.n. 91-95.

Qanungo quotes *'Imad-us-Saadat'* which is a later work written in 1807 A.D. at Luckhnow, when the fame of Bharatpur fort was at its peak after General Lake's unsuccessful expedition against Bharatpur. It appears that the impact of Bharatpur on the minds of the people was so dominant that Mir Ghulam Ali confuses Bharatpur with Thun. *Imad-us-Saadat* is mainly a history of Nawabs of Awadh, it throws sidelights on the early activities of Churaman and more confidently on Suraj Mal, whose associate Rao Radha Krishan was the informant of the author. Qanungo himself observes in his bibliography on the work 'Though his history is neither full nor methodical, it amply repays, perusal.' Strangely enough, Qanungo himself and Irfan Habib (*The Agrarian System of Mughal India*, 392) take Bharatpur for Thun on the wrong information given by *Imad-us-Saadat*, at p.55. Churaman built the fort of Thun not Bharatpur. Thun was captured from Churaman's son Muhkam Singh by Sawai Jai Singh on 9th November 1722 and no fort was built at Thun's demolished site again. It lies 11 miles west of Deeg. At present also the descendant of Thakur Churaman are inhabited in Jatoli Thun. In 1733 Suraj Mal captured *Fatehgarhi* of Khema Jat and built Bharatpur at that site during 1743 - 1750. U.N. Sharma, *Jaton ka Navin Itihas*, I, 198-199 f.n. 40-41, 304 f.n 100, 327; also Final Settlement Report Bharatpur State, III (1901) p. 25 for site of Thun. Also see, Growse, Mathura, I, 23; Tod. III, 1358; Gokal Chand Dixit, *Brijendra Vansh Bhaskar*, 20. —Ed.

some Hindu Chamars from the neighbouring villages, and settling them there, entrusted its defence to them. When his army grew to 14,000 men, he left one of his trustworthy brethren with sufficient men and materials of war in-charge of Bharatpur, (*Thun* ed.) and himself started on a plundering expedition towards Kota and Bundi where he looted many caravans and acquired a rich booty.[10] Being more enterprising than those who had preceded him, he not only increased the number of his soldiers, but also strengthened them by the addition of fusiliers (musketeers) and a troop of cavalry whom he shortly after set on foot . . . and having robbed many of the ministers of the Court on the road, he attacked the royal wardrobe and the revenue sent from the provinces [Fr. Ms.f. 41]. . . . About 1704 he recovered Sinsini from Mughal possession, but lost it again in October 1705. [Prof. J.N. Sarkar, *Modern Review*, October, 1923].

Greater opportunities came to the robberchief, when Aurangzeb closed his weary eyes in the Dakhin in 1707. Bahadur Shah and Azam prepared for a decisive fight at Jajau, not far from Samugarh, where Fortune had placed the crown of Hindustan upon their father's brow. Churaman collected his tribesmen, and hung about the neighbourhood of both armies, looking out for an opportunity to attest his timely zeal for the victor by falling upon the camp and baggage of the vanquished. He became eminently successful, securing at the end a very rich booty as well as a *mansab* of 1500 zat, 500 horse, bestowed upon him by the victorious Bahadur Shah. Churaman made an intelligent investment of his vast wealth by building forts, collecting men and winning over his enemies. But as the government of Bahadur Shah was fairly strong, he chose to be faithful to it,[IX] and render good services to justify his newly acquired rank as an imperial commander.[X] He accompanied Bahadur Shah to Lahor in 1711

10. *Imad-us-Saadat*, Pers. text p. 55.

IX. Contra see G.C. Dwivedi. 'that Churaman remained faithful for fear of Bahadur Shah's government being "fairly strong" is untenable. It was unquestionably weaker than the preceding one and even that failed to make Churaman faithful to the Mughals. *The Jats: Their role in the Mughal Empire*, p. 55, f.n. 14. —Ed.

X. Churaman joined the Empreror near Delhi. Qanungo altogether ignores this issue. See for clarification, G.C. Dwivedi, *The Jats: Their role in the Mughal Empire*, p. 57, f.n. 23. —Ed.

and there witnessed the battle of succession among his four unworthy sons in 1712.

Jahandar Shah, the eldest son of the late Emperor, a profligate fool, now disgraced the throne of Aurangzeb. He was old in years (about fifty at this time), but worse than a child in frivolity and frolicsomeness, a slave to him sweet-voiced concubine Lal Kunwar, and passing the few inglorious days (ten months) of his reign in midnight revelry and morning slumber, preferring fiddlers to soldiers, and loving to play at night the part of the Great Monkey, Hanuman, by setting fire to a mimic city of Lanka. A successful rebel who had carved out a principality for himself, could scarcely entertain any fear or respect for such a sovereign. Accordingly, Churaman retired to his own estates and gathered resources to make a fresh bid for fortune. When the news of Farrukh-siyar's march from Patna reached Delhi, Jahandar Shah induced Churaman by many far promises to join his army. Churaman had become the *de facto* ruler and law-giver of the Jats and other Hindu people, inhabiting the western bank of the Jamuna from Delhi to the Chambal, owing to the weakness of the imperial Government to provide security of life and property to the inhabitants. So, he was a man to be reckoned within those troubled times-his attitude practically determining the friendship or hostility of the whole rural population towards a particular candidate for the throne of Hindustan. He came with a large number of Jats and was present with Jahandar Shah's army at the battle which was fought outside Agra city. But, instead of rendering any help to the unfortunate Jahandar Shah, he rather contributed to his defeat by falling upon the imperial baggage at a critical moment of the fight (January, 1713).

Churaman marched away from Agra after plundering the baggage of both sides impartially. He seemed to have been aiming at independence, at least deferring his submission till the new Emperor should show more energy. He felt himself strong enough to hold out, because the Emperor was weak-minded and his Court corrupt and divided against itself. The majestic beauty and splendid physique of Farrukh-siyar, ill-suited his cowardly and vacillating nature: never did a more magnificent body clothe a poorer spirit. Early in Farrukh-siyar's reign Chabela Ram, the then *subedar* of Agra, made strenuous but unsuccessful efforts to humble the stiffnecked Jat chief. Samsam-ud-daula (Khan-i-Dauran), the next governor of Agra, reluctant to risk his reputation in a doubtful enterprise, tried conciliation. He secured Churaman's pardon from the Emperor, who summoned him to the Court. Churaman marched at the head of 4000 horsemen and was escorted with honour, befitting a raja, from Barahpula into the city. He was conducted to the Dewan-i-khas by Khan-i-Dauran himself, and appointed by the Emperor to the charge of royal high way (*Shah-rah*) from the neighbourhood of Delhi to the crossing on the Chambal. A wolf was left to watch over the flock; thereby loot was only legalised and made more methodical.

Churaman had been allowed by the Mughal Government to levy a toll on traffic along that portion of great road which was left in his charge. He made his collections so harshly and arbitrarily that an outcry soon arose against him from every quarter. A Jat tax-collector, as the proverb says, is indeed a sign of God's wrath; his penny breaks a head while the Baniya's hundred rupees hardly touch the skin. He behaved as if he were the absolute master of the whole tract traversed by this portion of the road. Even the *jagirdars* could not get their dues from the villages, except what Churaman pleased to dole out to them. The Emperor and his courtiers burned with rage, but no one was willing to undertake the task of punishing the rebel.

The rapid growth of the Jat power on the immediate border of his own state caused alarm as well as hatred of the ruler of Jaipur. Aurangzeb had employed Raja Bishan Singh Kachhwah to crush the ancestors of Churaman since that time a hereditary feud had continued between the Jats and their Rajput neighbours. Now Raja Jai Singh Sawai came forward to take command against Churaman, to the great joy of Farrukh-siyar. The Raja was liberally supplied with men and money; Maharao Bhim Singh Hada of Kota, Raja Gaj Singh Narwari, and Maharao Budh Singh Hada of Bundi also accomplished him. The campaign (November 1716–April 1718), opened with the siege of Thun in which Churaman was said to have gathered grain, salt, ghee, tobacco, cloth and fire-wood for twenty years! The prudent Jat had turned out empty-handed all merchants and traders–useless consumers of bread, with their families, before the siege began. The besieged made a sally and led by Churaman's son Muhkam Singh, and his nephew, Rupa, gave battle in the open. The Jaipur Raja claimed a victory which only enabled him to resume the blockade. But as success seemed doubtful, Adbus-samad Khan, the brave and energetic governor of Lahore who had won great fame by crushing the Sikhs, was recalled from the Punjab to reinforce Raja Jai Singh. However, owing to Court intrigue, he was not sent. Churaman had also allies outside, *viz.*, the *zamindars* and villagers who kept the imperialists in perpetual alarm by pillage and plunder. The siege dragged on for twenty months without any definite result. Party strife at the Court between the Hindustani faction headed by the Sayyid brothers, and the Turani faction led by the Nizam-ul-mulk proved the salvation of Churaman. The wazir, Sayyid Abdullah was hostile to the Jaipur Raja, whose success, therefore, he did not wish. Through a relation and agent of the wazir, Churaman made offers of submission by promising to pay a tribute of 30 lakhs of rupees to the imperial treasury, and another 20 lakhs to the wazir himself. Farrukh-siyar was helpless, like Sindbad the Sailor, with the two Sayyids upon his shoulders; so he reluctantly and ungraciously granted pardon to the rebel, brought before his presence, under the safe conduct of the wazir. From this time Churaman became an active and trusted partisan of the all-powerful Sayyids.

Churaman and the Sayyid Brothers

In February 1719, Farrukh-siyar was deposed, blinded, and put to death by the Sayyids who raised a consumptive youth, Rafiud-darjat, to the throne. The new Emperor was deposed after three months, and his elder brother Rafi-ud-daula succeeded him. This man was so fortunate as to die a natural death after four months. Then the throne was given by the Sayyids to Muhammad Shah in September 1719. However, the end of the Kingmakers was drawing near. A woman's curse rested upon one, and extreme insolence drew down Heaven's vengeance upon the other. Sayyid Abdullah had fixed his licentious gaze on Inayat Banu Begam, wife of the Emperor Rafi-ud-darjat. The unhappy queen, feeling her husband unable to protect her, cut off her beautiful locks and sent them to her tempter in order to escape dishonour. The vanity and infatuation of Sayyid Husain Ali had also gone beyond limit. He once boasted that upon whomsoever he cast the shadow of his shoe that man would become the equal of the Emperor Alamgir! Churaman followed the Sayyids like a shadow; he was with the army of Husain Ali at the time of Farrukh-siyar's deposition. Later on he accompanied him to Agra in the expedition against a pretender, Neku siyar, who had been proclaimed Emperor by the enemies of the Sayyids. He was assigned an important post in the siege of that fort,[11] and it was through his influence with the garrison that the fort was surrendered. After that he started for the Dakhin with Husain Ali when he marched against the Nizam-ul mulk (May 1720). For his faithful services, the Sayyid promised him the title of Raja, but this promise could not be fulfilled as Husain Ali was soon afterwards murdered by the Mughals with the connivance of Muhammad Shah. Large rewards were offered to Churaman to induce him to desert the cause of the Sayyids. Considering it foolish to incur the enemity of the Emperor for nothing, he accepted them and joined Muhammad Shah's army. The cunning Jat persuaded the Emperor to change his route which would have passed through his villages. Leaving his own villages at a distance, he led the army of the Emperor across the territories of his enemy Raja Jai Singh, and took it over high hills, thorny jungles, and waterless waste (Irvine's *Later Mughals*, ii. 68-69).

---

11. Another instance of Churaman's heartless treachery is given by Father Wendel:- "There having made an agreement with Neku-siyar to allow his brother Ali Zafar to pass with a large sum of money to Raja Jai Singh's country for raising troops and marching, when he would be summoned, to his succour, Churaman turned traitor to the unfortunate prince, seized the money (50 lakhs in gold), and sent by perfidious hand, Ali Zafar, to Husain Ali. [Orme MSS. p. 70 of Prof. J.N. Sarkar's transcript].

When Sayyid Abdullah advanced at the head of a large army against Muhammad Shah, Churaman went over to the minister with all his Jats. In this he was not certainly actuated by sentiments of devotion and gratitude to his old patron.[XI] The cynical Jat argued that "in case of the Sayyid's defeat, it would be much easier to secure pardon from Muhammad Shah, then it would be, in the reverse case, to save himself from the Sayyid's vengeance" (*Later Mughals,* ii. 81).

On the day of the battle (Nov. 1720), fought in the neighbourhood of Hodal, Churaman[12] with his Jats was employed to make diversion by attacking the camp and baggage of Muhammad shah. He threw himself heartily into this congenial task which meant a maximum of gain with a minimum of loss. Like a pack of wolves, the Jat fell upon the baggage camp from the west, south, and east in succession, and though driven back with difficulty, they carried off many oxen and horses and created much confusion among the camp followers. But in actual fighting, the day had ended in the virtual destruction of Abdullah's army. So, next morning, Churaman without caring for the favour or frown of either party, plundered both sides with strict impartiality, and made off with the booty to his own country.

Churaman now openly acted as an independent Raja though he did not assume that title for fear of exciting the jealousy of his kinsmen. He strengthened himself against the Kachhwahas by making an alliance with Raja Ajit Singh Rathor of Marwar and he sent assistance to the Bundelas to keep the Mughal Government busy in the east. But he committed an indiscretion and injustice by throwing his nephew Badan Singh into prison.

Badan Singh was released by the intervention of other Jats who began to be suspicious of Churaman's design. Family dissension afforded fresh opportunities to his enemies. Badan Singh fled for protection and assistance to Saadat Khan, subedar of Agra, who had already begun a campaign against the Jats. Muhkam Singh, son of Churaman, inflicted a crushing defeat upon Nilkanth Nagar, deputy of Saadat Khan. The Khan himself fared no better, and was accordingly removed from his office. Again Raja Jai Singh took the

XI. 'There is not enough ground to suspect his 'devotion and gratitude' to the Sayyid . . . . . Churaman's presence in the royal camp was a temporary device to avert a possible danger to his territory." For detail see, G.C. Dwivedi, *The Jats: Their role in the Mughal Empire,* 71-72. —Ed.

12. According to another account, "Churaman with his band fell on the baggage of Emperor and *that of Abdullah also,* and took a considerable booty in the very heat of the action." [Fr. MS., p. 73].

command against the Jats, to wipe off the disgrace of his previous failure. But by this time, old Churaman had committed suicide by taking poison (Sept.-Oct. 1721).[XII]

The story of his death runs as follows:-"One of his relations, a wealthy man died childless. The brethren sent for Muhkam, the eldest son of Churaman, and made him head of the deceased's zamindari, and gave over to him all his goods. Zul Karan, the second son of Churaman said to his brother, "Give me too a share in those goods and admit me as a partner." A verbal dispute followed and Muhkam made ready to resist by force. Zul Karan determined to have the quarrel out, gathered men together, and attacked his brother. The elders of the place sent word to Churaman that his sons were fighting which was not well . . . Churaman spoke to Muhkam. The son replied to his father in abusive language, and showed himself ready to fight his father as well as his brother. Churaman lost his temper, and from chagrin swallowed up a dose of deadly poison which he always carried with him, and going to an orchard in that village lay down and gave up the ghost. After a long time had elapsed, men were sent to search for him and they found his dead body" (*Later Mughals*, ii. 122).

Again did Raja Jai Singh Sawai appear on the scene to subdue the Jats. He began his operations with 14,000 horsemen, and the number by subsequent reinforcements rose to 50,000. The sons of Churaman were besieged in Thun, whose chief defence was a belt of impenetrable jungle. The imperialists gradually closed upon the fort by cutting the trees. Badan Singh who was with the army of Raja Jai Singh pointed out the weak spots and helped in the reduction of two fortified outworks. After conducting the defence for about two months, Mukham Singh lost heart, and secretly fleeing from Thun, took refuge with his father's ally, Raja Ajit Singh Rathor. On November 18, 1722; the imperialists entered the place. Badan Singh was installed as the chief of the Jats with the title of Thakur, by the ruler of Jaipur.

XII. G.C. Dwivedi conclude that Churaman died between 17th Sept. and 10th October, 1721. For details see, *The Jats: Their role in the Mughal Empire*, p. 76, f.n.11. Contra see Rajpal Singh, 'Churaman did not die in Zul-Hijja (sept.-Oct. 1721) as has been asserted by William Irvine (*Later Mughals, II, 122*) and undisputedly accepted by almost all the later historians. Several farmans preserved in the Rajasthan State Archives regarding correspondence between Delhi government and Jai Singh reveal that Churaman guided the destiny of the Jats till May 1724. Kapatdwara Records, Farman No. 26, 29 to 31, 34 to 39. Also see SIWANI-I-KHIZRI by Md. Umar, son of Khizar Khan that Author was present on the spot where Churaman's son quarreled and the Jat chief was made to take poison, cited by Rajpal Singh, *Rise of the Jat Power*, p. 47, f.n. 127. —Ed.

CHAPTER III

EXPANSION OF THE JAT POWER

Thakur Badan Singh, Founder of the Ruling House of Bharatpur

Thakur Badan Singh, father of Suraj Mal, started his career as a feudatory of Sawai Jai Singh of Amber (Jaipur), who had given him the lands and title of Churaman Jat in the reign of the Emperor Muhammad Shah. Unlike his notorious uncle, he was a quiet and politic man, having no taste for a predatory life. He set up a legitimate ruler, sincerely desirous of promoting the arts of peace. He believed more in the steady expansion and consolidation of his dominions than in erratic and slippery conquests. The task which he took upon himself was not a light one; it meant transforming a robber-chief's "sphere of influence" into an orderly principality with a regular government. In this however, he succeeded eminently after years of patient toil and tactful administration. We do not hear of any diplomatic activity or brilliant exploit of arms on his part. Nevertheless, it is clear that within a few years of his accession, he grew powerful enough to shake off his dependence upon Amber. Badan Singh, then uniting himself with the rebels of Mewat, carried raids into the territories of the Raja of Jaipur, who had to conciliate him by a grant of lands, yielding 18 lakhs of Rupees a year.[1] Taking advantage of the confused state of affairs, he made some acquisitions in the Bayana district and built a fort at Wair, which was given to his youngest son Pratap singh. His greatest achievement was the establishment of the authority of his house over almost the whole of the Agra and Mathura districts, partly by posing

1. Imad-us-Saadat, p. 55.

as the protector of the Hindus against Muslim misrule, but mainly by clever matrimonial alliances with some powerful Jat families of those places. He married the daughter of a wealthy and influential Jat of Kamar,[2] Chaudhuri Maha Ram and took another wife from the laird *(Zamindar)* of Sahar. These marriages made him virtually the master of the entire Mathura district.

In the eyes of the Mughal Government, Badan Singh was still a plebian rebel who deserved the severest punishment, if only the corrupt and effete Court of Delhi could inflict it. Håd Nadir Shah decided to stay in Hindustan a few months more, or made his intended pilgrimage to Ajmer[3] the Jat chief would have been the first to feel the weight of the Persian's arm. Since his departure the timid gaze of the Mughal Court was mainly fixed on the north-west. In the meanwhile, Thakur Badan Singh silently consolidated his authority over many outlying districts, without much difficulty. People welcomed him because he meant to rule and not plunder them like his predecessors. His one dear object was to secure the title of *Raja,* and for this, he was even ready to bow before the imperial throne, which he could otherwise have safely defied. But he was not successful, perhaps owing to the jealousy of the ruler of Jaipur, who affected to look upon the Jats as his subjects. It was perhaps from this time that the ruling house of Bharatpur openly laid claim to the Yadava lineage and the title of *Braj Raj,* a claim if not sanctified by past tradition, atleast justified by their complete sway over what is known as *Brij-mandal* or the Mathura region. Ajit Singh and Abhai Singh of Marwar, it is said, used to address Badan Singh as *Raja.* His ambition was certainly flattered, when he was invited to the *Ashvameda*[4] sacrifice of Maharaja Sawai Jai Singh, and the honour of a prince was accorded to his son suraj Mal. Undoubtedly, Badan Singh worked and lived in a manner to deserve that title. He kept Court with adequate grandeur.

2. Kamar [lat. 27°- 50'; long. 77° - 30'] is near Kosi in the Mathura district about 33 miles n.w. of Mathura. *Sahar* 18 miles n.w. [lat. 27° - 40'; long. 77° - 44',]. Growse, *Mathura* p. 23.
3. Irvine's *Later Mughals,* ii, 374.
4. Jawala Sahai's *History of Bharatpur.*

Several Muhammadan officers whom he had taken in service brought the requisite polish and dignity into his Court and served there as models of Court-life and teachers of etiquette to his rough tribesmen. His growing predilection for Islamic culture and aristocratic training became prominent in the education of his youngest and most beloved son, Pratap Singh.[5]

Badan Singh had some aesthetic sense and a taste for architecture too, which is testified by the remains of his numerous buildings and garden-palaces. He beautified the fort of Deeg with handsome palaces, which are known as the *Purana Mahal.* At Wair in the Bayana district, he planted within the fort a large garden with a beautiful house and reservoirs in the centre, now called *Phul-bari.* He also built palaces at Kamar as well Sahar, which are now in ruin, and dedicated a temple at Brindaban, known by the poetic name of *Dhir Samir.*[6]

Badan Singh lived to a ripe old age, which he spent in happy retirement at Sahar, leaving the management of his State to his most capable son Suraj Mal. He died on the 9th of Ramzan, 1169 A.H. = 7th June, 1756 (*Waqa,* 133) under the usual suspicion of being poisoned, though there was no imaginable ground for it.

Raja Suraj Mal: His character and early career

Raja Suraj Mal, the succesor of Thakur Badan Singh, was a strongly built man of "above the medium height, with a robust frame, inclining to corpulence in his old age, and a very dark complexion. His eyes were unusually sparkling, and all his appearance indicated more fire than one could notice in his conduct, which was very sweet and supple.[7]"

5. The author of *Imad-us-Saadat* tells us that this young man grew up (in airs and graces) a high-bred Muslim grandee with good manners and elegant speech. In the sytle of tying his turban, the fashion of his dress as well as his favourite dishes, he imitated the manner of Delhi. Bahadur Singh, son of this Pratap Singh, went a step ahead of his father. He took to the study of the Quran and read up to the Sura Jami. *Imad,* 55.
6. Growse, p. 139.
7. Father Wendel, Orme MS., p. 51.

He had little of book-learning, and none of the courtly grace of his youngest brother, being plain and unassuming in dress and manners. He possessed great political sagacity, a steady intellect and a clear vision. "Though he wore the dress of a farmer, and could speak only his own *Braj-dialect*, he was", says the author of *Imad-us-Saadat*, "the Plato of the Jat tribe." In prudence and skill, and ability to manage the revenue and civil affairs he had no equal among the grandees of Hindustan execpt Asaf Jah Bahadur[8] (the Nizam). He possessed pre-eminently all the nobler qualities of his race, energy, courage, shrewdness dogged perseverance and an indomitable spirit that would never accept a defeat. But in the pursuit of an exciting game, whether in war or diplomacy, he was of no more delicate conscience than most of his contemporaries. In an age of intrigue and unscrupulous diplomacy, he equally baffled the dissembling Mughal and the cunning Maratha. In short, he was a wary old bird that picked up grain from every net, without getting entangled in the noose.

Suraj Mal's first exploit, during his father's lifetime, was the capture of the fort of Bharatpur in 1732,[XIII] by a daring night-attack upon its lord, Khem Karan Jat Sogaria. At that time, the place was only a small mud-fort without any of the formidable fortifications with which its name was afterwards associated. His untutored genius turned it into an impregnable stronghold, and around it grew up a prosperous city vying in grandeur with the imperial capitals of Delhi and Agra. The fame of his just and wise rule attracted men of all classes, professions and creeds to his principality, which was the only spot where peace and security reigned in the midst of the chaotic plains of Hindustan. He early attached himself to Maharaja Sawai Jai Singh, the most powerful Rajput ruler of his time, in order to disarm the

8. *Imad*, p. 55.

XIII. The author mis-takes Bharatpur for *Fatehgarhi* or *Fatehpur* of Khem Karan Sogaria (also known as Khema Jat) originally from *Mauza* Tuhiya. Suraj Mal captured *Fatehgarhi* in a night attack in 1733. After demolishing it he built the impregnable fort of Bharatpur at that place. On January 1743 (Magh Sudi 5, Sam. 1799) the foundation of Bharthpur was laid and the construction completed in 1750. U.N. Sharma, *Jaton ka Navin Itihas*, I, 193, 325-330; II, p. 67; G.C. Dwivedi, *The Jats: their role in the Mughal Empire*, p. 90; Some people misunderstand '*Choburja*' as *Garhi* of Khema Jat. Ganga Singh, *Bharatpur ka Itihas*, I, pp. 131 - 135. —Ed.

Rajput jealousy and allow the infant Jat Power to grow unhampered under the shadow of Amber. Besides policy, an inherent sentiment of loyalty to the throne of Amber moved him to act thus. Suraj Mal's sincere devotion to the Maharaja was repaid with fatherly affection by that great ruler. After the death of the Maharaja, Suraj Mal, true to the dying wish of his beloved patron, stood faithfully by his eldest son Iswari Singh whose rightful claim to the throne was unjustly disputed by his younger brother Madho Singh in pride of the Sisodia blood derived from his mother. To sweep Iswari Singh off the throne of Amber Malhar Rao Holkar, Gangadhar Tatiya and the Maharana of Mewar advanced upon Jaipur with a huge army of Marathas and Sisodias, swelled by Rathor and Hada contingents from Jodhpur and Kota. Raja Iswari Singh, accompanied by Suraj Mal started from his capital with the levy of Amber and his Jat auxiliaries.

On Sunday, 20th August, 1749[XIV] both armies, joined in dreadful conflict at Bagru;[9] the contest was an unequal and unfair one: seven confederated rulers having combined against one prince. The Van of the army of Amber was led by Shiv Singh, the brave feudatory chief of Sikar; Suraj Mal was posted in the centre, and Raja Iswari Singh himself commanded the rear. The first day ended in an indecisive artillery duel. The second day closed gloomily for Amber, because the valiant Lord of Sikar, leading the Van died after an obstinate encounter. With the break of dawn on the third day, the eager enemy, confident of success, appeared in battle array. The army of Amber came out to meet them: the honour of leading the *harawal* (Van) devolved on Suraj Mal on this fateful day. The battle raged furiously throughout the line in spite of an autumn shower which failed to cool the ardour of the combatants. The clever Maratha chief Malhar sent Gangadhar Tatiya with a strong division to surprise the rear of Raja Iswari Singh. Gangadhar marched stealthily and fell upon Rao Sardar Singh Naruka, vassal of Uniara

XIV. **The battle of Bagru took place in August 1748 not in 1749. Scholars differ on exact dates. According to J.N. Sarkar 3rd of August and U.N. Sharma, 13 August 1748. On 20th August Suraj Mal returned to his country. Thus the duration of this conflict is 1st August to 20th August 1748. *Fall of the Mughal Empire*, I (1988 ed.), p.146; *Maharaja Suraj Mal Jat*, II, 154, 158; also see, P.C. Chandavat, *Maharaja Suraj Mal Aur Unka Yug*, 62-63. —Ed.**

9. **Bagru is a town on the Ajmer—Agra Trunk Road about 18 miles** south-west of Jaipur, (Rajputana Gaz. ii, 155).

who commanded the rear of the Amber army. He threw the rear division into confusion and pressed vigorously upon the artillery posted in the centre. The gunners were cut down and the cannon spiked: defeat stared Raja Iswari Singh in the face. Seeing everything lost, the Raja commanded Suraj Mal, his last hope to charge Gangadhar. The Jat chief bowed his head and without a moment's pause delivered a flank charge upon a stronger enemy. An obstinate struggle between the half-victorious Maratha and the stubborn Jat lasted for two hours. At last Gangadhar turned his back, and Suraj Mal restoring the broken rear, and leaving Sardar Singh Naruka in command there, returned to the Van to breast the surging tides of the hostile army. In that supreme hour of peril, the Jat chief fought with superhuman valour, "killing" says the enthusiastic native chronicler, "50 and wounding 108 of the enemy with his own hand." At last the darkness of night parted the combants. Suraj Mal triumphantly led back the army of Amber, after having snatched a victory from the jaws of defeat. Thr Rajput bard did not grudge the heroic Jat his due on this memorable occasion. The Bundi poet Suraj Mal commemorates the deed of his Jat namesake in the following spirited couplets:-

सह्यौ भलेही जट्नी, जाय अरिष्ट अरिष्ट।
जाठर तस रबिमल्ल हुव, आमेरन को इष्ट ॥
"बहुरि जट्ट मलहार सन, लरन लग्यो हरवल्ल।
अंगद है हुल्कर, जाट मिहर मल्ल प्रतिमल्ल ॥'

i.e., the Jatni did not in vain bear [the pain of travail].

The issue of her womb [Jathara] was Suraj [Rabi] Mal, the scourge of enemies, and the well-wisher of Amber.

Turning back [from the rear] the Jat began to fight with Malhar in the Van.

Holkar was the shadow [of night], and he the sun; the two champions well matched [in conflict].

Daylight brought the hostile armies again into conflict on the fourth day. In this way fighting continued for two days more, till at last the arduous struggle wore out the patience of the less persevering Maratha. Holkar proposed peace and Madho Singh had to content himself with the five parganas given to him as his appanage.[10]

---

10. Life of Maharaja Iswari Singh in *Hindi* (pp. 59-73) by Thakur Narendar Singh Verma, Vaidic Press, Ajmer.

Suraj Mal's first encounter with Mughals

In the reign of the Emperor Ahmad Shah, Saadat Khan, Amir-ul-Umra Zulfiqar Jang,[11] had been appointed governor of Agra and Ajmer. He entered into a league with Raja Bakht Singh Rathor, who had usurped the thorne of Marwar by ousting his nephew, Ram Singh. Though driven out of the capital, Ram Singh, with the support of the Raja of Jaipur, held out near Ajmer, waiting for the arrival of his Maratha allies. So the situation was full of danger for Bakht Singh who, therefore, sought the help of Saadat Khan. The Khan also required his assistance against Jats for recovering the greater portion of his Suba of Agra from their clutches. An understanding seems to have been entered into, to the effect that Saadat Khan, instead of marching to Agra by the Delhi-Agra royal road, should strike southwest from Delhi, through Mewat, unite his forces with those of Bakht Singh somewhere on the frontier of his principality, and thence turn towards Ajmer to crush Ram Singh: after the conquest of Ajmer, the subjugation of the Jat country would become easier, - so the Khan was made to believe. He began his march (1162 H.)[12]

11. In the original text of the *Siyar-ul-Mutaqharin* we do not find the name Saadat Khan (see original text. ii, 38), imported in the translation. This Saadat Khan has been confounded by the translator with his namesake, the uncle and father-in-law of Nawab Safdar Jang (*vide* vol. iv, index, p. 63). Burhan-ul-mulk Saadat Khan died during Nadir Shah's stay at Delhi (*siyar*, i. 316): the exact date being 10th March, 1739. The second Saadat Khan (Zulfiqar Jang) was appointed governor in the reign of Ahmad Shah who ascended the throne on Wednesday, 2nd Jamada 1., 1160 H. 1st May, 1747; Waqa, p. 35). He was created *Mir Bakhshi* by the Emperor Ahmad Shah on Thursday Raja 14, 1160 H. (11th July, 1747) on the very same day that Raja Bakht Singh was appointed *subedar* of Gujrat (*Waqa*, p. 38).
12. *Siyar's* date 1163 H. is wrong (*Siyar*, iii, 312). In that year Suraj Mal was, according to better authorities, fighting as an ally of Safdar Jang against the Ruhelas. The correct date seems to be *Safar* 1162 H. The translator of Siyar, iii, 311, 20th line, omits the date, "the end of the year 1162" (text, ii. 38). The text is also wrong. This should be the end of 1161, as is evident from *Waqa-i-Shah Alam Sani.*

with a well-equipped army of 15,000 horse, and arrived at a place, Nimrani, on the northern boundary of Suraj Mal's dominion. The Jat Raja was watching the movements of the Mughal army, without any intension of showing his hand first. But some soldiers of Saadat Khan picked a quarrel with the Jat garrison of a small fort[XV] and drove them out. This was construed by the Khan as a great victory, and he ordered his drums to be beaten in rejoicing. He became over-confident of his strength, and the sudden elation of an insignificant success changed his whole plan of campaign. He made a halt there, and recalled his advanced guards from the direction of Narnol. In spite of the earnest remonstrances of some of the officers of his army, he decided to conquer the Jat country first and then go to Ajmer. Saadat Khan ordered Fath Ali Khan to go out on a forage in force. The party started in the morning from their camp near Sobha Chand's *sarai*. While at noon the foragers with their convoy were about to return, the Jat army commanded by Raja Suraj Mal himself appeared. Fath Ali Khan, who was at a distance of two or three *kos*[13] sent urgent requests for reinforcement, but it came tardily towards the sunset.

Thinking a retreat by night before a stronger enemy dangerous, they sent word to Saadat Khan proposing to pass the night on the spot, expecting him to march with the whole army to their relief in the morning. This was objected to and this immediate return was insisted upon by the Khan. The Jats surrounded the retreating column; their mounted matchlockmen closed in small bodies and discharged volleys upon the confused Muslim troopers without dismounting. Such a mobile force as Suraj Mal's mounted matchlockmen could hardly be brought to the grapple in the darkness of night. A great many of the Mughals died helplessly, and the rest lost heart when Hakim Khan was shot dead and Ali Rustam Khan wounded – the two gallant officers who had brought reinforcements. The retreat became a panic-stricken flight. The main camp was also thrown into confusion by the rush of fugitives and the appearance of the advanced

XV. This small fort was Nimrana *garhi* (33 miles south-west of Pataudi), which was captured by the MirBakshi, Saadat Khan from the Jat garrison on 30th December, 1749. P.C. Chandavat, *Maharaja Suraj Mal Aur Unka Yug*, 70; G.C. Dwivedi, *The Jats: their role in the Mughal Empire*, 116 f.n.10 for references. —Ed.

13. This is omitted in the translation of the Siyar.

party of the enemy, close on their heels. A greater disaster was averted by the firmness and decision of Saadat Khan's more discreet captains, who did not hesitate to prevent by force their master's flight. The Lords of Lords writhed in agony in their grip till the panic subsided. "Luckily", says the author of the *Siyar*, whose uncle was an eye-witness of the affair, "as the Jat chief, for his own safety, did not wish to gain the evil repute of having captured or slain an Amir-ul-umra, he contented himself with besieging the camp for two or three days together, at the end of which he offered terms through Fath Ali Khan, an officer with whom he was acquainted. The Amir-ul-umra, considering it to be a great gain, consented to them." Suraj Mal sent his own son Jawahar Singh, to the Amer-ul-umra and concluded an agreement on several conditions, two of which were, that the dependents of the viceroy should not cut any *pipal* tree, nor offer any insult or injury to the Hindu temples in the country.[14] This victory over the Amir-ul-umra of the empire brought great prestige and self-confidence to Raja Suraj Mal. Soon afterwards he entered the political arena of Hindustan to play a bolder and more honourable role.

Suraj Mal's marriage with Rani Kishori

Raja Surja Mal followed his father's policy of extending the dominion of his house by politic marriages. He had his own son Nawal Singh married to a daughter of Sardar Sitaram, the powerful castellan of Kotman[15], and himself married to a daughter of Chaudhari Kashi, the head of a strong and prosperous Jat family of Hodal, 53 miles north-west of Mathura. This lady was the gifted queen Rani Kishori,[16] commonly known by her pet name, Hansia (the

---

14. For this campaign, see Siyar, iii 313-315 Perse text Part II, pp. 38-39. The translation is wrong in many places.
15. Situated in the Mathura district on the Agra-Delhi Trunk Road about three furlongs to the south of the boundary line dividing the Gurgaon and the Mathura districts.
16. I have not been able to find out the date of Rani Kishori's marriage. The descendants of Chaudhari Kashi stil occupy a respectable position at Hodal. Some of them, e.g., Chaudhari Ratan Singh, still serve in the Bharatpur State. The magnificant palaces, built by their ancestors, are now in ruins. Chaudhari Devi

smiling one), who figures prominently in the history of the house of Bharatpur. The story goes that one day while Raja Suraj Mal, mounted on a huge elephant, was passing through a street of Hodal, a group of girls, returning from the well, ran away terrified at the sight of the mighty beast; only one girl refused to move and stood gazing with unshaken nerve upon the strange animal and the gorgeous equipage of the princely retinue. The Raja, struck at the intrepidity of the girl, enquired about her, and demanded her in marriage from her relatives. Whatever may be the element of truth in this popular story, her courage and constancy in the face of grave disasters in later life are testified by authentic history. Her genius and resourcefulness saved the fortunes of Bharatpur many a time from almost inevitable ruin.

Singh Zaildar, Daulat Singh, Ratan Singh and Hari Singh are the most prominent living members of this house. The last-named gentleman is a personal friend of mine and entertained me very hospitably in the *mahal* or inner apartment of his ancestral palace.

CHAPTER IV

RAJA SURAJMAL, AN ALLY OF NAWAB SAFDAR JANG

Suraj Mal helps the Jats of Ballamgarh against the Nawab Wazir Safdar Jang

Already master of the Mathura district, Suraj Mal cast his eye upon the neighbourhood of Delhi and was waiting for an opportunity to extend his authority further south. The Jats of Ballamgarh, hard pressed by the faujdar of Faridabad, sought his help, and this embroiled him further with the Mughal Government. We may here breifly trace the history of the Jat feudal house of Ballamgarh. One Gopal Singh Jat of the Tewatia *got* (sept) settled in Sihi, a village three miles north of Ballamgarh, about 1705 and became wealthy and powerful by highway robbery on the Mathura Delhi road. He allied himself with the Gujars of Tiagaon (8 miles east of Ballamgarh; long. 77^0 - 30', lat. 28^0 - 25'.) and with their help killed the Rajput Chaudhari of the neighbouring villages. Murtaza Khan the local Mughal officer of Faridabad, instead of punishing the rebel, made peace with him by appointing him as Chaudhari of Faridabad pragana, entitled to a cess (rate) of one anna in the rupee on the revenue in 1710. After the death of Gopal Singh, his son Charandas succeeded him, and seeing how weak the imperial grasp was growing even in the nearer districts, withheld the revenue and set the authority of Murtaza Khan at defiance. However, Charandas was captured and thrown into prison at Faridabad. After some time, his son Balaram, duping[1] the Khan by a false payment of ransome, set him at

1. The story goes that Balaram promised to pay a large amount; in cash directly his father was freed. According to previous stipulations, Charandas was brought guarded to the side of a tank near

liberty, Father and son fled to Bharatpur, and securing the aid of Suraj Mal, killed Murtaza Khan (*Delhi Gazetteer*, p. 213).

This act of rebellious aggression remained unpunished till the accession of Emperor Ahmad Shah (1747). The Wazir wrote repeatedly to Balram and Raja Suraj Mal to give up the above mentioned *parganas*, but was put off with false pretences and evasive replies. This was sufficient to kindle the wrath of the wazir and to make him swear the utter destruction of the Jats. So he took the field against them in 1162 H. (January, 1749), almost simultaneously with the Amir-ul-umra, and captured Faridabad. Suraj Mal, elated with his recent success over one imperial army led by the commander-in-chief of the Mughal empire, was not in a mood to hear the proposals of the wazir to resign peacefully the places in dispute. He prepared to back the Jats of Sihi with all his resources and putting the forts of Deeg and Kumher in a state of defence, marched against the wazir (June, 1749). Fortune befriended Suraj Mal; the wazir, on receiving the news of formidable Ruhela rebellion in the immediate neighbourhood of his *suba* of Oudh, had to put off the settlement of his score with the Jats and return to Delhi. He fought these Afghans, and after quelling their disturbance, left his deputy Nawal Ray in charge of the districts wrested from them (beginning of 1750). Then he resumed his operations against the Jats, and sent an army against them. The Jast having got ready for fight, the wazir started against them during the rains (July 1750) and advanced as far as Khizirabad. About this time the news of a great disaster, viz., the defeat and death of Nawal Ray at the hands of Ahmad Khan Bangash, induced the wazir to make up his quarrel with Suraj Mal. A compromise was effected through the mediation of the Maratha vakil. In order to save appearences, Balaram,[2] with his wrists bound together,

Ballamgarh, and when the cart bringing the treasure had come up, Charandas was let go. He immediately made of on a fleet horse with his son. The other bags were found to contain copper coins (paisa) only. *Delhi, Gazetteer*, foot note, p. 213.

2. This Balaram is the builder of the fort of Ballamgarh or Ballabgarh. He is not the same man as his namesake, who was the brother

accompanied the Maratha envoy to the presence of the wazir, who graciously pardoned him and gave an implicit sanction to his illegal acquisitions. Raja Suraj Mal was given a *khilat* of 6 pieces, and his bakhshi one of two pieces. Mutual appreciation of merit and ability laid the foundations of a true friendship between the Nawab wazir and the great Jat, who ever after stood faithfully by his ally, even under most desperate circumstances.

Raja Suraj Mal joined the wazir in an expedition[3] against Ahmad Khan Bangash and the Ruhelas. The Nawab started on the 29th Shaban, 1163 H. = Monday 23 July, 1750 with an army of 70,000 horse. Suraj Mal with his Jats, occupied Farrukhabad, the capital of Ahmad Khan. A severe battle was fought at Pathari on Monday 22nd Shawwal 1163 H. (13 Sept. 1750). The wazir stood in the centre, mounted on an elephant; his right and left wings were commanded respectively by Suraj Mal Jat and Ismail Khan Kabuli. Both wings vigourously charged the enemy at a gallop and drove away Rustam Khan Afridi and some other Ruhela commanders, killing 6,000 or 7,000 Afghans. The battle began at nine and raged till the afternoon, the advantage being on the side of Safdar Jang. Ahmad Khan Bangash, seeing all lost, summoned his tribes men and urged them to make a last effort to retrieve their honour; "Otherwise", he said to them in the characteristic Pathan style "every Afridi [their braver comrades] will make water upon the beard of the

---

of Suraj Mal's wife, Hansia. This Balaram was killed on the 29th November, 1753 by one Aqibat Mahmud Khan as appears from the following entry (p. 83) in the *Waqa-i-Shah Alam Sani*: "On the 2nd Safar (1167 H.) Aqibat Khan, who went to Ballu Jat (Balaram) to settle the affair of his *jagir*, had an exchange of harsh words with Jat. He cut off the head of the said Jat and brought his head to His Majesty (Ahmad Shah)." This Aquibat Mahmud was the son of Murtaza Khan, whom Balaram had slain. However, Ballamgarh and Faridabad remained in possession of Suraj Mal who appointed Kishan Singh and Bishan Singh, sons of Balaram, as the *quiladar* and *nazim* of Ballamgarh. They retained their office till 1774. (See *Delhi Gazetter*, p. 213) This date, like all others, in the *Gazetteer* is doubtful.

3. *Waqa*, pp. 57-58; Harcharan Das, *Imad*, 49.

Bangashes."[4] The Afghans assembled in a grove of *palash* trees, and made a sudden rush upon the wazir's party. The wazir had dangerously weakened his division by sending reinforcements to his wings. But he neither pushed forward to keep touch with his commanders nor recalled them from pursuit. Nawab Safdar Jang severely wounded was brought into the camp. Next morning he began his retreat towards the imperial capital. The Afghans occupied almost the whole of his territories; the city of Allahabad was plundered; and its citadel besieged: Lucknow was saved only by the stubborn courage of the citizens. In the meanwhile, when the news of his defeat had reached Delhi, his enemies had turned the heart of the Emperor against him, and were plotting for his overthrow. But his timely arrival disconcerted their plan. The wazir again summoned Raja Nagar Mal, Raja Lachhmi Narayan, Raja Suraj Mal Jat, Ismail Khan Kabuli and others who were his well-wishers, to discuss the plan of a new compaign against the Ruhelas. He took into his pay the Maratha army of Malhar Rao Holkar for Rs. 25,000 per day, and the Jats of Suraj Mal[5] on a daily allowance of Rs. 15,000. On the 6th Rabi I., 1164 H. (Tuesday, 22 Jan. 1751) he started a second time against Ahmad Khan Bangash. Farrukhabad was sacked and the whole Ruhela country devastated with fire and sword. A thorn was planted in the side of the Ruhelas to torment them perpetually by giving the tract of country from Koel (Aligarh) to Kora Jahanabad to the Marathas[6] as *jagir*. He sent greetings to the Emperor on his victory over the Afghans on 9th Jamada, II. 1164 H. = April 24, 1751 [*Waqa*, p. 62]. This shows that this campaign was a short but sharp one, everything being finished within three months.

About a month after the wazir's departure from the capital, a great calamity had befallen the empire. Ahmad

4. *Imad*, p. 49; *Siyar*, p. 295. The author of *Gulsitan-i-Rahamat* says that Rustam Khan Afridi had actually been killed by Suraj Mal, and that Ahmad Khan concealed this from his followers.
5. *Ibratnama*, p. 41; *Bayan-o-Waqa*, p. 26; *Waqa-i-Shah Alam Sani*, p.61.
6. *Waqa*, p. 62. A good account of the Maratha activity during this campaign is to be found in Sardesai's *Marathi Riysat Panipat Prakaran*, p. 10-14.

Shah Abdali invaded the Punjab, entered Lahor on the 3rd of Rabi II. 1164 H. = Monday, 18 Feb, 1751 and threatened to march upon Delhi. The Emperor, as a compliment to Suraj Mal conferred a mansab of 3,000 *Zat,* 2,000 horse, and the title of *Rao* upon Ratan Singh, and that of 1,000 *Zat,* 1,000 horse upon Jawahar Singh (13th Jamada 1. = 29 March 1751) in addition to his former rank, making him in all a mansabdar of 4000 *Zat,* 3500 horse [*Waqa,* p. 70]. Repeated and urgent messages were sent to the wazir to come with all haste, bringing Malhar Rao Holkar and other Maratha chiefs with him. During the wazir's absence a lady of the harem, an eunuch, and a supple intriguer had acquired complete control over the Emperor's fickle mind. They induced him to accept the terms of the Durrani invader, who consented to retire on getting the subas of Lahor and Multan. On his return to the capital, the wazir justly resented this ignominious treaty made in his absence and without consulting him. He was bent upon punishing the evil-doers. The eunuch was to be the first victim of the wazir's wrath. Javid Khan was invited to a feast in the wazir's house and there murdered.

The Emperor Ahmad Shah, instigated by the queen-mother and the nobles of the Turani faction, dismissed Nawab Safdar Jang, from the office of the wazir, confiscated his estates, and removed him from the viceroyalties of Oudh and Allahadad. A civil war broke out between them; the ex-wazir, stung with the ingratitude of his sovereign, and unwilling to yield to him so tamely, laid siege to the capital and sent for Raja Suraj Mal Jat.[XVI] The Afghans, the natural enemies of Safdar Jang, joined the imperial army under young Ghazi-ud-din Imad-ul-mulk. The Jats, instigated by the angry Nawab, so thoroughly sacked old Delhi and its neighbourhood that the people still remember it as *Jat-gardi*[7] or Jat loot which takes rank in their memory, with two other classic loots the *Shahgardi* of Ahmad Shah Abdali, and

---

XVI. Suraj Mal received most pressing call for help from Wazir Safdarjang at Ghasira. Qanungo does not mention Suraj Mal's campaign(Feb 1753 - April 1753) against Bahadur Singh Bargujar of Ghasira. See for detailed description, Sudan, *Sujan Charitra,* 103-140, 146; for brief account see, *Tarikh-i-Ahmad Shahi,* 47a. —Ed.

7. *Imad,* p. 63.

the *Bhao-gardi* of the Marathas before Panipat. But the Mughals in the service of Safdar Jang deserted him to a man, and joined their Turani brethren under Ghazi-ud-din. His only hope now rested upon Raja Suraj Mal, and the Jat proved no broken reed to him in this hour of supreme need. Promises of high honours and threats of vengeance were treated with equal scorn by that faithful chief, who was determined to fight to the last for his ally, though his was clearly a lost cause. In order to terrify him, Ghazi-ud-din sent for Malhar Rao Holkar from the south. But this was equally unavailing; the clever Jat took advantage of the jealousy of the new wazir Intizam-ud-daula towards his ambitious nephew Ghazi-ud-din, whose motive he suspected and whose ability he dreaded. So successful was the diplomatic move of Suraj Mal that before the Marathas could arrive offers of peace were made from the Emperor's side; Maharaja Madho Singh Kachhwah, who came to Delhi about the end of 1753, was asked to mediate. The Jat Raja refused to sheathe his sword unless the Emperor restored the viceroyalties of Oudh and Allahabad, if not the office of wazir also, to Safdar Jang. At last peace was concluded on the above conditions, and the Nawab departed to rule his suba. Suraj Mal had saved his ally from almost inevitable ruin by drawing upon himself the implacable enemity of Ghazi-ud-din, the full force of which he was made to feel very soon.[8] [XVII]

8. For a detailed account of this civil war, see Tarikh-i-Muzaffari, pp. 65-75. *Bayan-o-Waqa*, pp. 270-280. Harcharan Das also describes this civil war in five pages. The general narrative given in *Tarikh-i-Muzaffari* is more authentic.

XVII. For a critical account of available sources of this civil war, see, G. C. Dwivedi, *The Jats: their role in the Mughal Empire*, pp. 130 - 137. —Ed.

CHAPTER V

SURAJMAL'S STRUGGLE WITH THE MARATHAS

Maratha invasion of Bharatpur

The Jats and the Marathas had met together for the first time in 1749, (1748. ed.) but then it was as auxiliaries fighting on opposite sides in the Kachhwaha War of Succession after the death of Maharaja Sawai Jai Singh. Three years later (1752) Raja Suraj Mal and Malhar Rao Holkar had fought shoulder to shoulder as hired allies of Nawab Safdar Jang in his war against the Ruhela Afghans. During the civil war between the Emperor Ahmad Shah and the ex-wazir Safdar Jang in 1752, Ghazi-ud-din Imad-ul-mulk had invited the Marathas to aid him against Raja Suraj Mal and Nawab Safdar Jang. In Oct. 1753, Raghunath Rao, with a large army under renowned chiefs, started on his first expedition to Northern India, having for its main object the plunder of the flourishing Jat principality, yet unvisited by them. Raja Suraj Mal had not given them the least provocation to justify a war. They crossed the Chambal at the ford of Dholpur and entered the territories of Bharatpur. The Jat Raja sent his *purohit* Rupram Katari as an envoy to Raghunath Rao to negotiate for terms, and in the meanwhile hurriedly put Bharatpur, Ramgarh (modern Aligarh) and his other forts in a state of defence, stocking them with provisions and war materials. He concentrated his main army at Kumher, midway between Deeg and Bharatpur, the best strategic position imaginable for the defence of the heart of his dominion. Raghunath Rao demanded the extravagant ransom (*khandani*) of one krore of rupees; Rupram agreed to forty lakhs at the utmost. The Marathas resumed their advance, and the envoy came back promising to procure a reply from his master. Suraj Mal wrote to Raghunath either to accept peacefully forty lakhs or to take to war; and with the letter he sent five cannon-balls and some gun-powder as samples of the hospitable fare he might expect in the Jat country. In January 1754 the invaders appeared before Kumher and the frowning look of that gaint fort dispelled their delusion. Raghunath in his avarice had overshot the mark, and now regretted his unjudicious demand. Somewhat cast down, he ordered batteries to be erected against the fort. With the imperial *risala* and *topkhana*, Ghazi-ud-din[1] joined the Maratha army and infused more vigour into the camp of besiegers.

Siege of Kumher (Jan. 1754–May 1754)

The Maratha batteries failed to make any impression upon the walls of Kumher and their main army was held at bay by the resolute enemy. One day, young Khande Rao Holkar,[2] the only son of Malhar, after taking his meal went, drawn by fate as it were, to an advanced battery and was struck down by a stray bullet from a Jat swivel-gun (*jazail*).[XVIII] Revenge nerved the arm of the Maratha, and the Jats began to feel its weight. Three months thus passed

1. He made a forced march of 22 *kos* from Hodal to Mathura in one day, (15th Rabi 11, 1167 = Feb., 1765). See *Waqa,* 85.
2. He was about thirty years of age at this time, The *Waqa* makes an entry, recording his death under the date 4th Jamada 1,, 1167 A.H. = Wednesday, Feb. 27, 1754.[XVIII] This corresponds with the time "*About a month and half* after the begining of the siege" by *Bhao Bakhar,* p.4.

XVIII. Date of Khanderao's death is 17 March 1754. See P.C. Chandavat, *Maharaj Suraj Mal Aur Unka Yug,* 113, f.n.6; G. C. Dwivedi though does not give exact date, also indicate middle of March not in the month of February. *The Jats: Their role in the Mughal Empire,* 147. The memorial of Khanderao is situated in Gangersauli Village near Kumher fort. —Ed.

away, and every day the prospects became gloomier for Suraj Mal. There was no power in Hindustan, bold enough to lift a finger to help him openly against the Marathas. Rajputana lay prostrate at their feet; the Emperor of Hindustan was hostile and powerless, and even the ally Safdar Jang was too afraid of the Maratha lance to move alone. The destruction of Suraj Mal appeared to be only a question of time.[XIX] Like a Rajput, the Jat calmly waited for that awful hour when the smoke of the horrible sacrifice of

XIX. Every ruler by diplomacy tries to win over the allies of his enemy- at the time of war against him. Surajmal also wrote to the Wazir Intizam-ud-daula and the Emperor against Imad-Maratha combine. The Jats also contacted Scinde whose estrangement with Malharrao Holkar was well known. G.C. Dwivedi observes- "But the rest of the version of Bhao Bakher seems to be overdrawn. The forts which in point of their strength evoked the lavish praise of all the contemporaries and which fifty years later were to baffle the mighty British for two long years, were not going to succumb to the Holkar's wrath only. Suraj Mal was a courageous man, he retained his habitual calm and poise even in most desperate situations. In the present case, Kumher, to use his own words, was "almost impregnable" and it contained provisions sufficient to last "more than a year". All this militates against his supposed increasing despair. The fact, as borne out by the contemporary sources, is that despite the enemy "deluge" the Jats made persistent forays and thus kept the enemy in "great alarm". There was no night when their raids were not sure, just as no day passed by when the enemy convoys were not attacked. Backed by the fort artillery they hovered round "as if there was no enemy in the environment of harming them at all". The Marathi letters and the Court history generally support this defiant spirit of the defenders. Thus, we learnt that Naro Shankar had to seek safety in flight before a Jat force from Deeg. Another letter eludes to an encounter having taken place between the Marathas and the Jat foraying party from Deeg. The later, however, disappeared when Dattaji arrived on the spot. On the night of 1st April 1754 (7th Jamadi II), Suraj Mal interviewed the Jaipur general, Natani, outside the fort of Kumher. Thereafter a Jat artillery force came out and attacked the enemy trenches in the plain. The battle was even with casualties on both sides. Again, on 30th April, a Jat squardon surprised Shivdeo, killing 41 Maratha soldiers and wresting his total sum of Rupees 29,500. Earlier (c. late in March) a Jat force from Wair under Bahadur Singh, fell upon a Maratha detachment and grabbed "a lot of money" along with a few (two or three) distinguished Maratha ladies of the Holkar's family. Malhar justly felt humiliated at this boldness. Suraj Mal was, however, courteous enough to send the ladies lack honourably. These sporadic instances suffice to belie the fancied despair of Suraj Mal and his imminent destruction." *The Jats: Their role in the Mughal Empire*, 147-148 f.n. 64-69. For diplomatic efforts by Suraj Mal see P.C. Chandavat, 115-116. —Ed.

his females (*Jauhar*) would ascend to heaven, giving signal to him to rush forth sword in hand to find an honourable death. Though equally indifferent to death the Jatni, bred in a freer atmosphere, with a wider outlook of the world and a deeper penetration of human character than the Rajput lady, proved to be more optimistic and resourceful. Hansia[3] (the 'smiling one', wife of Suraj Mal) roused the droping spirits of her husband, telling him to trust her and banish despair from his mind. She had heard of Jayaji Appa Sindhia, as a man, generous, straightforward, and chivalrous, who could be trusted more than any other Maratha chief; the mutual jealousy among the Maratha leaders, and their accessibility to bribe were also not unknown to her. In order to create division in the enemy's camp, she one night sent Tejram Katari, son of Rupram, with a letter from Suraj Mal and his turban to Jayaji Sindhia, to implore his protection and friendship by an exchange of head-dress. Jayaji made a noble response, accepted the pledge of Suraj Mal and sent him his own turban in exchange with an encouraging letter, and a leaf of the sacred *Bel tree,* taken from the offerings to his patron deity (*Bel Bhandar*), as the most solemn proof of his sincerity. The news of the incident leaked out and Holkar became despondent.[4]

Suraj Mal himself, spurred to exertion by his energetic wife, began to intrigue with the Emperor and the wazir Intizam-ud-daulah, who had viewed with misgivings the junction of Ghazi-ud-din with the Marathas. The timid Emperor also feared the dictatorship of Ghazi-ud-din no less than that of Safdar Jang. A mighty wicked spirit had been conjured up which might as well break the neck of the conjurers. He wrote letters to the Emperor as well as to the new wazir that Ghazi-ud-din by allying himself with the Marathas was bringing the empire to ruin. Who should stand across his path when he chooses to push aside his old uncle from the wazirat or deal harshly with His Majesty, if

3. The editor of *Bhao Bakhar* (p.5, foot-note 17) Sanskritises the name as *Anasua,* with unnecessary philological discussion. For a Jat girl, this is, however too learned and poetic a name beyond the comprehension of the countryfolk.
4. *Bhao Bakhar,* p.6.

no bridle is now put on his ambition and no check upon his sinister activities? Ghazi-ud-din had sent for some heavy cannon from the citadel of Delhi. But Intizam-ud-daula, who did not desire the success of his nephew, advised the Emperor not to send them. He shrewdly remarked that if the warlike resources of the Marathas, the vast wealth and strong forts, conquered from Suraj Mal, and the imperial topkhana were placed at the disposal of the turbulent and unscrupulous Ghazi-ud-din, his ambition would exceed all the bounds of imagination.

Suraj Mal and Intizam-ud-daula were busy in weaving a net of diplomacy round the Marathas and Ghazi-ud-din. The Emperor himself became a party to the conspiracy. Under the royal seal letters were sent to Maharaja Madho Singh of Jaipur, the Raja of Marwar; and Safdar Jang - who had all suffered much at the hands of the Marathas - asking them to unite their forces under the imperial standard and relieve Hindustan of these southern pests. Assurances being given by all, the actual plan of the intended attack was left to be devised by Suraj Mal. He suggested that the Emperor, under the pretence of hunting and visiting the crownlands in the Doab should reach Koel [Aligarh], and halt there till Nawab Safdar Jang joined him. On the arrival of the Oudh troops he was to march rapidly to the city of Agra where the Kachhwaha and Rathor Rajas would meet him with their armies. The plan was to form a cordon on the Chambal, so that the enemy might not escape. If the Marathas raised the siege of Kumher and marched upon Agra, Suraj Mal was to come close behind them and join the Emperor.

The Emperor started from the capital with his army, Court and harem, and by leisurely marches reached the neighbourhood of Sikandra.[XX] Nawab Safdar Jang also arrived at Mehdighat on the Ganges and encamped there expecting the Emperor at Koel. But the Emperor, instead of marching to Koel and putting himself in the shelter of its strong fort, delayed at Sikandra, enlisting new troops. In

XX. The author confuses *Sikandrabad* (21 KM west of Bulandshahar District) with Sikandra, the famous tomb of Akbar near Agra. Had the Emperor reached Sikandra the plan would have succeeded. For details of siege of Kumher see G.C. Dwivedi, *The Jats: Their Role in the Mughal Empire*, 145-150. —Ed.

the mean while Malhar Rao secretly left the siege-camp at Kuhmir with five thousand horses, intending to swoop down upon the unsuspecting royal quarry and appropriate the gain alone. The imperial camp was surprised; its treasures and equipages, and some of the ladies of the harem and the whole park of artillery fell into the hands of Marathas. The imbecile Emperor and his cowardly minister fled in disguise. The Marathas chased them towards Delhi and besieged the capital. Intizam-ud-daula put the city in some sort of defence, foolishly expecting help from the Rajput princes, Safdar Jang and Suraj Mal.[5] Ghazi-ud-din withdrew his army from the siege of Kumher and joined the Marathas. Still suspecting a combination of enemies, he invited the Ruhela chief-Najib-ud-daula to his assistance, promising him a high post and a liberal subsidy.

The fort was captured; the Emperor with his mother and other relations was made prisoners. Intizam-ud-daula was dismissed from office and the eyes of the Emperor were blinded by the order of Ghazi-ud-din. He himself became wazir and raised to the throne another prince Aziz-ud-din with the title Alamgir II. (10th Shaban, 1167 A.H. = 2nd June, Sunday, 1754), [*Waqa*, 91]. It was now too late for Suraj Mal to retrieve the situation. Safdar Jang was being watched by Najib-ud-daula, who was in league with Ghazi-ud-din. The rajas of Rajputana did not move, seeing that the plan had miscarried. Suraj Mal cannot be held responsible for the miserable fate of the Emperor, which the latter owned solely to his own negligence and want of discretion. Had he reached Koel encamped within its strong walls, surprise would have been impossible and his junction with Safdar Jang, who was waiting at Mehdighat, would have been easily effected. Such deplorable carelessness and lack of discipline prevailed in the Emperor's camp, that when Holkar fired some rockets at a distance to feel the pulse of the enemy, none in the imperial camp cared to go out and reconnoitre. Worse still they surmised that perhaps Aqibat

5. The best account of the counter-plot against Ghazi-ud-din and the intrigues of both parties are to be found in the *Tarikh-i-Muzaffari* [MS. 84-94] which differs considerably from the *Siyar* (text, ii. 48-49).

Mahmud, a lieutenant of Ghazi-ud-din might be burning some village. They contentedly went to repose, but lo! the thieves broke in and the brave lords and princes were soon in headlong fight. At any rate the immediate object of Raja Suraj Mal's diplomacy, viz., to turn away the Marathas from Kumher, was eminently successful. This unexpected success opened moralluring vistas of aggression to the Marathas. Standing behind the throne of the Great Mughal, the heart of the Maratha nation throbbed with a nobler impulse and they cast their wistful eyes upon the glimmering waves of the far-off Indus. The siege was practically raised when Malhar Rao and Ghazi-ud-din marched off towards Sikandra (bad). The Maratha army had already eaten up the supplies of the neighbouring country and scarcity pressed the besiegers more than the besieged. They dispersed in small bodies, leaving Jayaji Appa Sindhia before Kumher. Malhar Rao and Ghazi-ud-din, who still found themselves beset with many difficulties, forgot their old animosity and tried to win over so steadfast a friend and so redoubtable an adversary as Suraj Mal. Through the mediation of Sindhia, peace was concluded with him on the condition of the Jat Raja paying an indemnity of 60 lakhs. The Marathas evacuated the Jat territory, Raghunath Rao starting for home and Jayaji Sindhia for Marwar[6] (June 1754).

---

6. *Bhao Bakhar*, p.10. It is doubtful whether the stipulated sum was paid at all. Persian authorities and French MS, are silent about it.

CHAPTER VI

AHMAD SHAH DURRANI'S CAMPAIGN AGAINST THE JATS

1169 A.H. (Nov. 1756–April 1757)

Suraj Mal's struggle with the Abdali

Raja Suraj Mal was left undisturbed by the new Government of Delhi for about a year, as Ghazi-ud-din and the Marathas were busy in the Punjab. The Afghans were driven across the Indus, and again that province became a part of the empire. A quarrel soon sprang up between the wazir Ghazi-ud-din, and Najib-ud-daula (the Amir-ul-umra), who resented the dictatorship of his rival. The Emperor Alamgir II, being a nonentity, whose movements were swayed by the will of his keeper, the imperial camp had no room for two such equally ambitious and powerful grandees. Najib-ud-daula feared the alliance of the Marathas with Ghazi-ud-din, who might some day bring him to account with their help. He looked for protection to the Durrani Shah, and opened treasonable negotiations with him. Ghazi-ud-din made peace with Raja Suraj Mal as a counterweight to the alienation of the Ruhela chief. In the second year of Alamgir II's reign; Ahmad Shah Durrani again crossed the Indus (Rabi I., 1169; Nov. 1756), and marched rapidly upon the capital to punish Ghazi-ud-din. Antaji Mankeshwar and other Marathas in the pay of the wazir anticipated the Afghan freebooters, and after thoroughly looting the old fort, and the suburbs of the capital, fled at midnight. Ghazi-ud-din surrendered himself to the Shah in his camp at Narela. On his arrival at Delhi he was utterly fleeced, having to pay about one krore of Rupees and to lose the office of wazir. Ahmad Shah sat on the throne of Delhi and issued coins in his own name (8th Jamada I., = Saturday 29th January 1757). Raja Suraj Mal being nearest among the refractory chiefs, the wrath of the Shah turned upon him first with all its pent up fury.[XXI] Jawahar Singh, son of Suraj Mal, was watching the movements of the Afghan army from Ballamgarh[1] with five or six thousand troops. He cut off a foraging party of the Afghans, who had gone towards Faridabad. The Shah was extremely enraged, and that very night sent Abdus Samad Khan, with instructions to decoy the infidels into an ambush. The Jat prince almost fell into the trap, by chasing a squadron of the enemy's cavalry to their hiding place. He made his escape losing some followers and a part of the booty. The Afghans looted some villages and beheaded as many men as they could capture. On the 22nd Jamada I., = Saturday 12th Feb. 1757 Ahmad Shah left Delhi and marched against the Jats with the determination of conquering Deeg, Kumher and Bharatpur. A strong division of the army was sent ahead under the command of Jahan Khan (the Durrani general), and Najib-ud-daula, with these instructions, "Move into the boundaries of the accursed Jat, and in every town and district held by him slay and plunder. The city of Mathura is a holy place of the Hindus, and I have heard Suraj Mal is there; let it be put entirely to the edge of the sword. To the best of your power leave nothing in that kingdom and country. Up to Akbarabad (Agra) leave nothing standing." Not satisfied with this command to his generals the Shah directed the mace-bearers "to convey a general order to the army to plunder and slay at every place they reached. Any booty they acquired was made a free grant to them. Every person cutting off and bringing in heads of infidels should throw them down before the tent of the chief minister, wherewith to build a high tower. An account would be drawn up and

---

XXI. For discordant note see, G.C. Dwivedi, *The Jats: their role in the Mughal Empire* 167-168. Dwivedi concludes that grabbing the Jat wealth was the primary reason of the Afghan expedition'. – Ed.

1. Ballamgarh is written Ballabgarh in the modern atlas, 22 miles south-west of Delhi on G.I.P. Ry.; Faridabad, 16 miles south-west of Delhi.

five Rupees per head would be paid them from the Government funds." This was not a war but a scalp-gathering expedition on a big scale, worthy of a Red Indian Chief.

The campaign began with the siege of Ballamgarh,[2] as Jawahar Singh had taken his post there with two Maratha chiefs, Shamsher Bahadur and Antaji Mankeshwar. The fort was bravely defended for two days. On the third night the son of Suraj Mal and the Maratha leaders fled in disguise; a few men left in the fort to cover the flight, were put to death by the Afghans. Twelve thousand Rupees, some horses, and camels fell into the hands of the victors. Ahmad Shah at once sent out parties for making a vigorous search for the fugitives in the neighbouring places. But Jawahar Singh and the Maratha leaders, dressing themselves in Qizzilbash (Persian) clothes had gone through an underground chamber into the ditch of the fort, threaded their way through the Shah's troops, and hidden in some ravines near the Jamuna. For two days and nights they did not come out, even to drink water from the river.

The Shah halted for two days and ordered a general slaughter and plundering. An eyewitness, a Sayyid who was in the Afghan camp, thus describes their raids : "It was at midnight when the camp-followers went to the attack. It was thus managed: one horseman mounted a horse and took ten to twenty others, each tied to the tail of the horse, preceding it, and drove them just like a string of camels. When it was one watch after sunrise I saw them came back. Every horseman had loaded up all his horses with the plundered property, and atop it rode girl-captives and slaves. The severed heads were tied up in rugs like bundles of grain, and placed on the heads of the captives, and thus did they return to the camp . . . . Daily did this manner of slaughter and plundering proceed. It was a marvellous state of things, this slaying and capturing, and no whit inferior to the day of the Last Judgment. All those heads that had been cut off were built into pillars, and the men upon whose heads bloody bundles had been brought in, were made to grind corn, and then, when the reckoning was made up,

---

2. This was not originally intended by the Shah. He was prevailed upon by Ghazi-ud-din to besiege it.

their heads too were cut off. These things went on all the way to the city of Akbarabad, nor was any part of the country spared." [Irvine's translation of a Persian Ms., *Indian Antiquary,* Vol. xxxvi. p. 60]

Jahan Khan had also carried out to the letter his master's instructions. On the 28th February 1757, two days after the *holi,* he suddenly appeared before the doomed city of Mathura. The inhabitants had little apprehension of the terrible fate which was to overtake them in the midst of the gay rejoicings of the spring season. Mathura was an unfortified city, without walls and ditches, easily accessible on all sides. Suraj Mal had left there about 5000 troops, to defend the city against the Durrani generals. Though taken by surprise, they gave a good account of themselves. After an obstinate fight in which three thousand Jats fell in the defence, the holy city was taken by these Afghans and an awful carnage began. A detachment of the Shah's troops attacked Gokul lying to the south of Mathura. About four thousand warlike Naga sannyasis, ever ready to die for their religion, assembled there; two thousand of them fell after killing an equal number of Pathans. Gokul was saved;[3] the Musalmans turned back terrified by militant *Hindu* fanaticism. But they met with no resistance at Brindaban, the earthly paradise of an *effeminate* cult—the resort of females and unsexed males. And a terrible treatment was meted out to it by the followers of a sturdier faith.

That year the *holi* was played afresh by the Durranis with the blood of the Hindus; the whole city of Mathura burnt like a huge bonfire such as was never lighted on the merry moonlit night of the *holi.* Groans of outraged women and cries of mothers from whose bosom the fiendish soldiery tore away their children for slaughter, echoed through the burning streets. The blue current of the Jamuna of the poet's imagination flowed blood-red for seven days and yellowish for a week more. The devotees of the degenerate Vaishnavism, who lived in bowers beside the stream, dreaming of the frolics of the Divine Cowherd and hearing in ecstasy the tune of his amorous flute, met with a fit

3. See Sardesai's *Panipat Prakaran,* (in Marathi), p. 77.

retribution. The throats of the meek babajis were cut in the exact manner of Muhammadan butchers, in their dwelling places.[4] In each hut lay a severed head (of a *bairagi*), with the head of a slaughtered cow applied to its mouth and tied to it with a rope round its neck. [*Ind. Ant.* Vol. 36, p. 62]. The Musalman inhabitants of the city also did not fare much better at the hands of their co-religionists. They saved their heads but not their honour and property. The soldiers of the Shah so scrupulously enforced his order that those who declared themselve Musalmans had to strip themselves naked and show the sign of circumcision, before they were let off. At Mathura, about 14 days after massacre, a stark naked figure crept out of a heap of ruins and stood before the Mir Sahib, who penned this horrible account, asking for a little food. On being questioned he related the following story : "I am a Musalman; I was a dealer in jewellery, my shop was a large one. On the day of slaughter . . . . a horseman, drawn sword in hand, came at me and tried to kill me. I said I was a Musalman. He said "Disclose your privities." I undid my cloth. He continued "Whatever cash you have, give to me so that I may spare your life. I gave him my 4,000 rupees. Another came and cut me on the stomach with his sabre. I fled and hid in a corner" (*ibid,* p. 62). Brindaban met with a worse fate, as the Mir Sahib's description bears out. "Wherever you gazed you beheld only heaps of slain. You could only pick your way with difficulty, owing to the quantity of bodies lying about and the amount of blood spilt. *At one place,* we saw about *two hundred dead children in a heap. Not one of the dead bodies had a head . . . .* The stench and fetor and effluvium in the air were such that it was painful to open your mouth or even draw a breath. Every one held his nose and stopped his mouth with his handkerchief while he spoke" [*Ibid.* p. 62].

About the middle of March, Ahmad Shah reached Mathura and was gratified to see what his generals had done. Jahan Khan and Najib-ud-daula were exalted by the gift of *khilats* and commanded "to move on to Akbarabad where there are many wealthy men who were subjects of

---

4. *Bhao Bakhar,* 34.

the Jat." The city of Agra was also depopulated by a general slaughter and the fort invested. Fortunately an epidemic broke out in the Shah's army—150 men dying every day. It took one hundred rupees to purchase one seer of tamarind. The Shah made up his mind to march back to his country. Jahan Khan was called back from the siege of the citadel of Agra. His return march began on the 27th of March and by the 29th the Jat country was cleared of enemies. [*Ind. Ant.*, Vol. xxxvi, pp. 64-65]. The campaign of Ahmad Shah was a failure from the military point of view : Suraj Mal's strength remained almost unimpaired. Deeg and Bharatpur were not taken, nor was their proud owner brought to his knee. Only two or three undefended towns were captured and the civilian population massacred. He had failed to draw out Suraj Mal and make him fight. Suraj Mal's tactics were to play a waiting game till the heat of the Indian plains would drive the Abdali away or bring upon the scene the Marathas, who were reported on the banks of the Narmada. When the Durrani threatened to advance from Mathura upon Kumher, he amused him with the offer of a krore of Rupees as *peshkash*, if the Shah would postpone his march. A few days after, Suraj Mal now grown bolder at the Shah's distress, wrote to him bluntly, as advised by Rupram Katari, "I cannot pay more than ten lakhs as *peshkash*; let there be peace and amity between us by your acceptance of this; otherwise continuation of hostilities is decided upon."[5] Shah was glad to agree to this little, as his brave Afghans were dying by hundreds every day. A written agreement for paying ten lakhs was executed by Suraj Mal, and the Durrani army retreated to Delhi. But of this sum the Jat Raja did not pay a single penny.

Suraj Mal's alliance with Ghazi-ud-din and the Marathas

Scarcely had the Northern tempest abated its fury, when a deluge came from the south to overwhelm Hindustan. It stopped only at the foot of the Himalayas and the bank of

5. *Bhao Bakhar*, p. 38. For another version, see Wendel, 39; "His good fortune so willed it that he had no need to give a penny of what he had promised."

the Indus, threatening to engulf Islam in India; sweeping off momentarily all vestiges of the Durrani conquest, and submerging all the Muslim principalities in Northern India. The victory of the Shah was a triumph of Ghazi-ud-din's rival, the Ruhela chief Najib-ud-daula, whom the conqueror left as his deputy in charge of the person of the titular Emperor Alamgir II and the imperial city. The office of the wazir had been taken away from him and restored to his intriguing uncle Intizam-ud-daula. Ghazi-ud-din burnt with the thirst of revenge against the Emperor, the wazir, and the Amir-ul-umra, and to gratify it he invited the Marathas again. Raghunath Rao came to Hindustan second time (Nov. 1756–Oct. 1757), and infused a new life among the despondent Maratha chiefs. Delhi was recaptured and Ghazi-ud-din reinstated as wazir. Najib-ud-daula escaped the terrible vengeance of his turimphant rival by throwing himself upon the mercy of Malhar Rao Holkar, whom he called his god-father (*Dharma Pita*). Raghunath reconquered the Punjab, defeated the Durrani's general Jahan Khan, and his son Taimur Shah, and drove them across the Indus. A *de facto* Maratha dominion was established throughout Northern India.

Raja Suraj Mal swam cautiously with the current. He had now to make choice between the Abdali and the Marathas: between an enemy of his faith and his own unscrupulous co-religionists. His Pan-Hinduistic ideal inclined him to the Maratha cause, though their conduct inspired little confidence. But he was too prudent to join them in their offensive campaigns and thereby diminish his resources and earn the enmity of his Muslim neighbours. This informal Jat-Maratha alliance was of a purely defensive nature against the foreign Afghan invaders. The political views of the great Jat chief, expressed on many occasions during this period, deserve high admiration, and had the Maratha Government acted upon them their *de fecto* sovereignty in Hindustan would have remained long unshaken. Suraj Mal in the first place recognised the supreme necessity of doing away with the traitor Najib-ud-daula and crushing thoroughly the colonies of Ruhela Afghans before the Durrani should find time to come to their relief: in short, the prospect of any assistance from the traitors within to the invader from Afghanistan must be cut off. Raghunath Rao and Dattaji Sindhia were also of the same view, and would have killed Najib-ud-daula, but for the unwise and interested intervention of Malhar Rao Holkar. Secondly, Suraj Mal's desire was to make Nawab Shuja-ud-daula the wazir of the empire in place of Ghazi-ud-din. This was not at all dictated by personal prejudice. Ghazi ud-din was an isolated figure in Northern India; having neither territorial nor family influence, his position was extremely weak. On the other hand Nawab Shuja-ud-daula was practically the independent and hereditary ruler of a large and wealthy kingdom. This would bring the requisite strength for the maintenance of the dignity of the wazirat, without making him independent of the support of the Marathas. His family being of Persian origin, and of the Shia faith, he had no extra-territorial attachment like that of Ruhela Afghans to the Abdali, so as to make him dangerous and formidable like Najib Khan.[6]

The inevitable crash came a couple of years later. Najib-ud-daula besieged for about a year at Sukkartal, remained unsubdued owing to the scarcely veiled enmity of Holkar to other Maratha leaders. The racial sympathy of Ruhela leaders like Hafiz Rahmat Khan, Dundi Khan, and others, was with Najib-ud-daula and Abdali. But they could not hitherto move owing to the fear of Nawab Shuja-ud-daula. The designs of Holkar against Oudh having now become known. The Nawab became extremely alarmed and was driven to form a coalition with them to help Najib-ud-daula, though he was strongly averse to their proposal of inviting the Shah from Kabul. The unhappy Emperor Alamgir II found the throne of his ancestors not even the softest of chairs under the humiliating dictatorship of Ghazi-ud-din. He sent secret letters to the

6. Malhar Rao Holkar advocated and acted upon a contrary policy, viz., to uphold the power of his *dharmaputra* Najib Khan, and with Najib's help crush Nawab Shuja-ud-daula and conquer the kingdom of Oudh. This would, he thought, bring the whole of India from Attock to Rameshwar under the shadow of the Peshwa's umbrella, i.e., sovereignty! (*Panipat Prakaran,* p. 103). With leaders, so much deficient in farsight and statesmanship, no nation, however brave in war, did ever succeed in building up an enduring empire.

Abdali entreating him to rescue him from the galling yoke of his cruel wazir and restore to him Najib-ud-daula, the best of his gaolers. The Shah, in order to wipe off the past disgrace and avenge the defeat of his son and his generals, crossed the Indus for the fourth time (Thursday, 25th Oct., 1759)[7]. The wazir had his uncle Intizam-ud-daula and the Emperor, murdered, as they were suspected of being in secret league with the invader, and raised another prince to the throne under the title of Shah Jahan II (8th Rabi II, 1173 H. = Thursday, 29th Nov. 1759). The Shah steadily marched towards Najib Khan's territory and was there joined by all the Ruhela chiefs and the Nawab Shuja-ud-daula. But there was no unanimity in the Maratha camp. They were defeated in several small engagements; a panic set in among them. Dataji Sindhia raised the siege of Sukkartal on 11th Dec. 1759, and came to Delhi. Consternation and dismay prevailed everywhere; the imperial capital became deserted. Those who had anything, either honour or wealth, to lose, fled southwards, to the territory of the Jats, which became the hospitable asylum of both Hindu and Muhammadan fugitives. The Maratha chief also sent their wives and children to the protection of Raja Suraj Mal. And with them came the harem of the wazir of Hindustan, who did not hesitate to trust the honour of ladies to the custody of his generous foe. Suraj Mal had hitherto maintained an attitude of suspicious aloofness while the fortunes of the Marathas were in the ascendant. But at this critical stage, he was not deterred by the fear of the Abdali's vengeance from coming forward and standing by their side. The Jat had not forgotten the good done to him by Jayaji Appa Sindhia during the siege of Kumher, and was on the look out for an opportunity to return it. While Dattaji Sindhia was yet before the fort of Sukkartal, and Delhi was without adequate Maratha troops, Suraj Mal sent 5,000 Jats to reassure the people and aid in the defence of the city.[XXII] Seeing the overwhelming superiority

7. 3rd Rabi. I. 1173 H.; (*Waqa*, p. 135).

XXII. Qanungo does not take note of the Sindhia's invitation to Suraj Mal. 5000 Jat troops under Rup Ram Kataria joined Sindhia on 8th November, 1759, at Sukkartal not at Delhi. On 8th December Sindhia raised the futile siege of Sukkartal. On 20th December, 1759 he entrusted his family, heavy baggage and the disabled camp followers to the care of the Jats to be escorted to Delhi. On 4th January 1760 Rupram Kataria escorted them towards the Jat country. Rajwade, I, 143, 144, 147, 150; S.P.D., II 110; cited by G. C. Dwivedi, *The Jats: Their role in the Mughal Empire*, 178. —Ed.

of the enemy, every one advised Dattaji to retreat beyond the Chambal and wait for the arrival of reinforcements. But that noble hero, conscious of the responsibility of the new role which his country aspired (him) to play, resolved to demonstrate in the open field that Maharashtra would not shrink from paying the necessary price in blood for the dominion of India. He reached Delhi on the 3rd January 1760 and told Jankoji Sindhia to go home with the ladies. But the latter firmly refused, having resolved to stay and share the fate of his chief. Rupram Katari conducted the ladies to Suraj Mal's territory for safety. On the plain of Badli, about 8 miles from Delhi Dattaji gave battle to the Abdali in the first week of Jamada II, 1173.[8] Long and fierce was the conflict. Inspired by their brave leader, the Marathas reckless of life, fought with a dashing valour and perseverance never displayed before by that people in Hindustan. But the superior generalship of the Durrani and the greater staying power of the Ruhelas won the day. The Marathas left ten thousand men by the least computation dead on the field. The Jats carried Jankoji, wounded and disabled, and other survivors to the fort of Kumher.

The wazir Ghazi-ud-din Imad-ul-mulk, divining the probable issue, had left Delhi before the battle.[XXIII] Fallen from fortune he stood a suppliant at the gate of Suraj Mal's fort for an asylum which he despaired of getting any where else against the wrath of the victorious Shah. This was the same Ghazi-ud-din who, as Father Wendel and Ghulam Ali (author of *Imad-us-Saadat*) remind us, had shortly before armed All Hindustan to destroy Suraj Mal and sat as an implacable foe before those very walls whose protection he now sought. Suraj Mal came out and conducted his honourable guest in "with all attention and respect befitting

8. All Persian histories including *Siyar*, say that this battle took place in the month of *Jamadi-ul-Akhir* which begins on Jan. 20, 1760. *Waqa* makes no exact entry. It took place in the last week of January.

XXIII. According to Ali Muhammad Khan, Wazir Imad fled to Suraj Mal's fort Kumher after the defeat of Dattaji at Barari Ghat on 9th January 1760. He had already sent his family members there in November 1759. *Mirat-i-Ahmadi*, p. 905; cited by P. C. Chandavat, *Maharaj Suraj Mal Aur Unka Yug*, 159, f.n.2. —Ed.

his rank."[9] We are told that he richly furnished his best palace at Bharatpur for the use of Ghazi-ud-din, amply provided for the comfort, security and honour of the wazir and his family, and treated him rather like a master on a visit to the house of a servant. In the meanwhile, the Shah after making himself master of the capital, demanded one krore of Rupees from Suraj Mal as fine for his disloyal conduct. The Jat Raja was too prudent to supply the sinews of war to his enemy, whose next demand, as he knew would be the surrender of the fugitives. He banished all idea of peace with the perfidious invader and made up his mind to spend that sum more honourably in carrying on a war of defence. All Hindustan rejoiced over the fall of the Marathas, and the joy was shared even by the Hindus who had suffered rather more severely from their rapine than the Musalmans had done. Their character and conduct created no confidence among the people of Northern India. Their hand had been against everybody and now everybody's hand was against them. Rajputana had suffered so much at their hands, that Rajput princes, like Madho Singh of Amber, and Bijay Singh of Marwar, greeted the victory of the Abdali with as much joy as their unhappy descendants evinced forty years after, at the victory of Lord Lake over the same race.[10]

But Raja Suraj Mal who had suffered equally at their hands, viewed the situation in another light, and acted with greater foresight to gain higher political ends. It was not merely the sentiment of gratitude to the Jayaji Appa Sindhia that determined his conduct during this critical period. To him the annual Maratha raid appeared to be a lesser evil than the revival of a strong Muhammadan empire under a new dynasty, viz., that of the Durrani. He regarded the presence of the Marathas in Northern India as a great political necessity to keep out all foreign invaders and hold the balance between the Hindu and the Muhammadan powers.

---

9. Wendel, 51; *Imad*, 73.
10. The situation is graphically described in the contemporary Maratha letters :
माराठ्याचा हर्ष उड़न गेला, बहुत फिकिरींत पेडले, काल फिरला, जेरीस् आले जाटमाए जयाजी शिन्दयांचा कुम्भरील डपकार स्मरून. वरचेवर साह्य करीत हाते वाकी सर्व्व रजपुत सुहां मराठयांवर उडन आंचा वदनक्ष ह्मालावद्दल आनन्द मांनु लगले।

He was too much of a practical statesman to think of an exclusive and intolerant Hindu *swaraj* like the short-sighted Bhao. No one was more conscious—as we shall see hereafter—of the value of preserving the dignity of the Mughal imperial throne, as the only centre of attraction and the sole bond of union among newly risen Hindu and Muhammadan principalities. So far as we are in a position to infer from his attitude towards his neighbours, his aim was to establish a confederation of several practically autonomous States under the headship of the Mughal Emperor, having no other obligation than to combine under the imperial banner in times of common danger. He was willing to give the Mughal empire a new lease of life, *but not of power*, being averse to the idea of reviving the tradition and the formidable power that it had been in the days of Akbar and Aurangzeb, when aspiring smaller nationalities were mercilessly crushed under the dead-weight of the despotic imperialism of Delhi. Any attempt in that direction, he knew full well, could begin only with the destruction of the Jat Power. In his scheme, the Emperor was to remain only the dignified figurehead, all initiative and lead remaining with the wazir, who should not be allowed to become powerful enough to be independent of the support of the confederates or overthrow the house of Taimur, Suraj Mal fixed his choice upon Shuja-ud-daula, the wise and tolerant ruler of Oudh, to be the constitutional wazir of this confederated empire.

Ahmad Shan Durrani, after having put the affairs of Delhi in some order, started on 2nd February 1760 (14 Jamada II., 1173 H.) against Raja Suraj Mal, and on 7th February invested the fort of Deeg. But this seems to have been a mere demonstration, because we find him marching away towards Mewat on the 27th (*Waqa*, 170-171). Suraj Mal came out of his stronghold and made incursions into the Doab. The Jats plundered half of Koel and stormed the citadel of the town (March 17, 1760). The daily entries in the *Waqa-i-Shah Alam Sani* about the movements of the Durranis, Jats and the Marathas give us some idea of their tactics. While the Durrani was before Deeg, a Maratha detachment advanced from the direction of Rewari in order to draw away the Afghans in pursuit. Ahmad Shah chased them through Mewat, but they vanished in the desert tracts beyond Rewari, and another division of the Marathas apeared before Bahadurgarh (about 20 miles w. of Delhi), in the rear of the Abdali. When the Shah made one march towards Delhi they crossed the Jamuna and plundered Meerut and Sikandra.[XXIV] The Abdali started in pursuit and chased them towards Mathura and Agra. Again the Jats appeared in the Doab, plundering and conquering; in short they carried on a brilliantly planned running fight in concert with the remnants of the Maratha army (*Waqa*, 173).

Holkar and Suraj Mal, forgetting their old animosity, had become friends under the stress of adversity. Malhar Rao, who perhaps did not desire that his rival Dattaji should win the glory of defeating the Durrani, appeared tardily on the scene after the disastrous battle of Badli and asked Raja Suraj Mal to join him in giving another battle to the Afghans. But Suraj Mal refused to move until reinforcements came from the Peshwa. Holkar was once so completely surprised by the Abdali general Shah Pasand Khan at Sikandra[XXIV] in the Doab that his whole detachment was cut off, and he himself managed to flee with only his clothes on, riding upon a mare (*Siyar*, iii. 381). He never ventured to issue out again from Deeg where he had taken refuge in fear of the Abdali.

Aware of the impending danger that awaited him in Hindustan, the Shah hearing the reports of the vast Maratha preparation in the South, busied himself in forming a coalition of all princes, Hindu and Musalman, of Northern India, who had suffered so much at the hands of the southern robbers. He tried to convince them that his mission was that of their emancipation from the Maratha pest, and not one of conquest and new enslavement. He wished to detach Raja Suraj Mal and Ghazi-ud-din from their alliance with the Marathas, and for that purpose sent esteemed Ruhela chief Hafiz Rahamat Khan with proposals of peace[11] (*Tarikh-i-*

XXIV. Sikandra read as Sikandrabad in Bulandshahar District. – Ed.

11. In the month of Shawwal 1173 H., Hafiz Rahamat Khan went to Mathura to talk of a compromise with the Jat and Ghazi-ud-din, *Negotiations were cut off by the Jat* on the 23rd of Shawwal (8th June, 1760), when the Marathas approached (*Waqa*, 175). This corroborates the statement of the *Tarikh-i-Husaini*, the only Persian history which mentions the embassy of Hafiz-ul-mulk.

Husaini, 537). The fickleminded Ghazi-ud-din wavered, and Suraj Mal gave his guest complete liberty of action. News reached Delhi on 19th February (2nd Rajab, 1173 H.) that peace had been concluded between the Shah and Ghazi-ud-din Imad-ul mulk, the latter having been confirmed in the office of wazir (*Waqa*, 173). Throughout the eventful year of 1760 Suraj Mal fought the Shah not only with arms but also the subtler weapon of diplomacy and intrigue. The Durrani wanted to invest a sordid quarrel between himself and the Marathas over the carcase of the Mughal empire with the more attracting character of a Hindu-Musalman conflict for the dominion of India. The credit of Raja Suraj Mal lies in baffling this aim of Afghan diplomatic activity. He carried on a counter-intrigue with the son of his old ally, the Nawab of Oudh. Shuja-ud-daulah did not like the permanent establishment of the Durrani Power in India, because it would only make his natural enemies (the Afghans) too formidable for his safety. Suraj Mal almost achieved his end, but fortune befriended the Abdali. Those who follow the complicated threads of diplomacy, and the movements of the Nawab of Oudh during this period, cannot but hold that the junction of the Nawab with the Shah was a pure accident (*vide Kasi Rai Asiatic Researches*, Vol. III), Suraj Mal had at first allowed Ghazi-ud-din to swallow the bait of the Shah, but he now made him reject it by playing upon his fear. Though Ghazi-ud-din was a fugitive, poor and powerless, his adhesion was anxiously sought by both parties, as it carried a great moral value, and Suraj Mal bid as high as the Shah to secure it for the Marathas. He promised in a most solemn manner to procure his restoration to the office of wazir after the repulse of the Afghans. Ghazi-ud-din broke the newly made treaty with the Shah and waited for the arrival of the Bhao.

CHAPTER VII

SURAJMAL'S GREAT DISAPPOINTMENT

The Prelude to Panipat

India held her breath in painful suspense for the last six months of the year 1760. The two mighty war-clouds which had so long darkened the political horizon, were now gathering impetus for a more tremendous shock. A struggle between the foreign Afghan invader and the Marathas for ascendancy in Northern India was given the appearance of a great communal and religious war by the Durrani and the Peshwa. The Afghan monarch claimed the support of all Muhammadans as the champion of decaying Islam against the aggressive Hindu reaction; while the Maratha declared his mission to be to rescue his co-religionists from their agelong servitude under oppressive Muslim rule. Agents of the Peshwa visited the Court of every Hindu prince of Rajputana, but received a cold reception and evasive replies. If the periodical visits of the Marathas when moving under the shadow of the Mughal throne meant such misery and ruin to them—so the princes argued—what would be their fate under the undisputed sovereignity of the Southerners, relieved of the fear of the Abdali? No Rajput prince responded to the Peshwa's appeal; so little was the faith reposed in them even by their Hindu allies that Raja Suraj Mal dared not visit the camp of the Bhao without taking before-hand from Holkar and Sindhia the most solemn pledges of his safety.

The Peshwa Balaji Baji Rao sent his cousin Sadasiva, and his son Biswas Rao at the head one of the largest and best-equipped armies, numbering about half a lakh, that had ever crossed the Narmada to contend for the dominion of India. His parting words to his cousin were: "Take this nephew of yours to Hindustan and win over all non-Afghan nobles of the empire to our side. I shall soon follow you with another strong army; through the blessings of Shri Bhawaniji, I shall make Qandahar empty of living beings, and leave no seed of the Afghan race on earth. After that only one or two Musalmans like Shuja-ud-daulah and Jafar Ali Khan (Mir Jafar of Bengal) would remain to be dealt with. If they show hostility, their existence would be wiped out; if they submit, we shall keep them like pigeons stripped of their feathers (*manand kabutaran par buridah*). Then placing Biswas Rao on the throne of Delhi I shall go on a pilgrimage" (*Imad,* 78]. How far these high hopes were realised is now a notorious facts in the history of India.

After his arrival on the bank of the Chambal, the Bhao sent a high-flown letter to Raja Suraj Mal, requestin him to come without delay to the Maratha camp and unite [*Iamd.,* 78, 178]. Malhar Rao Holkar and Sindhia persuaded him to meet the Bhao at Agra. Suraj Mal went to the Maratha camp and was honourably received by the Bhao and other Maratha generals. From Agra they marched together to Mathura where the sight of Abdun-nabi's mosque inflamed the anger of the Bhao. He turned upon Suraj Mal and said to him. "You profess to be a Hindu; but how is it that you have kept this mosque standing so long?" Suraj Mal mildly replied: "Maharaj! of late, the Royal Fortune of Hindustan has become fickle in her favours like a courtesan; to-night she is in the arms of one man and the next in the embrace of another. If I could be sure that I should remain master of these territories all through my life, I would have levelled this mosque down to the earth. But of what use will it be, if I to-day destroy this mosque, and tomorrow the Musalmans come, and demolish the great temples and build four mosques in the place of this one? As Your Excellency has come to these parts the affair is now in your hands." The Bhao rejoined, "After defeating these Afghans I shall everywhere build a temple on the ruins of a mosque." However, a holy bath in the Jamuna, after the capture of Delhi, cooled his temper; the *faqirs* of the Jama Mosque shared his charity equally with the Brahmans (*Waqa,* 178).

Everything went on well for a few days and it was all love and cordiality between the Jats and the Marathas. But a coolness soon sprang up owing to a difference of opinion as to the plan of campaign against the Abdali. The Maratha commander-in-chief called a council of war at Agra, and there, Suraj Mal was asked to give his opinion as to the proper method to be followed in the impending campaign. The Jat chief replied: "I am a mere zamindar (peasant), and Your Highness is a great prince; every man forms his plan according to his capacity. Whatever appears advisable in my opinion, I shall submit to you. This is a war against a great emperor, assisted by all the chiefs of Islam. Though Shahan-Shah is a sojourner in Hindustan, his adherents are all inhabitants of this country and lords of large estates. If you are clever, the enemy is cleverer . . . . Undoubtedly it is proper that you should act with great caution and reflection in conducting this war. If the breeze of victory breathes upon the cow's tail (on your standard) it should be considered as written by the pen of destiny on your auspicious forehead. But war is a game of chances, holding out two alternatives . . . . It is wise not to be too confident and rest in too much tranquility. It seems proper that your ladies, the unnecessary baggage, and large cannon which will be of little use in this war, should be sent off beyond the Chambal, to the fort of Jhansi or Gwalior, and you yourself with light-armed war-like troops, meet the forces of the Shah. If victory is won, much booty would come to our hands; if the case is the reverse, we shall have our legs (unfettered by females and other impediments) to flee away on. If you are opposed to the idea of sending them to such a distance or consider it impracticable, I shall vacate any one of my four iron-like forts according to your choice where you may keep in safety your women and baggage, stocking it well with provisions, so that at the moment of decisive action your heart may not be weighed down and your hands fettered by anxiety about the honour of your ladies. And in this time of famine, the road for the supply of grain must be kept open, so that scarcity of grain may not cause hardship to the army. I shall wait upon your stirrup with my troops; and as my country has been free from the depredations of the enemy, supplies can be secured from that quarter . . . . It is advisable to carry on *an irregular warfare with light cavalry (jang-i-kazzaqana)* against the Shah, and not encounter him in pitched battles after the manner of kings and emperors (*jung-i-Sultani*). When the rainy season will arrive both sides will be unable to move from their places, and at last the Shah, who will be in a disadvantageous position (in comparison with us), will of himself become distressed and return to his own country. The Afghans, thus disheartened, would submit to your power" (*Imad*, 179-180). He further advised the Bhao that "one division of the army should be sent towards the *east*, another towards Lahor, so that by devastating those countries, the supply of grain to the army of the Durrani may be cut off.[1] We find Raja Suraj Mal and the Marathas in communication with the Sikhs of the Punjab, the most resolute enemies of the Abdali, and with Raja Balwant Singh of Benaras, who was a thorn in the sides of the Abdali's ally Shuja-ud-daulah, evidently with a view to prevent supplies being sent from Oudh and the Punjab to the Abdali's camp or to cause diversions in the rear and left flank of the invader.

All the chiefs of the Maratha army having praised his plan, declared with one voice that this was their opinion too. "We are ourselves predatory fighters (*kazzaq*); so this mode of fighting can bring no blame upon us. Our skill lies in flight, i.e., evading blows. If the enemy cannot be conquered by stratagem, it is not wise to be entangled in a difficult situation and throw ourselves into destruction." But the arrogant Bhao looked upon this mode of fighting as unworthy of a prince like himself—the cousin of the Peshwa, whose mere servants and agents had already achieved such brilliant exploits in Hindustan. He regarded this advice as the outcome of the senility of Holkar and other aged chiefs and the stupidity of the Jat upstart. All the chiefs thus disappointed and insulted went out, saying to themselves

---

1. Abdul Karim Kashmiri, the author of the *Bayan-o-Waqa*, corroborates the above statement, viz. Suraj Mal's advice "that no pitched battle should be fought with the army of the Durrani who has been joined by all the amirs of Hindustan." He says that Suraj Mal advised the Bhao to leave his baggage at *Akbarabad* (MS. p. 289).

that some great reverse would bring this fiery and rash leader to his senses and make him more attentive to the opinions of his lieutenants (*Imad,* 180-181). Suraj Mal's enthusiasm for his Maratha allies somewhat cooled down and an injurious misunderstanding was avoided only by the tact of the other Maratha chiefs. They induced the Bhao to be more considerate to the Jat chief whose adherence was represented to be of primary importance for the success of their enterprise.

Raja Suraj Mal, accompanied by Ghazi-ud-din, joined the Bhao with 8,000 Jats. The allied army reached Delhi in July, 1760[2] and laid siege to it. Ghazi-ud-din threw himself into the task of capturing the city with his characteristic energy and resourcefulness. When the imperial capital fell, he had his revenge upon the Mughals (*i.e.,* Abdalis) and the Marathas their plunder. So much booty fell into their hands, that none remained poor among them (Sardesai, *Panipat,* p. 162). Ghazi-ud-din brought out of the imperial seraglio a prince of the royal line, seated him on the throne, restored order in the city, and for the first few days discharged the duties of the wazir, which office was believed by all to have naturally reverted to him. But the Bhao suddenly signified his unwillingness to recognise Ghazi-ud-din as wazir. He confered the title of *Raje Bahadur* upon Naro Shankar, appointed him commandant of the fort, and governor of the capital, and formally invested him with the office of wazir. Raja Suraj Mal's word was thus violated: he strongly represented to the Bhao that the new appointment was unjust and injudicious, and prayed for the reinstatement of Ghazi-ud-din. Holkar and Sindhia supported the Raja's representation. But nothing could shake the haughty obstinacy of the Bhao. These disappointed chiefs remarked with grave concern: "Our prestige in Hindustan is gone. What will it lead to?" Suraj Mal came to his mentor, the priest-politician Rupram Katari, and told him that the Bhao had utterly disregarded their joint and earnest representation

2. The *Tarikh-i-Muzaffari* (MS. p. 180), gives the date of the Bhao's arrival as 9th Zihijja, 1173 A. H. = Wednesday, 23rd July, according to the *Waqa-i-Shah Alam Sani,* 10th Zihijja (p. 178).

to restore the office of wazir to Ghazi-ud-din : "It is no good staying here; some mishap may come. It is prudent to try by every means to draw our heads out of it." But Sindhia and Holkar were encamped close by, there was no way of escape. His mind became disturbed by anxiety.

The folly and perversity of the Bhao did not end there. The gilded silver ceiling of the *Diwan-i-am,* beautifully inlaid with jewels, attracted the greedy eye of the rude Southerner. At heart he deliberated "Here is this ceiling; I shall strip it off and melt it to pay the daily wages of my troops. And *in its place I shall make one of wood!* Having first decided he called Sindhia, Holkar and Suraj Mal to hear their advice about it. Nothing does so much credit to the heart of Raja Suraj Mal as the following passionate appeal to the Bhao to spare this last relic of imperal grandeur. He said "Bhao Sahib! this room of the Emperor's throne is a place of dignity and veneration. Even Nadir Shah and Ahmad Shah Durrani, who had laid their grasp upon many a precious thing of the imperial palace, spared this ceiling. The Emperor and the amirs are now in your hands. We shall not see this (disfiguring of the place) with our own eyes. It can bring us no credit but only the odium of disloyalty.[3] To this humble prayer of mine about it today, you should kindly pay due consideration. If you are short of funds, you have only to order me. I am ready to pay you five lakhs of Rupees (for sparing the ceiling)." The Bhao paid no heed to these words, thinking that he would get more by melting the ceiling. This heartless act of vandalism was committed under his orders, the ceiling was taken down and weighed; but to his great disappointment the bullion was found only worth three lakhs of Rupees. Raja Suraj Mal could restrain himself no longer; he went to the Bhao and bursting with honest indignation said, "Bhao Sahib?! you have destroyed (the sancitity of) the throne while I am present here, and thereby brought odium upon me (as well). Whenever I make any request on any affair, you disregard and reject it. We at heart profess to be

3. Suraj Mal, though a habitual rebel from necessity, always considered himself, like other virtually independent rulers of his time, a subject of the Mughal Emperor.

Hindus. Do you attach this much importance to the Jamuna's water which you touched (as a solemn proof of your alliance with me)?"

In October 1760, the Bhao having decided to march against the Nawab of Kunjpura (a place 78 miles north of Delhi, commanding a ford on the Jamuna), summoned his chiefs, Holkar, Sindhia, Suraj Mal and others, to consult them. Suraj Mal took this opportunity to vent his embittered feelings and with great bluntness said to the Bhao: "You have taken off the silver ceiling against our wishes. Replace it to its former position . . . . Give back to Ghazi-ud-din the office of the wazir, which of right belongs to him. Sindhia, Holkar and I myself are all embarrassed on this account, and our honour and good name have been affected by it. From this time, be kind enough to give greater consideration to our little requests. In that case you may consider me and all my resources at your disposal. I shall continue to help and supply you with provisions as before. You should not leave Delhi. Mature your plans from this place . . . . It is not advisable to be now entangled in the affair of Kunjpura." These wholesome but unpalatable words of advice fell like a sprinkling of clarified butter (ghee) into the smouldering fire. "What!" replied the Bhao in haughty disdain, "have I come from the South relying on *your* strength? I will do what I like. You may stay here or go back to your own place. After overthrowing the Ghilcha (the Abdali), I shall come to a reckoning with you." Hearing these harsh words, Sindhia and Holkar in dismay sat motionless and dumbfounded.

Suraj Mal, greatly disgusted and mortified, left the assembly and returned to his place, cursing his own folly in coming to the Maratha camp. He was virtually a prisoner and his position was one of great danger. Sindhia and Holkar had pledged their word of honour for his safety, and upon thier fidelity depended his only chance of escape. These two chiefs, now greatly concerned, met secretly and thus deliberated: "We have brought the Jat here by pledging our word of honour to him; the design of the Bhao is very bad. Balwant Rao and the Bhao have secretly planned to arrest Suraj mal Jat, imprison him and plunder his camp. Suraj Mal must be anyhow sent away in safety, so that the blame of faithlessness may not be laid on us. Let the master (the Bhao) do what he can (to punish us) on this account." Having deliberated thus, they sent for Rupram Katari, the vakil of the Jats, and advised him thus: "Do flee from this place to-night by any means. The encampment of the Bhao Sahib lies at a distance: without letting him know it, slip out in slience. The pledge of honour between you and us is thus redeemed; say not a single word to us after this"; saying these words the two chiefs pulled their own ears in repentance and made a silent vow not to compromise their honour and involve themselves in such difficult situations again for the benefit of such a haughty and faithless master.

Rupram Katari came back to the Jat camp and explained the whole situation to his master. Raja Suraj Mal found himself between Scylla and Charybdis, the Bhao on one side and the Durrani on the other. He said to Rupram, "If by fortune we manage to escape to-night, we incur the enmity of the Bhao. Should he succeed by chance in beating the Durrani, my ruin is inevitable. If he is in earnest, I shall find no refuge and none will be able to save me. Should I stay here, in fear of this future danger, I become a prisoner. Both courses are beset with difficulties. What is to be done now?" Rupram replied, "You know the proverb - Escaping one bad astral conjunction in one's horoscope means a further lease of twelve years of life. Both the Bhao and the Durrani are equally strong and equally implacable enemies. Who knows which of them would come out successful? Till then, in our own place we shall sit silent, holding our breath. Whatever is destined ahead for us by God must be good. Why do you trouble yourself now by the thought of the future (which is uncertain)? Let what may come afterwards; but to-night we must flee." Rupram's cool head and clear vision chalked out the right path for Suraj Mal, whose indecision might otherwise have brought down disaster on his head at this critical point.

When three hours of the night remained, the Jats silently struck their tents, packed their baggage, and marched off, with the connivance of Sindhia and Holkar, in the direction of Ballamgarh, the nearest Jat stronghold, 22 miles to the south of Delhi. Malhar Rao, whose policy was to run with the hare and hunt with the hounds, sent his Diwan Gangoba Tatiya to the Bhao, after Suraj Mal had covered four *kos,* to inform him that Suraj Mal without telling anything to anybody, had gone away; and that their forces had been sent in pursuit, and that the Bhao should send his own army to join them in the chase. Suraj Mal safely reached Ballamgarh; the Maratha troops who went in pursuit came back after plundering some bazars. The Bhao bit his lip in anger, and exclaimed in public, "God willing, if the Durrani is defeated, of what greater weight (the affair of) the Jat can be?"[4]

---

4. These interesting and accurate details are taken from *Bhao Sahib chi Bakhar* (in Marathi, pp. 114-121) of which the above sketch is a free translation. The learned Maratha historian Mr. Sardesai gives, on the authority of Kashi Rai four causes of the defection of the Jats: (i) the families of the Marathas were not sent to Gwalior; (ii) the wazirship was not given to Mir Shihab-ud-din (*i.e.* Ghazi-ud-din Imad-ul-mulk); (iii) the removal of the silver ceiling of the darbar room; and (iv) the management of Delhi was not given to them. (*Panipat Prakaran,* p. 166). The first point is undisputably true. The second is mentioned explicitly in the Maratha chronicles only, but not in the Persian histories, which however make certain statements leading to confirm this, as we shall see next. As regards the third, the author of the *Siyar* says : "What had so much shocked the Jat prince was this—They (the Marathas) stripped the imperial Hall of Audience of its wainscoting which was of silver, elegantly enamelled, and had sent it to the mint and without any respect for things held sacred by all mankind they had laid their sacrilegious hands upon the gold and silver vessels consecrated to the use of the monument of the sacred foot-prints, and of the mausoleum of saint Nizam-ud-din; nor did they spare Muhammad Shah's mausoleum, which they stripped of its incensory, candelabras, lamps and other utensils, all of solid gold, ... all of which were torn away and sent to the mint." (*Siyar* iii. 385-386). *For the last point, bearing against Suraj Mal, Mr. Sardesai gives no other authority,* and he silently passes over the treacherous design of the Bhao, which is attributed to him by the Persian historians as well as by the *Marathi bakhars.* The author of *Imad-us-Saadat* (Pers. text, p. 181) says that the Bhao demanded *two krores of Rupees* from Suraj Mal, and kept him under suspicious watch and that the Jat Raja owed his deliverance to Malhar Rao.

Panipat and its Sequel

The defeat of the Marathas at Panipat was not an accident but a foregone conclusion. They had been beaten by the Shah in the field of diplomacy, several months before their overthrow in the trial of arms at Panipat. Not to speak of winning the "non-Afghan Muslim nobles" as instructed by the Peshwa, the Bhao had made an enemy of the only powerful Hindu Raja who had come to serve him loyally and placed all his resources at the disposal of the Marathas. The value of Suraj Mal's adherence had hitherto been hardly appreciated by the Bhao; but *one day's hostility* of the Jat brought him to his senses. "Raja Suraj Mal, accompanied by Ghazi-ud-din Imad-ul-mulk, marched away to Tughlaqabad; grain became very dear (at Delhi), and next day the Marathas went to make a compromise with and pacify Imad-ul-mulk and Suraj Mal Jat."[5] (*Waqa,* 178). A large tract of the country about Delhi had been so completely ruined by constant ravages, that the Durrani became dependent on the country of the Ruhelas for his supplies and the Maratha army drew theirs from Suraj Mal's kingdom. The foolishness and treachery of the Bhao now dried up this inexhaustible source. So it is no wonder that the Marathas had to fight on an empty stomach at Panipat.

Raja Suraj Mal's position was so conspicuous and his attitude so important that even his neutrality was considered by both the parties as worth securing. He could not be persuaded to join the Marathas again. He thanked his star and the wisdom of his priest Rupram for his recent escape. The vigilant Abdali at once seized this opportunity to make an attempt to win over Suraj Mal. He knew that it was more easy for him to beat the Maratha army than to capture the Jat strongholds, and that his enemies could not be decisively crushed till they had been deprived of such an impregnable base of operations as the country of Suraj Mal. He had, without success, tried several times before to detach the Jat Raja from the Marathas. He now opened fresh negotiations with the Jat, through Nawab Shuja-ud-daula. "Raja Devi

5. The date is somewhat confused and indefinite. It was between Safar 14, and Rabi I. 15; 1174 H. (*i.e.* Sept. 25—Oct. 25, 1760).

Dutt, Ali Beg (of Georgia), and others came, on behalf of Shuja-ud-daula to the Jat for negotiating the terms of a compromise. The Jat agreed to it, wore the *khilat* sent by Shuja-ud-daula and the Shah, and exchanged oaths." The practical result of this treaty was to ensure only the neutrality of Suraj Mal, but not his active assistance on the Afghan side. In spite of the harsh treatment of the Bhao, the sympathy of Suraj Mal continued to be with the Marathas. He entered into this alliance with the Abdali only to provide against an emergency, and because complete isolation was too dangerous for any State in the then prevailig political condition of India.

Suraj Mal entertains Maratha refugees from Panipat

After the fearful wreck of the magnificent Maratha army at Panipat (14 Jany, 1761), the survivors fled southwards. In their hour of misfortune, the very peasants stripped them of their arms, property and clothes. Naked and destitute the Maratha soldiers entered the country of the Jats who welcomed them to their hospitable doors and provided medicine, clothes and food for their relief. If Suraj Mal had not forgotten the wrongs done to him by the Marathas, and befriended them in their hour of adversity, very few of them would have crossed the Narmada to tell the woeful tale of Panipat to the Peshwa. And this he did at the imminent risk of incurring the enmity of the Abdali staking his life and fortune at the impulse of a pious and noble sentiment which would have done honour to the stoutest heart of Rajputana in her heroic days. All Muslim writers[6] extol the generosity of Suraj Mal: the Maratha writers also acknowledge this: "At Mathura they entered the territory of the Jats. Suraj Mal, impelled by the Hindu religious sentiment, sent out his troops to protect them, and relieved their distress in every way by distributing food and clothes to them. At Bharatpur was the Jat queen, who showed much charity to the fugitives. Thirty to forty thousand men were fed here for eight days; the Brahmans being given milk, *peda*, and other sweetmeats. For eight days all were

6. *Imad*, p. 203; *Bayan-o-Waqa*, MS. p. 293.

entertained in great comfort. A proclaimation was made to the citizens that quarters and food were to be given to the fugitives in the manner most convenient to each. None was to be put to trouble. In this way the Jat spent altogether ten lakhs of Rupees. Many men were thus saved. Shamsher Bahadur[7] came wounded to the fort of Kumher; Suraj Mal tended him with the utmost care; but he died in grief for the Bhao" (Sardesai, *Panipat Prakaran,* 205). After relieving their distress, and pacifying their hearts, Suraj Mal gave one Rupee in cash, a piece of cloth, and one seer of grain to every ordinary man (common soldier and campfollowers), and sent them to Gwalior" (*Bayan,* MS. 293).

Did Suraj Mal Plunder Naro Shankar?

Francklin, presumably on the authority of Munna Lal, gives a completely wrong version of this affair which amounts calumny: "*It is said,* that he (Naro Shankar, the Maratha governor) was stopped in the way by order of Suraj Mal Jat, stripped of all his ill-gotten wealth and left to pursue his journey, in equal distress and terror, to Akbarabad" (*Shah-Aulum,* 23). This hearsay is opposite the truth, as we learn from the letter of a Maratha fugitive who was with Naro Shankar: "Naro Shankar and Balaji Palande, with two to four thousand troops had fled beforehand from Delhi. On the way they met Malhar Rao Holkar who had about eight or ten thousand troops with him. We are now staying with Holkar at Gwalior. At Bharatpur Suraj Mal took the greatest care of our safety and comfort. We stopped there for fifteen to twenty days. He paid us great respect and attention, and said with folded hands "I am one of your own household] your servant; this kingdom is your's and such other words. Alas! there are so few like him. He sent his chiefs to escort us to Gwalior' (Sardesai, *Panipat,* p. 193). In another letter, Nana Fadnavis remarked: "The Peshwa's heart was greatly consoled by Suraj Mal's conduct"

7. He was the son of Peshwa Baji Rao I by a Muslim concubine and professed the Muhammadan faith. The author of *Imad us-Saadat says that Suraj Mal built a masjid* and a house over his grave. (Pers, text, p. 203).

(*ibid*). Nothing more is required than a mention of these facts to wipe off this unjust stain upon the memory of the great Jat ruler. To believe Francklin in the face of this unanimous Maratha assertion to the contrary, is to act in defiance of the laws of historic evidence.

After the victory of Panipat Ahmad Shah, having entered Delhi in triumph, contemplated an expedition against Suraj Mal who had given refuge to the Marathas. The Jat Raja sent Nagar Mal to turn away the wrath of the Abdali (*Waqa,* 184), and hold out offers of submission. Suraj Mal, who knew well that the warworn Afghans would be reluctant to pass another summer in India, was not prepared to sacrifice much for peace. The negotiations were protracted from March to May, 1761. But during all this while, with cynical indifference to the presence of the Conqueror of Panipat at Delhi, he was engaged in capturing Agra, the second capital of the empire, from the Musalmans. After a siege of 20 days the conquest was achieved. Suraj Mal carried off 50 lakhs in the pillage of the city. (Wendel, Fr. MS., 46-47). Only five days before the Shah' departure from Delhi, "news arrived that the troops of Suraj Mal had forced the qiladar of Akbarabad to evacaute the fort, and entered it" (11 Shawwal, 1174 = 16th May, 1761; *Waqa,* 185). As a solace to the Shah, he paid one lakh of Rupees in cash and excuted a new bond for five lakhs to be paid *aferwards, i.e.,* never. The claim to the five lakhs promised by Suraj Mal in 1757 was tacitly dropped. The rainy season was coming in, and the Sikhs had risen in his rear; the Shah was only too glad to get this much from the stubborn Jat. On the 16th Shawwal (21st May, 1761) he started from the garden of Shalimar[8] (outside Delhi) for his country, leaving Suraj Mal to pursue with impunity his more ambitious designs of agression.

---

8. This Shalimar stood near Badli (9 miles n. w. Delhi on E. I. Ry.).

CHAPTER VIII

REIGN OF SURAJ MAL

Suraj Mal's conquest of Haryana

The battle of Panipat was followed by a comparative calm—a quiet of exhaustion; Northern India at least ceased for some time to be the battle-field of the Afghan and the Maratha. The rapidly rising Sikh commonwealth served as a break-war to the Abdali invasion, while in the south Haidar Ali and the Nizam kept the Marathas busy. An interregnum, if not anarchy, prevailed in the empire. At Delhi Najib-ud-daula watched over an empty throne and a widowed capital. The Emperor Shah Alam II was an exile in his own dominion, a protege and pensioner of Shuja-ud-daula. The ruler of Oudh had his eye upon the suba of Bihar and was busy in intrigues with Mr Qasim, the Nawab of Bengal who was preparing for a manly struggle to throw off the English yoke. The victorious Muslim coalition broke up owing to the irreconcilable enmity between Shuja-ud-daula and the Ruhela chiefs. Panipat had only shattered the extravagant dream of the Maratha but brought no permanent peace to Islam. The moment the Maratha was overthrown, the Jat came in and challenged her victorious champion who, weary and exhausted, shrank from the contest and retired beyond the Indus. The stubborn Jat courage revived confidence in the prostrated Hindu mind, and Islam was again thrown on the defensive.

"Suraj Mal wanted to seize these few moments of his enemies respite for carrying out his two-fold object which he had long in view; first to interpose a solid block of a Jat confederacy between the Abdali and the Ruhelas, extending from the Ravi to the Jamuna; secondly to expel Najib-ud-daula from Delhi, restore his protege the ex-wazir Ghazi-ud-din to his former position and power, and through him control the policy of the empire. But he decided not to attack Delhi first but simply cover it during his contemplated campaign. The tract of Haryana dominated by powerful Muslim jagirdars presented a dangerous gap between the Sikh commonwealth and his own principality. Barred in the south and west by the Rajput predominance and in the east[1] by the Ruhela power, he sought the expansion of his dominion in this tract and the districts around Delhi, mainly inhabited by the Jats.

This was a move in the right direction for more reasons than one. The Jats of the Jamuna were being drawn as if by racial instinct towards the Jats of the Five Rivers. The two branches of one mighty stream which had bifurcated at Sindh in the dim days of hoary antiquity, now turned to meet again moved by the impulse of common blood as well as common political and religious interests. The Jat ruler was alive to the danger which was sure to arise from the consolidation of the Ruhela ascendancy at Delhi and the consequent growth of another Rohilkhand on his northern frontier (Mewat), driving a mortal wedge between it and the Sikh territory. The possession of this tract would, above all, enable both the Jat and the Sikh to make a firm stand with their backs upon one another, and fight confidently against the Ruhela and the Abdali. Suraj Mal sent his eldest son Jawahar to conquer Haryana while another army was sent under his youngest son Nahar Singh to establish his authority in the Doab, and watch the movement of the Eastern Ruhela chiefs. Jawahar directed his attack upon

1. Suraj Mal's territory in the east touched the possessions of the Ruhelas, the districts of Koel (Aligarh), Jaleswar and Etah formed part of his kingdom. "On this side of the Jamuna from the gates of Delhi to the Chambal, there was no other government than his own, and towards the Ganges the condition was almost the same. After the reduction of Agra fort, he had not more to do for the extension of his dominion on the south. He then turned his thoughts to west of Delhi. He had also destined that country (Haryana) to be made a kingdom for his son Jawahar Singh" (Wendel, 45, 48).

Farrukhnagar, held by a powerful Baloch chief, Musavi Khan. But he having failed to capture it, Suraj Mal himself came with all his forces and big artillery and laid siege to it. Two months passed away and Musavi Khan being hard pressed, consented to surrender it "if Suraj Mal would take an oath on the Ganges water not to hinder his departure."[2] But the Jat on this occasion made the same unscrupulous use of the sanctity of the Ganges as that of the Quran by some Muslim rulers.

The Baloch chief was made a prisoner and sent to Bharatpur. Sin prospered for a while only to make the retribution more terrible and shocking. Rewari, Garhi Harsaru and Rohtak had already fallen into the hands of Suraj Mal.[3] He now turned his arms against Bahadurgarh, about 12 kos to the west of Delhi, the strong-hold of another powerful Baloch chief Bahadur Khan. In his distress, the Baloch chief appealed for help to Najib-ud-daula, who, however judged it inexpedient to provoke a war with Suraj Mal, before the arrival of the Abdali.

---

2. Wendel 49, the *Waqa* (p. 198) make entries which tell us that Najib Khan was coming to relieve Musavi Khan. But on the 19th Jamada 1, 1177 A.H. (Nov. 25, 1763 A.D.), news reached him at Safdar Jang that "Suraj Mal Jat, having *deceitfully* (*aj-rah-i-dagha*) imprisoned Musavi Khan Baloch, captured Farrukhnagar by forcing the garrison to evacuate it." This seems to suggest that Musavi Khan was seized *before* the capture of the fort—perhaps during negotiations.
3. All these places remained possessions of his house till they were recovered for the Emperor Shah Alam II, by Mirza Najaf Khan; after defeating Raja Nawal Singh Jat. Their positions, Rohtak, lat. 28°-55', long. 76°-35'; Rewari, 28°-10', 76°-40'; *Garhi Harsaru* 28°-35', 76°-55' about 8 miles east of Farrukhnagar. It is said that in an assault upon Garhi Harsaru, Suraj Mal's elephant, urged against the huge wooden gate of the fort turned back exhausted and unsuccessful. Sardar Sitaram, the Jat Ajax, seeing this, rushed forward with an axe and hewed down the gate with great intrepidity. This is one of his numerous feats of strength remembered by his descendants, still living in the ruined castle of his, Kotman.

Death of Suraj Mal

But a breach between Suraj Mal and Najib-ud-daula was unavoidable. About this time another division of the Jat army under the command of Nahar Singh, (the youngest son of Suraj Mal), Balaram and other renowned commanders, was carrying on war in the Doab, wresting many remarkable places from the officials of the Mughal Government. Suraj Mal, knowing his chances of success greater, was eager to come at once to a reckoning with Najib-ud-daula, while it was the policy of the latter to postpone the trial of issue till the Abdali would be in a position to come to his aid. The Ruhela chief dissembled and employed suppleness; but the shrewd Jat would not let this opportunity slip away, and determined to strike a decisive blow at his enemy at the moment of his weakness. "The Jat prince, finding from this cautious behaviour of Najib-ud-daula that he was afraid of a war, became the more daring and he demanded the *faujdari* of the Gird or Circuit (the governorship of the districts around the capital)." [*Siyar*, iv. 30].

Najib-ud-daula knew what it meant; it was like a demand for the surrender of the outer approaches of a stronghold to the enemy. With Suraj Mal[4] in possession of the Belt round the capital, Delhi would become only a spacious prison for him and the descendants of Timur.

The Afghan chief unwilling to see matters come to a rupture sent Yaqub Ali Khan (brother of Shah Wali Khan, wazir of Ahmad Shah Abdali), as envoy "to endeavour by mild words to bring matters to a pacification, so as to smoother the seeds of tumult and war." He took with him as a present two pieces of beautiful Multan chintz, painted in yellow and pink. If we are to believe the author of the *Siyar*, the present proved more acceptable than the message

---

4. Abdul Karim Kashmiri, author of the *Bayan-o-Waqa*, says; "After seizing the persons of Musavi Khan and other Baloch chiefs and sending them to Deeg, he sent words to Najib-ud-daula, telling him that he should leave the capital and cede to him the Mian Doab. Although Najib Khan compelled by necessity, offered to cede Sikandra(bad, ed.) and other parganas, Suraj Mal was not satisfied." [Bayan, MS., 302.]

of peace.[5] Yaqub Ali went to the Jat for negotiation on the 14th Jamada II, but returned unsuccessful after an absence of four days (17th Jamada II, 1177 A.H. = 23rd Dec. 1763 A.D.; *Waqa,* p. 199).

Driven to hostilities by the unjust demands of the Jat, Najib-ud-daula, with an army of ten to twelve thousand horse and foot, and accompanied by his two sons Afzal Khan, Sabita Khan, and also by some other Ruhela leaders of note, such as Mahmud Khan Bangash (*Siyar,* iv. 31), crossed the Jamuna [19th Jamada II=24th Dec., 1763] to give battle to the "proud uncircumcised." Suraj Mal leaving his son Jawahar at Farrukhnagar to look after the recently conquered territories, had, several days before, crossed the Jamuna. Both armies now took up positions on the banks of the Hindan (a small tributary of the Jamuna), about seven kos, east of Delhi. The Jat army entrenched themselves and planted their guns on the other [eastern] bank of the Hindan. In the earlier part of the day several petty engagements took place in which the Jats had the better of the encounter. Towards the closing hours of the day, Suraj Mal crossed the Hindan with six thousand troops and attacked the Muslim lines. An action took place in which about 1,000 men were slain on both sides. In the heat of action Suraj Mal Jat with thirty horsemen only fell upon the centre of the Mughals and Baloches and was slain" (Sunday, 19th Jamada II, 1777 A.H = Dec. 25, 1763 A.D. *Waqa,* p. 199). So admirable was the discipline of the Jat army, that though the news of Suraj Mal's death spread through the ranks, not a single soldier was shaken. They stood on their ground as if nothing had happened, while the Musalman army broke and fled to their camp. Afterwards the Jat army left the field with the mastery

---

5. According to the *Siyar,* Yaqub Ali was abruptly dismissed on the very day of his arrival, "with words that if he came for a pacification only he had better not come at all [*Siyar,* iv. 31]. There is no truth in it as is proved by the more definite and authentic entry in the *Waqa.* However there is no doubt that Suraj Mal's demand was extravagant and his attitude towards Najib-ud-daula was haughty and unyielding. Father Wendel briefly remarks "But Suraj Mal demanded war"....(Orme MS., 49).

of victors [*Siyar*, iv. 32]. This was too great an event to be believed by the enemy. "His corpse did not come into their hands. The news of his death was not verified at that time. Najib Khan remained standing on his ground throughout the night for the safety of his army. At midnight the Jats retreated from the opposite bank of the Hindan. Not a trace of the Jat army was to be found, and then only was the news of the death of Suraj Mal believed.[6] Najib Khan returned to the capital." [*Bayan*, MS. p. 303.]

Raja Suraj Mal, "the eye and the shining taper of the Jat tribe—the most redoubtable prince in Hindustan for the last 15 years"—thus disappeared from the stage of life leaving his work half-done. His was a towering personality and a transcedental genius to which homage has been paid by every eighteenth century historian. "He was," says Father Wendel, "in one word, wise, politic, valiant and grand, above his birth and to the point of being admired and feared by foreigners." [Fr. MS. 51]

---

6. Najib Khan's caution is perhaps justified by the saying in the country-side "Don't believe a Jat to be dead till his thirteenth day [*Shardhdha* ceremony] is over!"

CHAPTER IX

LEGACY OF SURAJ MAL

Raja Suraj Mal and his family

Raja Suraj Mal was about 55 years old at the time of his death. He had virtually exercised the sole management of the affairs of the State for over twenty years before and after the death of Badan Singh. By his four wives, he left five[1] sons: Jawahar Singh, Ratan Singh, Nawal Singh, Ranjit Singh and Nahar Singh. The first two were born of a lady, popularly reputed to have been a Rajputni, possibly of *Gaurua* caste, the third was the son of a Malin (gardener class) mother, the last two were born of the women of his own tribe.[2] But the mother of none of these enjoyed the particular

1. Wendel says four; but it is a common fact of history supported by the authority of persian histories that Ranjit Singh, who succeeded his brother Raja Nawal Singh, was also a son of Suraj Mal. This makes the number five. The narrative of Wendel though extremely valuable as a contemporary history, is vitiated by some inaccuracies about well-known facts.
2. Col. Tod says that Jawahar and Ratan Singh were born of a wife of *Koormi caste* (an agricultural tribe inferior to the Jats). But father Wendel who lived at the Court of Jawahar Singh, and knew him intimately asserts that they were born of a wife of the Gore caste (French MS., 51). Elsewhere he adds, "There are men who claim that the Gorees are a little more noble than the Jats, and that they are a *species of decayed Rajputs*, either fallen into decadence or mixed, but always one degree higher than the Jats as regards their extraction" (*ibid.* p. 74). This exactly tallies with the notice of the *Gaurua caste, whom (Sir H.M. Elliot calls "an inferior clan of Rajputs"* (Memoirs of the Races, i. 115). The author of *Imad-ud-Saadat* maintains that Jawahar's mother was a *Rajputni* (Pers. text p. 56). "It has been asserted that the *Gaurua* of the Mathura and Gurgaon districts is only a *Rajput who practises karewa* (marrying elder brother's widow). [*Gaz. N. W. P.* Old series, vol. viii, 1, p. 73]

affection of the old Raja, who loved most dearly his masculine and barren wife the famous queen Rani Kishori, popularly called Hansia. Jawahar was fortunate enough to be adopted by this lady, whose influence and affection shielded the rebellious youth from the worst effects of the wrath of his father. He and his brother rose to high rank, as mansabdars of the Mughal Court. But Ratan Singh, addicted to pleasures in early youth, grew up a voluptuary without any ambition for power or martial fame. Nawal Singh and Ranjit Singh were youths of mediocre abilities, and were little heard of during their father's lifetime. Nahar Singh, the youngest, whom Suraj Mal thought of leaving as his successor and whom the Jat chief had already begun to initiate in the arts of government, was a boy of dull and narrow out-look and of weak intellect. Nahar [the Lion] resembled a lamb in character and presented a sad contrast to his eldest brother. He was a typical "good boy," obedient to his father's will, respectful to his superiors, devout and religious, with great reverence for the Brahmans, unostentatious and docile, fit for anything but ruling men and administering a State in stormy times. Jawahar feared neither God nor man, and would defy both in the pursuit of ambition and revenge. Possessed of great military talents and administrative capacity, subtle, active and audacious he was a born ruler of men; yet Suraj Mal rightly divined that this son of his would bring ruin upon the Jats.

The relation between Suraj Mal and Jawahar could never be cordial, as between a self-made miserly millionaire and his young, foppish son who looks upon his father as no better than a peevish and overbearing steward, and makes grievance of the salutary checks laid upon his own extravagance. Theirs were two different types of mentality incapable of understanding each other. Suraj Mal, in spite of the change of his former condition and the immense wealth he had piled up had not at all given up the primitive simplicity of his race in what concerned his own mode of living. He however, made a decent provision—very liberal according to his standard—which, he thought, ought to suffice for the maintenance of his son in dignity and affluence. But young Jawahar was extravagant and would always press for a larger allowance from his father. He soon created a circle of his own, and had a Court and train of which the expenses amounted far above what Suraj Mal had given him. Though brought up in a rude provincial town amidst a peasant population, his equipage, his fashion, his diversions all suggested an Amir of the Empire and the courtly airs of Delhi which he had not failed to observe well. Suraj Mal way greatly displeased, and in many ways tried to make his son understand the extreme aversion that he felt for his conduct. These remonstrances the more frequent and pressing they were, the more they soured the spirit of Jawahar. Already at a young age, Jawahar had commenced to nourish very high hopes and to indulge in outbursts of a fiery and enterprising spirit. Suraj Mal employed the military talents of his son in many expeditions, where he acquired great fame. He made his son commandant of Deeg, hoping that would satisfy him. But contrary results followed. A party opposed to Balaram, Mohan Ram and other influential chiefs of his father's Court, soon gathered round him there, and he persuaded himself that Balaram's group were turning his father's mind against him. Suraj Mal rebuked his son, for allowing himself to be guided by evil advisers, whom it was necessary for his own good to dismiss. But these paternal remonstrances were treated with usual indifference. What was worse Jawahar prepared for an armed revolt.

Jawahar Singh resolved to set himself as an independent ruler at Deeg and defend it to the last against his father. With the assistance of his desperate associates, he took possession of the city and did, in truth all acts of war. Suraj Mal, having tried in vain to make him return to his duty, had no other expedient than to go and besiege his son in person. In order to come most quickly to a conclusion with his son, he threatened to apply extreme rigour to the wives and children of those that followed his party. Jawahar put up a stiff resistance. Not content with defending Deeg against the efforts of his father, he resolved to try issue on the plain. He came out and attacked his father's troops; a fierce struggle ensued under the walls of the fort. After a while, the rebels were forced to turn their backs; but not their Maloch-like leader. Jawahar who rushed into the thickest of the fray, and fought with ardour and courage befitting a nobler cause, was brought to the ground at last covered with wounds—a sword-cut, a lance thrust and a musket shot. Suraj Mal, who would rather see Deeg lost than his own son dead—hastened out of breath to snatch him away from the hands of those who in spite of all the prohibitions and cries of the father, hurried to give him the death blow. His life was saved; but owing to the three wounds, his right arm became weak and he limped in after-life [Wendel, 34-36].[3]

A dark cloud hung upon the mind of Suraj Mal; the prospect of another civil war and family dissensions after his death made the closing years of his life extremely unhappy. He saw with alarm the rise of a strong party, headed by his most powerful chiefs, Balaram, Mohan Ram and others, who were bent upon opposing with arms, if necessary, the succession of Jawahar. He knew the character of his people which his son did not and cared not to understand. Jawahar gave himself the airs of an aristocrat and never failed to bring home to the mind of his nearest kinsmen and relatives, his own superiority and right to rule them by reason of his birth. Nothing was more offensive to the Jat, who, like the Afghan would not fear to tell any pretender to his face, "What art thou that I am not? What shalt thou be that I shall not?" Besides, the character of the prince was least calculated to create confidence in others. He was harsh, cruel, vindictive, and dissimulating to a degree. The pen of a sympathetic observer could depict him

---

3. In all fairness to Jawahar Singh, it is proper to add to following remarks of Father Wendel: "Although it is not other than very true that Jawahar Singh had been dragged into this wicked affair partly by his own spirit, and partly by the counsels of the persons he had about himself-nevertheless it was certain that mostly, the *aloofness of Suraj Mal* towards him and a *certain indigence* to which on certain occasions the son found himslf reduced with all his comrades by the miserliness of his father, or the wickedness of those who according to his [Suraj Mal's] orders, supplied the money for the maintenance expenses of Jawahar Singh, obliged him to take that measure of last violence." *This rebellion took place in 1755 before the invasion of Ahmad Shah Durrani.*

as no better than as a second Mihir-kula, a man who "has up to the present time caused it to be seen that he is never more satisfied than when he has occasion to make war against someone, *i.e.*, to render others unhappy, and cause to flow before his eyes a river of human blood" (Wendel, MS., 34]. He never forgave any injury or insult, and never failed to retaliate. All the old chiefs became apprehensive of the safety of their offices, wealth and lives under his regime. To have crushed these powerful associates of his cabinet and battlefield, in order to smooth Jawahar's path to the throne would have been, for Suraj Mal, the undoing of his life's work. So he decided to deprive such a son of his birth-right, rather than see the Jat power perish, although he esteemed silently Jawahar's resolution and bravery, and judged him to be *solely worthy* of succeeding him.

But it was too much to expect that Jawahar would sit idle, and tamely submit to this injustice and be disinherited. So Suraj Mal proposed to create for him another kingdom outside the hereditary dominion of his house which he meant to leave to his more tractable son Nahar Singh. This suggested the scheme of the conquest of Haryana and the formation of a buffer State where the exuberant energy and military genius of Jawahar would find ample occupation in holding his appanage against the Ruhelas and the Abdali. It was undoubtedly a wise policy, and the site chosen for the contemplated kingdom was excellent. Haryana, which was and still is ethnologically a Jat country, accepted Suraj Mal's rule with alacrity and welcomed it as a release from the unbridled tyranny of a Muslim military aristocracy.

At the time of Suraj Mal's death the possessions of the Jats consisted of the districts of Agra, Dholpur, Mainpuri, Hathras, Aligarh, Etah[4], Meerut, Rohtak, Farrukhnagar, Mewat, Rewari, Gurgaon and Mathura, apart from the original principality of Bharatpur. "The right bank of the Ganges forms its [of the Jat kingdom] eastern boundary, the Chambal the southern, the suba of Agra included in the

---

4. Etah—Agra Division, bounded on the north by the river Ganges, on the south by Mainpuri district, on the east by Badaun district and the west by Jalesar pargana of the Agra district, lies between long 78°-29' and 79°-19' and latitude between 27° and 28°.

territory of the Raja of Jaipur the western, and the suba of Delhi the northern; its length is about 100 kos, east to west and 70 kos, north to south [*Le Nobab Rene Madec,* sec. 45]. As regards the finance of the State, Father Wendel says, "Opinions differ on the subject of the treasure and property which he [Suraj Mal] left to his successor. Some estimate it as 9 (nine) krores, others less. I have enquired into his annual revenue and expenditure from men who managed them; all I could learn as more credible is that all his expenses were not above 65 lakhs a year nor below 60, and he had at least during the last 5 or 6 years of his reign, not less than 175 lakhs of revenue annually. He added 5 or 6 krores of silver to his ancestor's treasure . . . . To-day [after the accession of Jawahar Singh] up to 10 krores are in the treasury of the Jats . . . Much is buried—not known where. Suraj Mal fruitlessly dug at Deeg a large tract of land to recover part of the hoard of Badan Singh. This has given that city a tank and citizens have thus got water to their advantage! Notwithstanding the common opinion regarding the treasure[5] of the Jats, I always believe that there is not so much money in their hands" [Wendel, 51, 52]. Years have not at all affected—but rather magnified—the popular belief, about the fabulous wealth of the house of Bharatpur. The secret vaults of its treasury are still supposed to contain many rarities and choice plunder of Delhi and Agra, which few can hope to see.

"Besides the treasure, Suraj Mal left to his successor nearly 5,000 horses, 60 elephants, 15,000 cavalry in his pay,

5. *Imad-us-Saadat* is the only Persian chronicle which gives, though incidentally, a hint about the wealth of Suraj Mal. Rao Radha Kishan (informant of the author Ghulam Ali), who had been for a long time a trusted adherent of Suraj Mal says that, Suraj Mal made to him a prophecy about the issue of the Third Battle of Panipat and in the course of the talk said, "I who possess *territories, yielding one krore and a half,* and have *in my treasury five or six krores of rupees,"* have been made to part company with him [the Bhao] for nothing (*Imad,* Pers. text. 72). This is substantially a correct estimate.

more than 25,000 infantry (besides those in fortresses), [*ibid.* p. 55]. The author of the *Siyar* says 'He [Suraj Mal] had in his stable twelve thousand horses, mounted by so many picked man, amongst whom he had himself introduced an exercise of firing at a mark on horseback, and then wheeling round in order to load under shelter, and these men had by continual and daily practice become so expeditious and so dangerous marksmen, and withal so expert in their evolutions, that there were no troops in India that could pretend to face them in the field. Nor was it thought possible to wage war against such a Prince with any prospect of advantage." [*Siyar*, iv. 28]. Suraj Mal as we learn from the *Memorie of Jean Law*, the French freelance captain, was also on the look-out for Europeans for training his infantry regiments in European discipline, so much admired by all his contemporaries. The party of M. Law[6] was attacked by 10,000 cavalry under Rao Durjan Singh (a relative of Suraj Mal and commandant of a small province of Atrauli[XXV] in the Doab), on 23 March, 1758, while he was encamped on the eastern bank of the Kalini river. His intention was to capture the Europeans and send them prisoners to Suraj Mal, who had been long desiring to have such people in his service. Fortunately, however, they escaped and the desire of the Jat Raja remained unfulfilled.

6. See *Memoire of Jean Law* (pp. 312-313), edited by Alfred Martineau. The *Kalini river* of the text is evidently the *Kalindi* river, a tributary of the Ganges, flowing through the *tehsil of Atrauli* (16 miles to the north-east of Aligarh on the Ramghat Road).

XXV. Atrauli had never been a province big or small. From the days of Akbar upto 18th Century, it remained a *mahal* or sub-division of the *sarkar* of Koil of *Suba* of Agra. During the 19th Century it became a Tahsil sub-division of Aligarh district. J.M. Siddiqui, *Aligarh District; A Historical survey*, p.113, f.n. 7. —Ed.

CHAPTER X

MAHARAJA SAWAI JAWAHAR SINGH BHARATENDRA (1764-1768)

Jawahar's accession to the throne

After the death of Suraj Mal, the baronial party, headed by Balaram, brother of Rani Hansia proceeded to place Nahar Singh on the *gadi* of Bharatpur, as desired by the late Raja. But one bold and well-judged stroke of Jawahar's policy brought about a dramatic change of the situation. He sent a messenger from Farrukhnagar with a stern warning to his brother and the nobles, reproaching them with cowardice and unworthy scramble for gain. This was no season, so they were told, to think of giving successor to the illustrious dead but to exert themselves to propitiate his departed soul, crying for his slayer's blood. He would not claim at present, he said, his own birth-right, but would go with the small force that remained with him against the enemy, and afterwards see who deserved most to succeed his father. This threat disconcerted the chiefs and so dismayed Nahar Singh, by nature timid and cowardly, that he fled the following night. With his family and partisans, he retreated to Dholpur (which had been given to him as an appanage during Suraj Mal's lifetime) to wait for a more favourable time to recover his legacy. Balaram gave up all hopes of resisting Jawahar's claim to the throne and thought it prudent to submit. Jawahar Singh returned to Deeg, and was installed there as master and sovereign of the Jat territory.

Weakness of Jawahar's position

But his position was as yet one of peril and uncertainty. The submission of the old chieftains was nothing more than a tardy recognition of his title. They retired to their own estates unwilling to participate in the work of the new government. Balaram, the leading chief, general of the cavalry and governor of Bharatpur (where the State treasure was deposited), shut up the gates of the fort in the face of Raja Jawahar Singh, and would not reveal to him the secret sites of Suraj Mal's treasure in other places. Nahar Singh was at Dholpur ready to lend himself to any intrigue for his brother's overthrow, and Bahadur Singh (son of Suraj Mal's brother, Pratap Singh), who held the fief of Wair, refused to acknowledge the authority of the new Raja and was making preparations for asserting his own independence. Nothing but a military success, grand enough to capture the imagination of the people, was likely to check the disruptive forces in the State, and consolidate the rule of Raja Jawahar Singh.

He dissembled for the moment and behaved as if he had forgotten and forgiven the faults of his father's nobles in consideration of their helping him to the throne. Sentiment and interest alike demanded that a retaliatory expedition should be undertaken to avenge the death of Suraj Mal on Najib-ud-daula. The ex-wazir Ghazi-ud-din, who had been living at Bharatpur as a pensioner of the Jats since 1760, also fanned the flame of Jawahar's wrath in the hope of regaining his exalted office and bringing about another revolution at Delhi. But none of the Jat chiefs approved of this design, and the proposition was generally rejected. Jawahir Singh set little value on the armed help of his chiefs, if he could only get money. In spite of his turbulence and ingratitude, Rani Hansia loved Jawahar, her adopted son, with all the tenderness and warmth of an indulgent mother. She could not but respond to the passionate appeal of Jawahar and furnished him, without the knowledge of her brother Balaram, with large sums for the expenses for the expedition.

The War of Revenge

Towards the end of October[1], 1764, a formidable Hindu

1. Pers. Record i. 352. This news was brought from Delhi to Calcutta in 16 days, on Nov. 11, 1764.

army, second only to that which Maharashtra had sent forth in 1760 to assert her dominion in Hindustan—appeared before the gates of Delhi, to demand satisfaction for Suraj Mal's blood, and to undo the effects of the Muslim victory at Panipat. Jawahar Singh brought against Najib-ud-daula 60 thousand troops and 100 pieces of cannon of his own, 25 thousand Marathas under Malhar Rao Holkar, and some 15 thousand Sikhs—both as hired allies,[XXVI] to ensure a rapid success. Doubtful of the issue but determined to fight it out to the last, the brave Ruhela chief had prudently removed beforehand his family and treasure to the strong fort of Sakkartal[2] in Saharanpur,[XXVII] and throwing entrenchments

---

XXVI. The writers have given varied figures regarding the strength of Marathas, Sikhs and the Naga Gosains, hired allies of Jawahar Singh that participated in the siege of Delhi against Najib. For details see, Rajpal Singh, *Rise of the Jat Power*, p.163-164, f.n. 27-34. —Ed.

2. Also called Sukkartal, situated in the confluence of the Solani river and the Ganges at its highest navigable point.

XXVII. Sakkartal (Sukkartal) is now in Muzaffar Nagar District. In the reign of Akbar, the entire district of Muzaffar Nagar belonged to *Sarkar* of Saharanpur with the exception of *pargana* kandhla in Delhi *Sarkar*. At that time present Muzaffar Nagar area was known as *Sarvat*. In the reign of Shahjahan, Sarvat and Khatauli were bestowed upon Saiyed Muzaffar Khan, in whose honour the town Muzaffar Nagar was founded. In 1824 the district was formed by creating a sub-collectorship at Muzaffar Nagar. In 1826 sub-collectorship was converted into regular district. According to 1838-1840 and 1860-1868 settlements, some villages from Meerut were transferred to Muzaffar Nagar. *The Encyclopaedic District Gazetteers of India*, central zone (Uttar Pradesh), Vol. 6, (Ed. S.C. Bhatt) p. 875; for location of Sarvat see, Irfan Habib, *An Atlas of the Mughal Empire*, Map (political), 8A.

Najib-ud-daulla was appointed *Faujdar* of Saharanpur on 21st November 1753. After that he ejected the local zamindars around. At the time of Jawahar Singh's expedition against him in 1765 Sukkartal was in Najib's *Jagir*. Najib built three forts at Pathargarh(1755) in Najibabad,Sukkartal 17 miles east of Muzaffarnagar and Gausgarh(1765) 22 miles north west of Muzaffarnagar. A small tributary Solani river falls in Ganga at Sukkartal. Thus Sukkartal has Ganga on three sides with torturous ravines; on the fourth side the ground was so uneven that the approach to Najib's defence line was extremely difficult, particularly in rainy season. Due to strategic situation of Sukkartal fort Najib sent his family members there. Marathas also could not defeat him in 1759 because the natural surroundings of Sukkartal enhanced the strength of the fort. Iqbal Husain, *The Rise & decline of Ruhela chieftaincies in 18th Centuary India*, p.96, f.n. 32, p. 216; also *Tarikh-i-Shakir Khani*, 84 b cited by Iqbal. —Ed.

around the city of Delhi stood ready for a long siege. He summoned other Ruhela chiefs to his aid and sent urgent entreaties to the Abdali, informing him of the perilous situation. Delhi was closely invested; the Marthas were posted to the north of the city, and the Sikhs to the north-west, while Jawahar planted part of his army on the eastern bank of the river and the rest before the Delhi and Ajmer gates. The fiery Jat, impatient of delay, sent a challenge to Najib Khan, to come out like a man and fight in the open instead of hiding himself in a corner. He chivalrously withdrew his army five or six *kos* off the city in the direction of Faridabad (about 16 miles, south of Delhi), to allow the Afghans to come out unmolested. Lashed to fury Najib-ud-daula sallied out and gave battle to the Jats (15th Nov., 1764), who, however proved stronger and drove the Afghans back into the city, each side lost about a thousand in killed and wounded. Jawahar Singh, accompanied by Holkar and other chiefs, crossed the Jamuna and plundered Shahdara, and planted batteries on the side (17th November). The day after the loot of Shahdara, the troops of Najib Khan owing to the heavy cannonading of the enemy left the sandy plain [*reti*] below the fort and went inside; shells began to fall into the city[3] (19th November). Three months passed away in distress and hardship. All attempts of the Afghans to cut their way through proved futile. On the 12th of Shaban, 1178 A.H. (4th Feb., 1765), Najib fought another battle with the Sikhs and the Jats on the ridge near Nakhas [cattlemarket] and Sabzi-mandi [the well-known fruit and vegetable market of Delhi]. The action began with a heavy musketry fire; a large number of men were killed and wounded, and again the Afghans had to retire discomfitted (*Waqa*, 204). No choice was now left but starvation or surrender; shops were closed and the utmost exhortation of the Government failed to pacify the people. The very next day, the inhabitants of the Old and the New city rushed into the Jat camp, begging for a supply of corn to save them from starvation. This was a virtual surrender of the city—the defenders retired within the citadel.[4] There was no prospect of relief coming from

3. The battle, loot and bombardment took place within the first 26 days of Jamada I, 1178, on Thursday, Saturday and Monday (*Waqa*, 198-199).
4. Pers. correspondence i. 372; the date 9th Jan., 1765 is evidently wrong there.

any quarter whatsoever; the Sikhs were ravaging Saharanpur and other possessions of Najib-ud-daula and there was little chance of the Abdali coming.[5]

Treachery of Malhar Rao

When complete success seemed almost within his grasp, Raja Jawahar Singh was baffled by his faithless ally, Malhar Rao, "Who spoiled the affair" as Father Wendel says, "by showing greater slackness and open partiality for Najib Khan. He proposed peace at a time when the Ruhelas could not have delayed any longer in offering unconditional surrender, and at last obliged Jawahar Singh to consent to it" [French MS., 59]. Najib Khan opened negotiations for peace; "Sujan Misra, Raja Chait Ram, and the nephew of Rupram,[6] (the family priest of the Bharatpur Raj) went to Malhar Rao to talk of peace and returned (14th Shaban; 6 Feb., 1765). About two *gharis* before sunset, Nawab Zabita Khan started, and going up the Jamuna, brought with him Gangadhar Tatiya and Rupram to Najib-ud-daula [*Waqa*, 201]. The two parties evidently came to an agreement but it is not known on what terms. On the 17th Shaban (Feb. 9), Najib-ud-daula went to pay a visit to Malhar Rao in his camp; and thence [after the interview with Holkar] they proceeded to the camp of the Jats, and towards sunset returned to the city bringing with them large quantities of grain loaded upon pack horses. [*Waqa*, 201]. On the 20th of Shaban, (12th Feb.), Raja Jawahar Singh marched away to Okhla, 5 miles south of Delhi. [*Waqa*, 202]. Malhar Rao had the reward of his treachery to his ally.

---

5. The Abdali crossed the Indus in Oct., 1765 about 7 months after the conclusion of peace between Najib Khan and Jawahar Singh. So the report of his coming could in no way terrify the Jats and influence the negotiations between two parties.
6. Rup Ram figured prominently also in the reign of Suraj Mal. The Marathi chronicles mention him several times with his title Katari. He "having acquired great reputation as a Pandit in the earlier part of the last [the eighteenth] century, became *Purohit* to Bharatpur, Sindhia, and Holkar, and was enriched by those princes with the most lavish donations the whole of which he appears to have expended on the embellishment of Barsana and other sacred places within the limits of Braj his native country" [Growse's *Mathura*, 178].

On the 21st of Shaban (13th Feb) he paid a visit to Najib-ud-daula who presented him with an elephant, two horses, and nine plates of jewels and bestowed one hundred and twenty-nine robes of honour to his companions [*ibid.* 202]. On the 22nd of Shaban (14th Feb.), Jawahar Singh received a visit from Zabita Khan who had brought with him an elephant and a robe of honour on behalf of the Heir-apparent, Jawan Bakht" (*ibid*). Here the affair ended. That he was not pleased with the compromise which was in a sense forced upon him by the untrustworthy Maratha chief is evident from the fact that he departed earlier from the capital without returning the visit of Najib-ud-daula as courtesy required. He went away to Deeg, bearing a grudge against Malhar Rao who, the Jat knew, had him spend without much benefit 160 lakhs of Rupees. "He had no other gain from this expedition" as Father Wendel says "than to have under his command the chiefs and the army and to make himself more respected by his people."[7] (French MS., 59).

Jawahar Singh crushes the refractory chiefs

After his return from the expedition against Delhi (March, 1765), Raja Jawahar Singh thought it high time to make himself master of his own household first, and to crush the enemies within, before he should indulge in the vision of foreign conquest. He suspected, not without reason, a secret connection between Malhar Rao and his discontented chiefs who had reluctantly accompanied him to Delhi, out of fear and shame. Two old chiefs, Balaram, commander of the cavalry, and Mohan Ram, general of the artillery had almost monopolised all power in the State: the treasure and army of Suraj Mal were in their hands and their relatives occupied all the important public offices. Besides the memory of old

---

7. The above account has been mainly reconstructed from the account of Father Wendel and the *Waqa*. Harcharan, the author of *Chahar-Gulzar-i-Shujai, says that at the very beginning* Najib Khan made proposals of a compromise which was rejected by Jawahir Singh remembering the enmity arising out of his father's blood. He then approached Malhar Rao and through his mediation peace was effected. Najib Khan visited Jawahar Singh in his camp and *offered apologies to him.*

grievances, and their intrigue to set him aside from succession, the idea of getting enriched at one stroke by killing these *golden geese* entered his mind. The notorious German captain Somru, having quitted the banners of Shuja-ud-daula, sought service and safety in the Court of Bharatpur (April, 1765). Here was a man after Jawahar's heart, a capable soldier without a conscience, who would unhesitatingly carry out with skill and thoroughness any dark design of a good paymaster. The reputed wealth of Bharatpur attracted many veteran mercenaries discharged from the service of bankrupt princes. Having recruited a powerful corps of foreigners who could be trusted more than the Jats, Raja Jawahar Singh proceeded to chastise the inimical nobles (*circa* July, 1765).

"Fortified with these helps, he believed himself strong and secure enough to demand with much firmness, satisfaction from those of his kinsmen whom for a long time past he had desired to seize. It was probably with this design that he came to Agra where having summoned those whom he wished to seize, and commanded his foreign troops to guard well the roads, he caused to be arrested Balaram with the others in different places, and *on the same day* all persons appertaining [attached?] to them were seized. Balaram and one other chief with him, full of hate and spite at what had happened to themselves, and probably to prevent a greater ignominy, cut their own throats with their swords shortly after, the one face to face with the other. The others were conveyed under strong guard as prisoners to Bharatpur where afterwards they ransomed themselves with the money which was demanded of them on the account of Suraj Mal whose affair they had had in their hands . . . Certain [of the chiefs] let themselves be rather killed than give up money, although they had the reputation of having much wealth and were already convicted of malversation in the administration . . . . Not to speak of Balaram and his riches, Mohan Ram alone was estimated to possess nearly 80 lakhs in cash, without reckoning the property and other wealth that he was master of . . . . He let them cut his head off after many tortures and cruelties rather than deliver the least part of that which he in truth, owed, and which he could not fail to have very well guarded" (Fr. MS., 61-62). Thus

Jawahar Singh revenged himself upon the old nobles of his father. This bloody affair proved a great mistake and a sorry failure as a means of recovering Suraj Mal's treasure. "He was very ill-advised, all spoiled by haste and harshness. A slow and pleasant method of extraction would have been more fruitful. All that Jawahar Singh could seize was not more than 15 or 20 lakhs" [*ibid*]. This was a political blunder too, which ultimately brought about the downfall of the house of Bharatpur. "This conduct of Jawahar Singh at the beginning of his reign sent", says Father Wendel, "consternation among his relatives and dismayed entirely the Jats in general, at the same time that it soured their spirits and *removed totally their attachment to his person.* And although for many reasons of State he was almost obliged to act in that fashion, it was, however, very hasty and unreasonable" [*ibid*, 62].

Next came the turn of Jawahar's rebellious cousin, Bahadur Singh who held the fief of Wair[8], "a man" as Father Wendel says, "so courteous for a Jat and of a spirit above most of his race." He had served his uncle Suraj Mal very faithfully and was rewarded with several additions to his appanage. He was wealthy and powerful, possessed a good and numerous artillery, and had in his pay a considerable army. After the death of Suraj Mal, Bahadur Singh believed that he had at least as much right to the dominion of the Jats as Suraj Mal or Jawahar Singh, and showed, by his activity and conduct that he desired to govern Wair as a *master* and not at the pleasure of another. "And in spite of the fact that Jawahir Singh had indicated to him his displeasure, he did not cease, but commenced to fortify more and more the place which was well fortified, increase the garrison, munitions and provisions, and put himself in a state to defend it against whomsoever would contest it. Jawahar Singh marched in midst of the rainy season [August, 1765] against *Vaer* [Wair] and invested it on all sides. Bahadur Singh defended himself valiantly for three months; the besiegers underwent great hardship, because that year the

---

8. Wair is within the territory of Bharatpur, lying about 12 miles north-west of Bayana, situated in lat. 27° and long. 27°-15'.

rain fell in a deluge. Partly by false peace proposals, and partly by the treachery of some chiefs within, the fort was carried by assault and Bahadur Singh seized and carried off prisoner to Bharatpur (November, 1765) whence he was released at last with Musavi Khan [of Farrukhnagar], at the birth of a grandson [of Suraj Mal][9]. But two Rajputs (who were known to have instigated Bahadur Singh in that war against Jawahar Singh and had afterwards forbidden him to admit proposals for a compromise, which he was about to make)—were by order of Jawahar Singh, in a manner that has not yet been seen or practised among the Jats - as a warning to others, impaled on the road to Bharatpur, and there remained a long time as an awful spectacle to the passers-by". [Wendel, French MS.,[10] 63-64]. This expedition cost Jawahir Singh more than 30 lakhs, rather a heavy drain on the State treasury. But it was not to be the last.[XXVIII]

---

9. The grandson, referred to in the text, is Kheri Singh, born to Jawahar's younger brother Ratan Singh. Raja Jawahar Singh being without issue and also without the hope of having any one, adopted this child. It was on this occasion that these political prisoners were set free. The exact date of the birth of Kheri Singh is nowhere mentioned. This can, however, be inferred from an entry in the *Waqa*, dated 23rd Ziqada, 1179 (May 3, 1766), on which date, Afzal Khan, son of Najib, had an interview with Nawab Musavi Khan [*Waqa*, 208], presumably after his release. So the child was born and the prisoners were set free probably in the month of April, 1766.
10. The original MS. contains a long account of the siege and sack of *Wair*, considerably abridged here to suit the narrative.

XXVIII. For siege of Wair see, Wendel's Memoirs (Hindi) *Hindustan Mein Jat Satta*, p. 183-185; U.N. Sharma, *Maharaja Jawahar Singh Aur Uttradhikari*, chapter III, subtitle 4. —Ed.

CHAPTER XI

REIGN OF RAJA JAWAHAR SINGH

Overthrow of Nahar Singh

While Jawahar singh was engaged in the siege of Wair[XXIX] (July-November of rains 1765), Nahar singh (the youngest son of Suraj Mal) was making preparations at Dholpur to strike a blow for the *gadi* of Bharatpur. It was quite apparent that his turn would come next, should Jawahar succeed in crushing Bahadur Singh. About this time Malhar Rao Holkar was on the other bank of the Chambal, carrying on hostilities against another Jat principality, Gohad.[1] Nahar Singh commenced a correspondence with the Holkar in order to buy Maratha support and with the latter's aid to raise himself to the Raj. Jawahar Singh and Malhar Rao had an old score to settle ever since the Delhi expedition of 1764. The cunning Maratha had made a fool of the Jat by taking his money and at the same time baffling his object. But he had soon to repent his trickery when Jawahar, who was anything but a saint himself, bluntly refused to pay the unpaid half of the stipulated sum of twenty two lakhs, alleging breach of faith on the part of the Holkar. Malhar Rao seized this opportunity of making his claim good, and eagerly accepted the proposal

---

XXIX. The exact dates of operation Wair are not available. It began in the middle of August 1765 and ended in the first week of November 1765 in three months of the rainy season. U N Sharma, *Maharaja Jawahar Singh*, chapter III. —Ed.

1. Gohad is situated to the north-east of Gwalior. This principality was bounded on the west by the Gwalior territories, on the east by the Kali Sindu river, on the north by the Jamuna and on the south by the hills of Sirmur [?] See Rennell's atlas.

of Nahar Singh, whom, as usual the Holkar made his *dharma putra* (God-son), because Nahar Singh was rich enough to pay a good price for this paternal affectation.

Malhar Rao sent his troops across the Chambal and garrisoned the fort of Dholpur along with the men of Nahar Singh. Jawahar Singh summoned his brethren of Punjab, the Sikhs, to his aid, and arrived quickly on the bank of the Chambal to carry war into the enemy (December, 1765). One division of the Maratha army which had penetrated into the Jat country was surrounded and captured. Dholpur was next besieged and when it fell into the hands of Jawahar Singh, many Maratha chiefs who had taken shelter there during the retreat, became prisoners of war. Flushed with this success, Jawahar wanted to pursue Malhar Rao and clear Malwa of the Marathas. But the Sikhs refused to keep the field any longer as summer had already set in and they had suffered a good deal from the intolerable heat and scarcity of water. "Nahar Singh who had already retired to the army of Malhar lost his estate ... and was afterwards abandoned by the Marathas to whom he wished to deliver the country.... He took refuge at Chopor, the citadal of a petty Rajput Raja on the further side of Karauli, where he at last ended his life in despair by swallowing poison. His family retired to the protection of the Raja of Jaipur, where they *are at present* (i.e., 1768), having carried the most part of their riches and probably the knowledge (of the whereabouts) of the great part of the treasure of Suraj Mal, of whom Nahar Singh the destined successor, had been the confidant."[2] (Wendel, Fr. MS., 65).

---

2. The *Imad-us-Saadat,* is the only Persian chronicle (Pers. text, p. 56) which notices the death of "the good natured" Nahar Singh by self-administered poison. On the 10th December, 1766, the news came from Jaipur that "Nahar Singh *is dead of his disorder.* This news has been received with utmost concern by Maharajah Jawahar Singh. All the cavalry officers who were in the army of Nahar Singh immediately returned to Jawahar Singh to consult what was most advisable on the occasion" [Pers. Cor. ii. 6]. The death took place evidently on the 6th or 7th of Dec. 1766.

Jawahar fights Raghunath Rao, 1767

The unrealised dream of Suraj Mal, namely to build up a great Jat confederacy extending from the Chambal to the Ravi dominating the whole of Northern India appeared to become well-nigh an accomplished fact by the establishment of more intimate relations between Jawahar Singh and the Sikhs, the recent victory of their united forces over the Marathas under Holkar, and the successful resistance of the Sikh commonwealth against the Abdali. Success opened new vistas of aggression to Jawahar who thought of widening the confederacy further so as to include the Jats of Northern Malwa, and raise a stronger barrier to Maratha invasion. The brave Rana Chattar Sal of Gohad had been carrying on for years a heroic struggle against the Marathas. The obstinate courage and undaunted spirit of the race shone no less brilliantly in Malwa than in the Punjab or Bharatpur. But they were losing ground every day, being only a handful, however brave, compared with the locust hordes of the South. Should the Marathas succeed in over-throwing the Rana of Gohad, their full strength, Jawahar knew too well, would be pitted against him. "Proud of success over Malhar, Jawahar Singh resolved to give *himself* [of his own accord?] help to the Rana [Chattar Sal] Jat, his ally, and thus finish the Marathas beyond the Chambal and outside his own country" [Wendel French MS. 65].

The Peshwa Madhu Rao viewed with alarm the growth of this formidable coalition and sent Raghunath Rao in the autumn of 1766, to retrieve the prestige of the Maratha armies in Hindustan. His army, together with those under the Holkar exceeded 60,000 horsemen, and had a choice artillery of more than 100 pieces. Raghunath began with the siege of Gohad, and made certain haughty demands upon Jawahar Singh, who was about this time suffering from a dangerous malady. As soon as he recovered, he "marched anew with the design to attack the Marathas, if they would not give up, of themselves the claims which they thought to have against him. But treason lurked in his own camp, which frustrated his object. Raghunath Rao seduced two of his principal chiefs, Anup Giri Goswain and Umrao Giri Goswain, (the leaders of the Nagas), from their allegiance to the Jat Raja. The traitors promised to make Jawahir Singh a prisoner in his camp and hand him over to the Marathas, and they were to get, as a reward, certain territories in the direction of Kalpi. The spies of Jawahar Singh gave their master timely warning of this plot. At midnight Jawahar Singh got his troops ready and suddenly fell upon the camp of the Goswains. The traitors escaped with difficulty, but a considerable number of their followers were taken prisoners and their camp thoroughly pillaged. About 1400 horses, 60 elephants, 100 pieces of cannon, and other valuable booty, fell into the hands of Jawahar Singh. The dependents of the household of these two Goswains who were at Agra, Deeg and Kumher were brought to one place and kept under watch [*Chahar Gulzar-i-Shujai* MS.][3]. About this time (Feb., 1767) Ahmad Shah Abdali made some progress in the Punjab and threatened to advance upon Delhi. Raghunath Rao and Jawahar Singh, who were equally interested in keeping the Abdali out of Hindustan, made up their quarrel in the face of this common danger. They met in friendship and adjusted their claims; the terms of the treaty were as follows:

1. The Maratha prisoners at Bharatpur, are to be released.

2. Jawahar Singh should execute a new agreement to pay up the balance of 15 lakhs of Rupees, due to Malhar Rao, after the conditions of the original agreement had been fulfilled [by the Marathas]

3. Raghunath Rao cedes to Jawahar Singh a small tract of the Rajput country, lying contiguous to the territory of the Raja on a yearly quit rent of 5 lakhs of Rupees [Pers. Cor. ii. 4-7)

The treaty was a make-shift arrangement, neither party meaning to respect it if its violation would bring greater advantages. The fear of the Abdali wore away towards the

3. Harcharan Das, author of the *Chahar*, makes some confusion about the date which he puts as 1179 A.H., the correct date being 1180, A.H. He estimates the gain of Jawahar as more than two krores, which, however, Wendel with perhaps greater accuracy puts as 30 lakhs. Nevertheless the account of Harcharan is substantially correct, and is corroborated by the version of Wendel, (French MS., 66).

middle of the year (1767) when the Sikhs considerably regained their ground. Jawahar Singh projected a campaign in the rainy season. "The country of the Raja of Atter[4] and Bhant had been formerly tributary to the Marathas.... Jawahar Singh, seeing the Maratha parties so, weak, imagined that he had there as much right as they, and took it into his head, without any other reason, to make the conquest.... This enterprise also led him much further than he had proposed to himself. Going with superior forces to that side, he seized in the rainy season (July-Sept. 1967) all the dominions of the Marathas and other petty zamindars as far as Kalpi. If he had as much skill in preserving the recently conquered country, as he had success in seizing them, he could have been praised for his enterprises and would have been entirely glorious: but it is just this in which he failed more, namely in wisdom and moderation" [*French MS*., 66].

Raja Jawahar Singh and the English

A revolution of the greatest magnitude had in the meanwhile taken place in Bengal, and a new and foreign power, the English, now emerged as the most potent factor in the politics of Northern India. They paid at Gheria and Udaynala, the necessary price in blood for the kingdom of Bengal, which had been handed over to them by her treacherous sons at Plassey (1757). A high spirited and able prince who tried to do his duty fell a victim to the commercial greed of the English East India Company. Mir Qasim fled from his lost kingdom to Oudh. His new protector, the Nawab wazir Shuja-ud-daula, appeared in the field to dispute the fairprize with the victors. On the morrow of the battle of Buxar, the English merchant Company appeared with a monarch's sceptre before the astonished people and princes

4. Atter is situated north-east of Gwalior and due north of Gohad. Bhant is difficult to identify. It is perhaps the same place as Binde of Rennell's atlas, lying close to Atter and to the south-east of it. The territory of the above mentioned Raja was perhaps the tract between the Chambal and the Kali Sindu rivers near their confluences with the Jamuna. These two places lie on the west and east of long. 79° and on lat. 26°-30'.

of India. The wazir of the empire bowed before it and received back his lost territories with an assurance of protection from his generous enemies. The homeless Emperor recognized the rising power and set up a melancholy Court at their fort of Allahabad, with the found hope of shining in borrowed light.

But the new masters of Bengal could not repose in peace so long as Mir Qasim was at large plotting against them, from his refuge among the Ruhelas. He had sent *vakils* to Ahmad Shah Durrani imploring his aid against the English. To this were added the urgent entreaties of Najib-ud-daula who was being crushed between the two millstones, the Jat and the Sikh, by their concerted pressure. The Bengal Government had every reason to fear an Abdali invasion on a grand scale against them, resulting in another Panipat on the border of their territory. The Ruhelas were bound both by interest and racial sympathy to the Abdali. Shuja-ud-daula could hardly be relied upon because the ruler of Oudh was to profit most by the extinction of the English Power in Bengal. Less reliable were the Marathas who found in the territorial ambition of the European merchants, the greatest obstacle to their national aspirations both in the north and the south. The Bengal Government did not fail to notice that there was only one Power in Hindustan with a well-organized government and a powerful army, namely the Jats of Bharatpur, who were likely to prove their surest allies; because situated as both powers were, one had nothing to gain by the destruction of the other, on the other hand both were equally interested in keeping back the Durranis and the Marathas. Raja Jawahar Singh could be of great service to the British in more than one way. First, he could keep the Abdali busy in the Punjab by backing the Sikhs. Secondly, should the invader threaten to march against the English, he could create a diversion in his rear or possibly draw off the invader to the siege of the Jat forts, giving time to the English to organize resistance. Thirdly, he could place the Emperor Shah Alam on the throne of Delhi and maintain him there with English help: a friendly Emperor on the throne of the Mughal capital and a powerful ally in possession of the surrounding tracts would mean the domination of the whole empire by the British. If the Emperor would leave the English protection and turn hostile to them, Raja Jawahar Singh could equally check his anti-British designs. Such were the great possibilities of an alliance between the Jat and the English.

But the first approaches of alliance made by the English Government were not received with much eagerness by the Jat. The Governor of Bengal wrote a letter to Raja Jawahar Singh (19 Aug., 1765), requesting him to dismiss the notorious Somru who had taken shelter and service with him; on his fulfilling that condition, the prospect of a defensive alliance was held out to him (Pers. Cor. i. 427). Raja Jawahar Singh had no hostile design against the English in affording refuge to Somru, who was entertained simply because the Raja had the need of a European captain to organize an infantry brigade for him. He did not like the mandatory tone of the Governor's letter; and as there was no enemy at his doors, he chose to take no serious notice of it. Clive foresaw the necessity of creating against the Abdali and the Maratha, a confederacy admitting the Jats and the Ruhelas also to the advantages of a defensive alliance with the English. He advocated this scheme in the congress at Chapra, but the majority was opposed to him on the ground of the heavy responsibilities it was likely to impose on the Government of Bengal. At the beginning of the year 1767, the Durrani king invaded the Punjab with a firm resolution to root out the Sikhs, and then to reinstate Mir Qasim on the throne of Bengal. He inflicted several defeats upon the Sikhs, penetrated as far as the Sutlej, and threatened to advance upon Delhi. The progress of his arms created a stir among all the native powers and none was more alarmed than the Bengal Government. The emergency which Clive had foreseen now arose. His successor Mr. Verelst asked the wazir, who had some influence with the Jats, once his father's allies, to open negotiations[5] with them afresh.

---

5. The correspondence which passed between the Bengal Government and the wazir, reveals how eagerly the English sought to win over Raja Jawahar Singh. (Letters Nos. 201, 234, 255, Pers. Cor. ii. pp. 69, 77).

At this time Raja Jawahar Singh with the Abdali on one flank and Raghunath Rao on the other, was himself equally anxious for an alliance with the English. He now entered with alacrity into the scheme of a combined resistance to the Abdali.

Impressed by the fidelity of the English to their engagements, Jawahar wished to cement the proposed defensive union with them by a regular offensive and defensive alliance. He had made approaches through Muhammad Reza Khan and sent a letter to him by the hand of one Srikrishan, a dependent of his, requesting the Khan "to use his influence with the gentlemen of Calcutta to seal a vow of friendship and alliance with the writer [Jawahar Singh], so that he may be able to make war successfully with the Shah and obtain success . . . . [bringing about] the tranquility of the people of God and the settlement of the affairs of Hindustan . . . . [the writer] asked to be considered now as invariably attached . . . . [to the English] and determined to preserve with them a union in which there will never be least failure . . . . Should it be thought advisable, the writer will place His Majesty Shah Alam on the throne of Delhi and proclaim *Ghazi-ud-din Khan wazir,* [the writer] makes *one proposal beforehand,* namely, that *the fort of Ranthambhar should be placed in the writer's hands"* (*ibid,* p. 87, letter No. 296, dated April 12, 1767). The Governor of Bengal wrote in reply directing the Khan that "Raja Jawahar Singh may be informed that if he is really sincere in his desire to enter into an alliance with the English, he should send a trustworthy *vakil* to Banaras, where the writer [the Governor] is going, and where the subject can be thoroughly discussed" (*ibid,* p. 91; letter No. 315, dated 20th April, 1767). Accordingly Jawahar Singh appointed one Don Pedro De Silva as his *vakil* (*ibid,* p. 129). The wazir informed the Governor that he "does not place dependence on the Ruhelas or repose any credit in them; but Jawahar Singh can be relied upon to some extent. Writer imagines that he [Jawahar] will gladly embrace 'our' alliance . . . . If Jawahir Singh is inclined to enter into an alliance and compact, and give his firm and unshaken promise to take up the sword for the service of the English Company, and if the writer, and the

English engage to give him assistance should the Shah invade his territories, in what terms could an answer be returned to him? Hopes that the Governor will ponder over this question and inform the writer of his sentiments in order that he may act agreeably thereto" [*ibid,* p. 99, letter No. 346, dated April 25, 1767]. Jawahar had kept the Shah in good humour by professing loyalty and obedience to him. His *vakil* waited upon the Shah on the 17th of February 1767, and a special envoy, Karimullah, son of Raja Jawahar Singh's head munshi Yahya Khan went soon afterwards with presents of various sorts to the Shah's camp (Pers, Cor. ii. 26, 32). There cannot be any better proof of the sincerity and honesty of the Jat Raja than the fact that after the date (12th April) of his opening negotiations for an alliance with the English, he kept no correspondence with the Shah which might be construed as a proof of bad faith towards them.

Assured of English help against the Abdali, Jawahar did not hesitate to provoke the hostility of the Marathas. Immediately after the conclusion of this alliance, he began to occupy some places taking advantage of the temporary retirement of the Marathas. The Governor in a letter to the wazir expresses his anxiety at the conduct of his new ally and asks him "to keep the eye of observation on the movements of those restless people [the Marathas], while Jawahar Singh enforces his pretensions to those districts which once acknowledged the authority of the Marathas" [*ibid,* p. 145].

About this time a war broke out in the Deccan between the English Government and Haidar Ali who was joined by the Nizam of Hyderabad, of late an ally of the English. The Marathas also seeing the Madras Government very hotly pressed by their enemies, contemplated hostility against the English. Raja Januji Bhonsla made certain irritating demands upon the Governor of Bengal, who very courageously resented them and wrote to the envoy of Januji to tell his master that "it will not be difficult to convince him [Januji] that the English are not less formidable enemies than sincere friends." (*Ibid,* p. 152. letter No. 583, dated Sept. 27, 1967). As the Abdali had retired to his country, virtually defeated by the Sikhs, the Marathas were thinking of reconquering

Hindustan. It was rumoured that Raja Januji and Raghunath Rao had united their forces for invading Hindustan. The Peshwa Madhu Rao also felt the pulse of the wazir through his *vakil* who wrote a letter: "It is rumoured here that the Europeans are not on good terms with the wazir and give him innumerable troubles. If so . . . the wazir will . . . . favour him with letters for Sri Mant [Raghu Nath Rao][6] and Madhu Rao, the writer's gracious Master. [The *vakil*] tells him [the wazir] to send a deed under his seal making over the suba of Bengal to the Marathas, that they may collect revenue there" (*ibid,* p. 181; letter No. 667, Nov. 1767). The wazir forwarded the letter to the Governor and wrote in reply to the Maratha *vakil* that there was the most perfect friendship subsisting between the English and his Government. Apprehensive of a serious Maratha invasion of Hindustan the defensive union which had been formed against the Abdali was now set in motion by the English Government against the Marathas. The Jats had already begun hostilities and the wazir was firm in his attachment to the English. The Marathas became discouraged by their state of isolation in Hindustan and consequently gave up their aggressive designs. Raja Jawahar had received letters from the Governor for re-adjusting their old alliance to meet the new exigency and build up a more solid confederacy to preserve the peace of Hindustan against all enemies, including the Marathas. The Raja signified his regard for the friendship of the English and sent Padre Don Pedro to Calcutta "to communicate to the Governor the secrets of his heart" (*ibid.,* p. 171; letter No. 642, Oct. 31, 1767).

Jawahar's Pilgrimage to Pushkar [Nov.-Dec. 1967]

Raja Jawahar Singh had reached the very summit of his power and glory by a series of brilliant victories. Proud of his army and wealth, he thought he could with impunity, insult and oppress his weaker neighbours who appeared like so many pigmies to his delusive vision. Angry providence soon hurled him down from the pinnacle of fortune and

6. Somewhat confusing because Sri Mant in the Maratha correspondence is generally applied to the Peshwa himself.

humbled his pride. "Delivered from all the troubles which the Marathas could give him, and also in a certain degree above them, feared by the Ruhelas, and respected, beyond what he could claim, elsewhere, master of a vast country flourishing and tranquil, he knew not," says Father Wendel, "how to taste long the advantages of his good fortune or rather he himself thought to interrupt it and wished to invert by his own hands the high fortune, which up to the present had not ceased to follow him; in spite of the efforts which often he had made himself to banish it." [French MS., 67].

Jawahar owed his misfortune to the unhappy issue of a quarrel which he himself most wantonly provoked with Maharaja Madho Singh of Jaipur. As close neighbours the rulers of Bharatpur and Jaipur had causes enough for bad blood. The latter could not be expected to watch with satisfaction the growth of the new born Jat Power, a permanent menace to his State. It was nevertheless true that the Bharatpur principality could not in its infancy have lived and prospered without the patronage of Maharaja Sawai Jai Singh, and this was gratefully acknowledged by Jawahar's father and grand-father who always showed more out of goodness than fear—proper respect and homage to the ruling house of Jaipur, as to a superior and patron. But the accession of Madho Singh—against whom Suraj Mal had fought on behalf of Maharaja Iswari Singh—disturbed this cordial relation; the haughtiness of the new ruler offended the Jat chief, who ceased to attend the darbar of Jaipur on the day of the Dashera. As human nature goes, patrons become enemies when their patronage is no longer required; so this coldness developed into bitter enmity when Jawahar succeeded his father, and haughtiness was pitted against haughtiness. Raja Jawahar Singh believed too seriously in his reputed Yadava descent to feel, like his ancestors, any diffidence, due to consciousness of a less exalted birth, in claiming equality with the Rajput ruling houses of the Solar and Lunar races. Once, it is said, some advisers of the Raja, told him that he ought to show defference to the Maharaja of Jaipur, at least in consideration of his descent from Rama, who bridged the ocean. "Well," replied Jawahar, "if his ancestor threw a bridge across the ocean my ancestor [Shri Krishna] held up Govardhan hill for seven days on his little finger!" His father and grand-father were content to be addressed as Braj-Raj [King of Braj, *i.e.*, the Mathura district] as a compliment to their sovereignty over that tract. But Jawahar, as if to pique the ruler of Jaipur, assumed the lofty title of Maharaja Sawai Jawahar Singh Bharatendra [Lord Paramount of India, Fr. MS., 71] and, vying in splendour and magnificence made his Court outshine that of his neighbour. "In short", as Ghulam Ali, the author of *Shah Alam Nama* says, "Jawahar raised his head to the stature of Maharaja Madho Singh" (Pers. MS., p. 3). The ruler of Jaipur who had not the power to resent it, bore the humiliation in silence. But his aggressive adversary at last compelled him to take up arms for preserving the honour of his house and the sanctity of the soil of Amber.

No incident of the history of the eighteenth century is so green in the memory of the country-side, and nothing is so much distorted by national prejudices as the armed pilgrimage of Jawahar Singh to Pushkar through Jaipur territory—the fierce battle of Mawda (Maonda), and his inglorious retreat. The Jat attributes the disaster to the intrigue of the Rao Raja Pratap Singh the founder of the Alwar State—*who* having quarrelled with his suzerain, Madho Singh of Jaipur, fled for protection to Suraj Mal, and afterwards incited Jawahar Singh against his overlord. He is said to have treacherously deserted Jawahar and directed the Jaipur army to attack the Jats when entangled in a difficult pass. The Rajput version on the other hand is that Jawahar Singh demanded the surrender of the wife of Nahar Singh, which the Maharaja of Jaipur declined because the lady feared ill-treatment at the hands of Jawahar. She afterwards swallowed poison,[7] lest a calamity should befall her protector on her account. The brave Naruka chief whose patriotism prevailed over his sense of gratitude for the hospitality of the Jat, came over to the army of Jaipur and fought for upholding the honour of his country. No more authentic account of it can be found than that in the unbiased narrative

7. Appendix, p. 111, *Life of Maharaja Sawai Iswari Singh* (in Hindi) by Thakur Narendra Singh Verma, Vaidic Press, Ajmer.

of Father Wendel, who penned it within twleve months of its occurrence.

"The Jats . . . . had for many years past some quarrels (with the Raja of Jaipur) regarding a small tract of country[8] not far from Deeg, where there was always subject for misunderstanding, as ordinarily happens on the frontier between different territories. It went at last to the extent of having troublesome consequence by an open rupture which appeared inevitable. This affair, however, had been, or seemed about to be settled by compromise. Jawahar Singh proud of his forces[9] and riches and puffed up by his fortune, did not cease to treat haughtily the Rajputs and their Raja, and also with a certain insolence which was neither seasonable nor decent for him . . . . He at this time took the fancy to go and make a pilgrimage to the Pushkar lake in Marwar territory, close to Ajmer and to have also an interview with the Rathor Raja of that country, with whom he commenced a sort of limited friendship . . . . Having then with this design assembled all his forces, more to make a show than from necessity, in spite of the dissuasions of others, he began the journey of more than 70 kos outside his own country with a numerous[10] army, as if he was going to fight against all the Rajputs and conquer their territories" [French MS., p. 67].

With banners unfurled and drums beating, the Jat proudly set his foot upon the soil of Amber and marched

---

8. This refers to Kama (long. 77°-20' lat. 27°-40'), situated about 15 miles north-west of Deeg. Kama was for a long time a bone of contention between the two States. Raja Ranjit Singh Jat got it from Mahadji Sindhia and since then has been in possession of the Bharatpur Rajas.
9. Jawahar Singh had a large and well-disciplined army led by able European captains. Somru had been in his employ since 1765 and M. Rene Madec, the renowned French general joined his service in the month of June or July of the year 1767 (*Le Nabob Rene Madec*, p. 45]. The restless mind of the Raja hit upon this adventure as an opportunity to test the minds of his army upon the Kachhwahas.
10. Harcharan, author of the *Chahar-Gulzar-i-Shujai* gives an exaggerated estimate of Jawahar's army: "Sixty thousand horses, one lakh of footmen, and two hundred guns."

triumphantly towards the holy lake, doing great damage to the Rajput territory. A momentary stupor had seized the Kachhwaha, but the heir of Man Singh and Mirza Raja Jai Singh could not long bear the defiant flourishes of the enemy (challenging him to a trial of strength). The whole of Amber, peasants and lords, rose to their feet to strike a blow for her honour. Maharaja Madho Singh, whose fiery Sisodia blood had been cooled down by old age and misfortune, was roused to a sense of his honour by his feudal chiefs. They said to him in indignation and sorrow, "Will you suffer to be thus insulted by a man whose father and grand-father were the tenants of your house and who stood with folded hands before your ancestors?" "By no means" replied the Raja "so long as the seed of Kachhwahas remains on earth." The *levy en masse* of Amber was ordered. Dalel Singh and other Rajput chiefs with twenty thousand horsemen and an equal number of infantry occupied the road by which Jawahar was expected to return.

Raja Jawahar Singh had reached the holy lake and after finishing his ablutions there, he halted for some days and sealed a vow of friendship by the exchange of turbans with Raja Bijay Singh Rathor, who met him there. The Rajputs were watching his return march; but his army being a large and powerful one, they did not offer him a pitched battle. Jawahar Singh avoided the direct route, and tried to make his way through Tornawati, a hilly country, thirty miles north of Jaipur. Rao Raja Pratap Singh who had been for several years a refugee at Bharatpur, now deserted Jawahar Singh, and joined the forces of Jaipur. He counselled an attack upon the Jat army while it was threading its way through a defile and the famous battle of *Maonda* was fought on *the 14th Dec. 1767.*

This battle has been the theme of many a stirring ballad; each side claiming the victory and extolling the heroism of their respective chiefs. The memory of this ancient feud still causes some heart-burning to both peoples. M. Madec who had accompanied Raja Jawahar Singh to Pushkar, and fought for him on that occasion, has left the following account of this event. "The latter [Raja of Jaipur], piqued by the insult, followed the Jats, with his army, on their return. He had

16,000 cavalry. Near Jaipur the Jats had to traverse a defile. They made their baggage go ahead, in such a way as to cover them. They hoped to escape the pursuit of their enemies, but were overtaken and attacked at a disadvantage. The Jats routed them by a counter-march. The artillery and infantry of the assailants were too slow. The Jats took advantage of it to enter the defile, preceded by their baggages at a distance of three leagues. The Raja of Jaynagar engaged in pursuing them in the gorge, and overtook them in the middle. The Jats then made a half-turn to offer battle.

They engaged towards noon. The enemy cavalry put at the very first, that of the Jats to the rout. The latter saved themselves by falling back upon their baggage, crying out that all was lost; the peasants then plundered a great part of the baggage. But the party of Madec and that of the German Sombre, who laboured in that affair with all the bravery and prudence of a great soldier, restored the battle and defeated the Raja of Jaynagar. Nearly 10,000 men fell in the two armies together, among them nearly all the generals of the enemy's army. The victors, deprived of their baggage, of which they could not find even the fragments, were themselves put to great hardship. They had to abandon a part of their artillery[11] on account of the state of the road" (*Le Nabob Rene Madec*, pp. 49, 50).

---

11. **Wendel thus describes the plight of the vanquished: "The fortune of the Jats remains shaken and the result has been entirely fatal to them. They have returned home despoiled, stupefied and overthrown, and Jawahar Singh, having left there all his train of artillery (70 pieces of different calibres), tents and baggage" [*French MS, 68*]. Suraj Mal the bard of Bundi, commemorates this episode thus :**

    ताबत छत्र अरु तोप कोस लुट्टे कच्छबाहन।
    भरतनेर गये जट्ट मारवाय सिपाहन।।
    जित्ते कुरम जोध नाग जट्टन गिनि नाहर।
    समरु बेहुन्नु संग जाय पकरेहिं जवाहर।।
    संस्कृत भुजंग ससिमान सक १८२४ हमतक यह जंग हुब।
    जयनेर विजय जट्टन भजन भइ विदित आव्रज भुब।।"

On that fateful day Jawahar Singh fought with his accustomed vigour and tenacity, and maintained his ground till the darkness of evening brought him respite. Dalel Singh, the brave commander-in-chief of the Jaipur army fell in the fight with three generations of his descendants and none but boys of ten remained to represent the baronial houses of Jaipur. The aggressor, however, was overthrown and once more it was proved that God is not always with the heaviest battalion as tyrants believe.

Jawahar's struggle with his numerous enemies

Maharaja Jawahar Singh now presented a sorry figure, shorn of his power and splendour, derided by enemies, and deserted by friends. "Now is the moment," was the exultant cry that his enemies raised from every quarter. At the first report of his defeat, the country beyond the Chambal rose against him, and it was lost as suddenly as it had been gained. Maharaja Madho Singh entered the Jat territories with 60,000 soldiers and took ample vengenance by ravaging them. Nawab Musavi Khan Baloch of Farrukhnagar (who had been released a year before from his confinement at Bharatpur), and the Ruhelas were ready to co-operate with the Rajputs. His unprincipled allies, the Sikhs began desolating his two outlying provinces (Wendel, 69; *Le Nabob Rene Madec,* 50). The Emperor Shah Alam II was invited by Maharaja Madho Singh either to come in person, or if that was not possible, to send some English commander with a battalion of European troops to reinforce him. "Now is the opportunity" he wrote, "which Your Majesty should seize . . . . your old and hereditary servant and the other Rajas in his confederacy are ready in allegiance with their levies.... The royal seat of Akbarabad will fall to Your

---

The Kachhwahas captured the Umbrella of Royalty, guns and treasure. The Jat, after having his soldiers slaughtered, fled to Bharatpur.As the king of beasts looks upon the elephant [as his prey] so did the *Kurma* [Kachhwaha] warriors look upon the Jats. Had not Somru been in the company Jawahar would have been captured . . . . The battle took place in the year 1824 [of the *Vikrama era*]. This victory of [the ruler of] Jaipur, and the defeat of the Jats became known to the furthest limit of the land of *Braj*.

Majesty." [Pers. Cor. ii. 224]. The Emperor sent—though he disavowed it afterwards—"a royal mandate to Raja Madho Singh to advance and take possession of the fort of Agra, after effecting a junction with Musavi Khan's forces who was to proceed from Delhi [*ibid*, 234].

Every one counselled Jawahar to make a compromise with the Rajputs; but the Jat preferred breaking to bending and to abide by the chances of a war than to sue for terms from his victorious enemy. He decided to carry on war by buying over the Sikhs. He paid them 7 lakhs of Rupees to keep them away from plundering his territory and opened negotiation with them to enlist into his service 20,000 of them. The lethargy caused by the late defeat was shaken off, and warlike preparations commenced in earnest. M. Madec got an increase of Rs. 5,000 to his monthly allowance for increasing his corps. [*Le Nabob Rene Madec*, p. 50].

Meanwhile a plot was being hatched by Nawab Shuja-ud-daula to crush Jawahar's power. The wazir suggested to the Emperor a comprehensive and plausible plan, which, if acted upon, would have brought about the extinction of the Jat power. He asked the Emperor first to dissuade the Sikh sardars from assisting Jawahar Singh by the offer of the same amount of subsidy on behalf of Madho Singh and the grant of royal favours; secondly to send a prince of the royal line with *farmans* to the Ruhela chiefs to unite them under him and conquer that part of Jawahar Singh's territories that lay on the left of the Jamuna and bordered on the Ruhela possessions—the conquered territories were to be left in the Ruhela hands in order to ensure their loyalty. The wazir most enthusiastically offered his services to carry out his plan against Jawahar Singh: "Whenever His Majesty thinks fit to call upon the writer [Shuja-ud-daula] *he will perform what he has represented.*" [Pers. Cor. ii. 234, 235, letter No. 835, dated March 2, 1768]. In short Jawahar's enemies were drawing a net around him, which appeared too strong for him to break through. At this critical moment the attitude of the Bengal Government became the decisive factor. Leaving active hostility out of account, if the English had even secretly countenanced this scheme, the Emperor, Shuja-ud-daula, Najib Khan and all the Ruhelas would have been in full march against Jawahar Singh whom even the Sikhs could not have saved. But the Bengal Government, with an integrity and firmness rare in the politics of the eighteenth century, stood true to their alliance with Jawahar, and vigorously checkmated all the hostile designs of his enemies. The Emperor and Shuja-ud-daula dared not move without the consent of the Governor of Bengal. When Madho Singh found no response to his appeal from any quarter and saw the Sikhs coming to the assistance of Jawahar Singh, he made peace with the Jats and retired to his own country before the arrival of the dreaded cavalry of the Punjab.

Death of Jawahar Singh

Reverses failed to teach any moderation to Jawahar Singh. Strife was the very breath of his nostrils and without it life seemed to have had no charm for him. "The war having been ended on this side [against Madho Singh], it broke out on another. The Jat Raja sent Madec to besiege a fort where another Rajput clan was entrenched. In a month and a half Madec succeeded in climbing one of the bastions, but the assault failed on account of his being abandoned by the Indian troops who were frightened by the terrible fire of the defenders. He clung to the foot of the breach for making a second attack. The garrison in fear capitulated. [*Le Nabob Rene Madec,* 50].

Never did the fierce will and the untiring energy of Raja Jawahar Singh shine forth more brilliantly than during the 6 or 7 months following his reverse in Rajputana. With great rapidity he mastered a desperate situation and brought it back to normality. The late reverse appeared to have done little injury to him, and he was up again on his legs. His arms were recovering their wonted lustre and his territories their erstwhile prosperity. He threw himself heart and soul into re-organizing his army, and particularly increasing the European corps and the field artillery. His authority was re-established everywhere in his dominion and his name respected and feared abroad. His neighbours trembled at the prospect of a more tremendous outburst of his wrath; fortunately for them the swift hand of destiny silenced this unspent volcano.

The story of Jawahar's violent death (July, 1768) runs as follows : "It is said that Jawahar Singh formed a friendship with a soldier whom he admitted to very great intimacy and showed him regard and honour exceeding proper limits and raised him from a low to a high rank. The degree of this man's companionship made him superior [in status] to other courtiers. By chance, some improper acts were done by him, and Jawahar Singh forbade the soldier to come to his private audience and bedroom, disgraced and humbled him, and made him contemptible in his own eyes and in those of the public. This man, being roused to a sense of honour sought for some means of killing Jawahar Singh. One day Jawahar Singh with a small party rode out for hunting. This soldier, at that time, took horse and arrived with sword and shield, and at a place where Jawahar Singh was standing carelessly with a few men, he struck him down with his sword crying out "This is the punishment for the disgrace and insult you did to me." This event happened in the month of Safar, 1182 H. (June-July 1768).[12]

Popular tradition, as recorded by Growse (*Mathura,* 25), attributes the murder of Jawahar to the instigation of his enemy, Maharaja Madho Singh of Jaipur. The sudden death of Jawahar Singh within 8 months of his quarrel with the Raja of Jaipur who undoubtedly benefited by this event, possibly gave colour to this unjust calumny which has no foundation in truth, or documentary proof. As regards the murder of Jawahar Singh the author of the *Siyar*[13] says: "He gave a chobdar named *Sada,* predominant authority over the whole body of his *sardars,* and thus made them all

12. *Chahar Gulzar* MS.: this date, though not very definite, is undoubtedly correct. From a letter of the Emperor to the Governor of Bengal, dated 27th August, 1768, we learn that Jawahar died before that date (Pers. Cor. ii. 299).
Don Pedro De Silva formally announces the death of Jawahar Singh and the accession of his successor Ratan Singh, to the Government of Bengal on 7th Sept., 1768 (*ibid.* p. 304).

13. The translator of the *Siyar* puts it thus: "He put one *Haidar,* a chobdar of his own at the head of his affairs and army: a measure that lost him the heart of his troops, and shocked his commanders to such a degree that one of them resolved to fall upon him and put him to death. This man having a favourable moment, killed

extremely oppressed—they instigated one to slay Jawahar Singh. A short time after his occupying the throne of his father he was killed treacherously." [Pers. text, *Siyar*, iv. 34]. M. Madec, who was in the service of Jawahar Singh at the time of his death, does not accuse anybody: stating simply that the Raja was murdered by an unknown man, who beheaded him with one stroke of his sword [*Le Nabob Rene Madec*, 50].

Character and policy of Raja Jawahar Singh

Raja Jawahar Singh lacked neither the soldierly qualities nor the administrative capacity of his father. Apparently engrossed with the exciting game of war, he was never remiss in his attention to the details of the civil administration, or indifferent to the promotion of the arts of peace. His Court was splendid and magnificent, the best market in Hindustan for the valour of a soldier, skill of an architect,[14] and the flattering harp of a native bard. He paid his troops more regularly and more handsomely than his father, and there was no occasion when he did not generously recompense good services. "His finances were in the best order and his people the least imposed on in the country and he had political views" which appeared very wise to His European military chief [*Le Nabob Rene Madec*, 51]. He left behind him not a set of turbulent and rebellious military chiefs, but a numerous and well-disciplined army, commanded by loyal officers, who faithfully obeyed even a contemptuous voluptuary like Ratan Singh, his successor.

him upon his very *Masnad!*" (Eng. trans. iv. 34). Sada is perhaps the more correct reading, because Abdul Karim Kashmiri, author of the *Bayan-o-Waqa*, says that "Jawahar Singh was slain by an oppressed *Brahman*" (MS. p. 302). However it is likely that Mustapha, the translator, who used only one manuscript, quite naturally preferred the reading, Haidar, to Sada, a rather obscure name. But he cannot be excused for his want of fidelity to the original text which is little likely to have varied so greatly. Those who put implicit faith in translations should take a warning from this.

14. A detailed account of the buildings of Jawahar Singh along with those of Suraj Mal and other Jat Rajas will be found in a subsequent section. *The Jat style of Architecture.*

His clemency spared his younger brothers, though he knew them to be so many thorns in the path of his adopted minor son. At times, he could rise to the height of generosity and forgive his worst enemies, as we find in the release of Bahadur Singh and Nawab Musavi Khan Baloch—dangerous political prisoners—on the occasion of his nephew's birth. Friends remembered him as a knight-errant, bold, magnificent and open-handed, and enemies as a man, capricious and obstinate, a narrow bigot and blood-thirsty tyrant—a comet in the political sky of Hindustan.

Raja Jawahar Singh, unlike his father, had little control over his passions, no respect for antiquity and tradition, no catholicity of heart. At any rate, tradition, no doubt prejudiced to a great extent, associates his name with the despoilation of the relics of the Mughal imperial grandeur. He is said to have seated himself on the black marble throne of the Emperor Jahangir—a sacrilege which made the proud seat of the Great Mughal, to burst in pique as it were, leaving a crack which is still to be seen! It was perhaps during the regime of Jawahar Singh, the strongest and most vindictive among the Jat Rajas that "The Great Mosque of Agra was changed into a market: the grain merchants had orders to expose their goods for sale there. The butchers' shops were closed. They [the Jats] made very severe prohibition of the slaughter of oxen, cows and also of kids [?] . . . . All public profession of the Muhammadan religion was interdicted under very harsh treatment. The *muazins* were ordered to cease their functions. One man gave the *azan* but the Government of Agra pulled his tongue out."[15] Though it is but human to retaliate, it was certainly unworthy of the son of Suraj Mal who had honoured the bones of a Muslim

15. *Le Nabob Rene Madec,* 47. M. Madec says: "I saw, some years ago, that unfortunate man, who begged alms, supplied with a letter from the *mullahs* of the Great Mosque of Agra, in which they attested that the faithful one, exercising the ministry with which he was charged, had been so cruelly treated by the idolators" [*ibid*].

It is doubtful whether some deception was not practised upon the credulity of the stranger, which is, by no means uncommon to this day. M. Madec does not specify the name of Jawahar Singh but says *"When the Jats became possessors of Agra,"* the known character of Jawahar Singh warrants the above inference.

refugee—Shamsher Bahadur, by building a mosque over it at Deeg. [*Imad,* 203].

Jawahar Singh too prematurely and too violently changed what was more or less a tribal confederacy into a centralized State, and rendered himself a despot with the help of mercenary troops. He crushed life out of the State and the people; the one ceased to grow of itself, and, the other, cowed by mercenaries and relegated to a secondary position, lost their vitality and spirit. Suraj Mal built up a structure which reflected faithfully the political instinct and tradition of his own people. But to the eye of Jawahar Singh, it appeared antiquated, inelegant, lacking in sympathy and compactness, unworthy of a *Prince,* though comfortable for a Jat. As in society Jawahar regulated his life according to the then up-to-date fashion of a Prince or an Amir, discarding the old simplicity of his father, so in politics he breathed the atmosphere of imperialistic Delhi. People to a certain extent imitated the fashion of the Prince, and one could see [the vices, maxims, etiquette of] Delhi near Deeg, Kumher and Bharatpur as some of our countrymen see to-day London in Bombay and Calcutta. With the new society established in these places, the customs, dress, buildings, language and all in general, had changed, among the Jats.[16] Jawahar seemed to move with the spirit of the time when he set about transforming a feudal confederacy into a centralized, despotic Government of the Mughal type. But as he was eager to make himself master of his own household, so was every Jat, who resented autocracy and whose innerself remained the same, in spite of all his outward polish. Without making a tactful compromise, he removed every powerful opponent to his fierce will and thereby recklessly destroyed a considerable amount of national energy and efficiency. If the Jats were the ancient Yadavas, Kansa (the uncle of Shri Krishna, who usurped despotic authority over the Yadava confederacy with the help of mercenary fighters, and oppressed his kinsmen) was perhaps reborn among them in the person of Maharaja Sawai Jawahar Singh Bharatendra!

16. Wendel, French MS., 40, 41. He adds: "It must be confessed that at the same time [in spite of considerable polish] one may always notice their naive rusticity in the midst of the very brilliant fortune with which they see themselves surrounded" [*ibid,* 41].

CHAPTER XII

CIVIL WAR

Raja Ratan Singh Jat
(1182 A.H., May 1768—April 1769)

The glory of the Jats departed with Raja Jawahar Singh and confusion fell on their kingdom when his iron grip no longer held the tribe together. His younger brother Ratan Singh, an imbecile and profligate youth, succeeded him, and reigned, according to the author of *Imad-us-Saadat,* for ten months and thirteen days. The few months of his rule were uneventful and spent wholly in ignoble diversions. Four thousand dancing girls surrounded his person; with them he started, a few days after his accession, for Brindaban [Madec, 51] to enjoy the rainy season there in gay revelry. All the scenes of the mythic past were acted once again by this reputed descendant of the Divine Lover of Braj, perhaps in a more magnificent manner. He never returned to his capital; his life tragically ended there at the hand of a Gosain named Rupanand.

M. Madec, the French Captain, was also in the retinue of Raja Ratan Singh during this pilgrimage. He was impressed very much by his magnificent *fetes* on the Jamuna, and his extravagant piety. He says, "The Raja had another weakness [besides his passion for women]—namely that for magicians, enchanters, and alchemists. He had taken away one of these last [=alchemists] to the festivity at Brindaban. For a long time the alchemist kept the Raja deluded by pretending to have made gold. Finally the Raja pressed him and threatened [to kill?] him in case he did not show it to him. The deceiver promised to the Raja to make it in his presence, if he should remain alone with him far from indiscreet people. When the Raja consented to it, the magician drew out a dagger and opened the belly of his master.[1] Before dying, the latter called the highest chief of the nation and motioned to him his minor son" [Madec, 51]. Abdul Karim Kashmiri, the author of the *Bayan-o-Waqa,* gives an almost identical description of this event, "Raja Ratan Singh went to him and pressed him hard saying, 'If you do not prepare the sample [*lit.* first fruits] of gold [*lit.* alchemy]. I shall kill you.' The darwesh declared 'The sample [*namuna*] is ready; it will be shown towards the latter part of the night.' Ratan Singh owing to his curiosity and eagerness kept himself awake throughout the night. The *Bairagi* sent word that the Raja should have privacy *i.e.,* be alone, and that he was bringing the sample. Ratan Singh ordering his attendants to go out sent for the Bairagi. When he was found alone, the Bairagi despatched him with one blow of a dagger" [*Bayan* MS., p. 302]. Harcharan's details about this affair are rather confusing, but he gives the date of the incident correctly, *viz., Ist Zihijja, 1182 A.H.,* [8th April, 1769], which is borne out by a more accurate authority, the *Waqa-i-Shah Alam II* (*Waqa,* 225).

The regency and civil war

After the sudden death of Raja Ratan Singh at Brindaban, a great assembly of the chiefs was convoked at Deeg, by Dan Sahi, who had been entrusted with the person of the infant heir. The child, Kheri Singh, was seated on the *masnad* and Dan Sahi assumed the regency, with their approval. But as

1. We learn from a letter, entered under the date, the 1st of August, 1769, sent by one Raja Parsudh Ray: "Ratan Singh Jat has been assassinated by the hand of an alchemist, and has been succeeded by his son Kheri Singh, an infant of a year and a half. Dan Sahi has been appointed Regent." [Pers. Cor. ii. 386]. This corroborates the notice in the French Memoirs. Ratan Singh died perhaps in *April, 1769;* because the wazir informed the Government about his death in a letter entered under the date 11th May, 1769 (Pers. Cor. ii. 357). The *Waqa* says: "On the 5th Zihijja 1182 A.H., [April 12, 1769], news reached that Raja Ratan Singh Jat, has been killed at his camp in Sri Brindaban by Gosain Rupanand with the blow of "Katar". Sada Sukh and Khushhal Ray cut off the head of the Gosain" [*Waqa,* 225]. We thus find the calculation of *10 months and eleven days of the Imad to be fairly accurate.*

soon as they were back to their provinces, they refused to submit to the regent, who had no more right to rule than any other person among them. This discontent was fanned by the intrigues of Nawal Singh and Ranjit Singh, half-brothers of the late Raja. While M. Madec, who supported the regent Dan Sahi, was absent from Deeg trying to reduce the provinces to submission, a revolution was carried into effect by these two brothers [Madec, Sec, 61], who overthrew his regency. But they quarrelled over the coveted office of regent. Nawal Singh being the elder had a better claim, but the younger preferred the decision of the sword. The turbulent nobles, keen about securing their own independence, formed factions and kindled the flames of civil war [beginning of 1770, A.D.]. Ranjit Singh, unable to contend against his brother, turned a traitor to his house and purchased the assistance of the Sikhs to crush him.

M. Madec took the side of the elder brother and led an army against Ranjit Singh, who had shut himself up in the fort of Kumher. He laid siege to it when 70,000 Sikhs, invited by Ranjit Singh, came to its succour [Madec, 52]. He raised the siege in order to go and encounter the Sikhs. One morning Madec went out with 500 men, 2 guns and one elephant on which he was mounted, to reconnoitre the enemy's position and incautiously pushed too far ahead. He was hemmed in by the Sikhs [*ibid* 52] and was only saved by the arrival of Jat reinforcements. Nawal Singh inflicted a defeat upon the Sikhs [Pers. Cor, iii. 43], but fearing the advent of Marathas bought them [Sikhs] off by the payment of a large sum of money. The Sikhs departed for their country, leaving the traitor to his fate (March, 1770).

The Maratha interference in the civil war

Within a decade from the third battle of Panipat the Marathas recovered from the shock of that great disaster. But they became none wiser by their late overthrow and drew no lessons from it. Towards the end of 1769, Visaji Pandit, Ramchander Ganesh, Tukoji Holkar, Mahadji Sindhia and others crossed the Narmada with a large army to reassert the dominion of their nation in Hindustan. The energy and enthusiasm of these chiefs like those of their predecessors were more conspicuous in harassing the helpless Rana of Gohad and in tormenting the worn out and afflicted Rajput rulers than in fighting their sturdier opponents. Instead of playing the noble role of strong peace-makers among the warring peoples and princes of Hindustan, they chose to play the part of mischiefmongers, fomenters of treason and civil strife. While the sons of Suraj Mal were fighting out with swords their claims to the regency, the Marathas were watching the struggle with satisfaction from Karauli, the seat of their operations against the Raja of Jaipur. When Nawal Singh, the elder and more legitimate claimant to the regency, well nigh brought the civil war to an end by defeating the unjust pretensions of his younger brother Ranjit and appeasing the Sikhs, the Marathas entered the Jat country, began pillaging the neighbourhood of Bharatpur and instigated Ranjit Singh to re-open[2] the fratricidal war (middle of March, 1770). They acted as if Maharashtra had sent them this time not to avenge the slaughter of her sons and the dishonour of her daughters led away into captivity from the field of Panipat, but to destroy those who risked their all to save and relieve the misery of her fleeing children. They sent an invitation to Najib-ud-daula—who was the author of all their misfortune and shame—to come and join them in crushing the Jats once for all. The Ruhela chief, who had retired to his safe retreat at Najibabad for fear of Maharaja Jawahar Singh and his Sikh allies, eagerly seized this opportunity of extracting one thorn with another, and with a powerful army reached as far as Sikandrabad in the Doab. The piety which Rani Kishori acquired by feeding the fugitive Maratha Brahmans with milk and sweets indeed brought a swift return.

The Marathas ravaged a considerable portion of the Jat territory and every where appointed officials in the name of Ranjit Singh. Unwilling to risk a pitched battle with the army of Nawal Singh, formidable on account of the presence of Somru and M. Madec, the Marathas concentrated their forces under the shelter of the fort of Kumher, 13 miles

2. "The Marathas . . . *entered into correspondence with Ranjit Singh* . . . . Consequently he met them at a small distance from the fort of Kumher, his residence." [Pers. Cor. iii. p. 41].

south of Deeg. Nawal Singh who was encamped at a short distance from the town of Deeg, tried in vain to bring the enemy to an engagement. On the morning of the 9th Zihijja [April 5, 1770 A.D.], he "sent a challenge to the Marathas to quit their position under the walls of the fort and give him battle." At noon news reached him that "Tukoji Holkar, and Jai Ram were on their way to meet Najib-ud-daula." In the afternoon tents were ordered to be struck, baggages were sent ahead to Govardhan (about six *kos* east of Deeg), and Nawal Singh with his army started in that direction. The resolution was too sudden; scarcely any *risala* was ready and many soldiers went to Deeg to procure their necessaries.

Two high roads run almost parallel west to east from Deeg and Kumher, gradually diminishing the distance in between, till they meet at Mathura. The army of Nawal Singh was moving along the northern road, while the Marathas who also began to march eastward took the southern road. These two roads are joined by a cross path running from Govardhan to Sonkh, the distance being not more than 5 miles. Somewhere between these two places, the hostile armies came within a distance of two *kos* from each other. Till then Nawal Singh had no idea of giving battle on that day; but the proximity of the enemy tempted two of his chiefs to offer fight. One of these was Dan Sahi, brother-in-law of Nawal Singh and a dashing cavalry officer, very proud of his *risala* of horse composed of Rajputs and Bhadauriyas; the other was Gosain Balanand the brave leader of the impetuous Naga *sannyasis.* But Somru and M. Madec objected to this proposal on the score of the lateness of the hour. Nawal Singh was carried away by the rash exhortation of Dan Sahi and ordered an attack. The Marathas formed themselves near the fort of Sonkh to meet the onset. A fierce battle ensued which went on even after nightfall. Dan Sahi led a gallant charge at the head of 2,000 choice horse; but before he could be effectually supported the Marathas with their artillery and rockets forced him to fall back with heavy loss. After a short artillery duel both the parties came to a close fight with swords. Ganga Prasad and Jud Raj led the division under the personal command of the regent. But Nawal Singh lost his head as well as heart in the heat of action. He alighted from his elephant, and mounting a horse retired behind the impenetrable lines of Somru's sepoys. Even there he trembled for his life, he threw away his insignia of royalty less he should be recognised by the enemy, and fled into the fort [Govardhan?]. The issue of the fight was still hanging in the balance; several *sardars* of rank immediately afterwards went in search of their faint-hearted chief into the fort and urged him in vain to show himself in the field, telling him that the fortunes of the battle might still be retrieved by their steadiness and courage. But no assurance could stimulate his carven heart. The true Jat fought well, but the Maratha fought better in the darkness of the night. The squares of Somru and M. Madec very bravely stood repeated and determined charges of the enemy. Worn out and exhausted, and deserted by their timid master, the army of Nawal Singh at last broke and fled. "Never was a greater number of *sardars* killed and wounded in any battle. As to the rank and file it [was] computed that 5000 horse and foot were wounded and 2000 killed. All the artillery was left on the field except two light pieces which Somru [had] brought off. The army was so completely broken that numbers returned after wandering about seven *kos,* from the battle-field. Had it not been for the intrepid behaviour of Madec and Somru in covering the retreat, not a single man would have escaped the sword of the Marathas [Pers. Cor, iii. 52-53].[3] Nawal Singh stood a siege, barricading the

---

3. Madec's division was almost annihilated. He alone lost 1400 men, and had not more than the wounded and the guard of the camp left at Deeg. [Madec. sec.: 56]. This shows that the number of the killed must have been greater than that reported by the English news-writers. The *Waqa-i-Shah Alam Sani* has an entry under the date 13th Zihijja, 1183, A.H. "News reached . . . . that on the 8th, a great battle was fought between Nawal Singh and the Marathas . . . . Nawal Singh at first fled to Garhi of *Aring* [5 miles *east* of Govardhan, eight miles north-east of Sonkh, in a *contrary direction*] after-wards to Deeg." [*Waqa,* 224]. Thus, we notice one day's difference between the dates given by the *Waqa* and the Pers. Cor. Harcharan gives an accurate and fairly detailed account of the civil war between the two Jat brothers. The author of the *Bayan-o-Waqa,* only notices it briefly (p. 305).

gates of Deeg. The Marathas who had also lost a considerable number of men contented themselves with watching him from beyond the range of the fort guns.

A formidable coalition was now set on foot to crush the Jat power altogether. Najib-ud-daula joined the Marathas, and with their aid began to conquer the possessions of the Jats in the Doab. Ghazi-ud-din Khan[4] hurried from his retreat at Farrukhabad and united with the Marathas. Repeated petitions were sent to Shah Alam II to repair to his capital; but he was restrained by the opposition of Waren Hastings. Thus the Jats for the second time escaped utter annihilation from a combination of their relentless enemies through the silent and faithful services of their English allies. The Marathas made Mathura their head-quarters and began, in concert with the Ruhelas, a systematic conquest of the Jat country in the month of *Muharram* 1184 *A.H.* (May 1770, A.D.). Najib-ud-daula captured *Shikohabad, Saadabad*[5] *and other parganas belonging to the Jats [Waqa,* p. 229]. Next he proceeded to Koel [Aligarh] and took possession of the Jat territories there in the name of the Emperor. [*ibid,* p. 230]. Nawal Singh was saved from almost certain destruction by the disunion and jealousy which sprang up among his enemies after their first success. The Marathas themselves were divided into two parties, led respectively by Tukoji Holkar and Ramchander Ganesh on one side, and Visaji Pandit and Mahadji Sindhia on the other. Tukoji was in favour of an alliance with Najib-ud-daula, but Sindhia and others distrusted him. The appearance of Ghazi-ud-din in the Maratha camp and Sindhia's support of him created a distrust in the minds of the Emperor and Najib-ud-daula. Nawal Singh took advantage of this situation to send his *vakils* to the Ruhela chief, to negotiate a secret and separate peace with him. In the first week of Jamada I, 1184 A.H. (last week of August, 1770 A.D.), Najib secretly made up his quarrel with the Jats [*Waqa,* 232]. More fortunate for Nawal Singh was the interception of a letter from Najib-ud-daula to Hafiz Rahamat Khan Ruhela, which contained some

4. Ghazi-ud-din had fled from Bharatpur disgusted with the conduct of Jawahar Singh (Wendel).
5. Shikohabad is a pargana in the Mainpuri district on E. I. Ry. (lat. 27° 10" long. 78° 40"). Saadabad is a tehsil of Mathura, 28 miles east, south-east of Mathura (lat. 27° 30" long. 78° 5").

reflections on the Marathas. Consequently a coolness sprang up between Najib-ud-daula and Ramchander Ganesh. The Marathas under the cloak of friendship prevented him from leaving their camp, and sent for the vakil of Nawal Singh Jat to talk of a compromise. A treaty of peace was concluded [17th Jamada I, 1184 A.H.[6] *September* 8, 1770], on the following terms: (i) Nawal Singh should pay 65 lakhs of Rupees in all, *exclusive* of the revenues accruing from the provinces conquered by Najib and the Marathas, (ii) out of these 65 lakhs, he should pay down 10 lakhs in twenty days, 15 lakhs in two months, Rs. 7,50,000 in the month of Phagan, and the remaining half in three years, (iii) he should pay an annual *nazarana* of 11 lakhs to the Marathas, (iv) a jagir of 20 lakhs should be settled upon Ranjit Singh [Pers. Cor. iii. 97-98].

---

6. The *Waqa-i-Shah Alam II says*: "News reached that on the 17th Jamada 1, 1184 A.H. [September 8, 1770] Najib-ud-daula holding *darbars* day and night settled the affairs of the Jats with the Maratha chiefs, gave *khilats* to the Maratha chiefs, and took leave of them leaving Nawab Zabita Khan at their camp." [*Waqa,* 232].

CHAPTER XIII

REGENCY OF NAWAL SINGH

Difficulties of Nawal Singh

A mutilated State, a factious nobility, a demoralised army, a depleted treasury and an anticipated revenue were the legacy of the civil war to Nawal Singh who now became the *de facto* Raja of Bharatpur, though nominally a Regent for his infant nephew Kheri Singh. Prospects abroad were equally gloomy for him. The interregnum at Delhi had come to an end. The exiled Emperor Shah Alam II re-entered the imperial city in Nov. 1771. Though the Emperor was weak, incapable and vacillating, the empire showed signs of recovery under the able administration of Mirza Najaf Khan, the last of the great foreigners who graced the Court of the Timurids. With the re-establishment of the legitimate authority of the Mughal Emperor, the Jat Raja stood revealed as the arch-rebel and usurper. The dispossessed Muslim Jagirdars of the Doab and Haryana, the shaikzadas of Mewat—whom Suraj Mal had expelled from their estates, looked up to the Emperor to restore their rights to them. Mirza Najaf Khan was preparing a formidable army to subdue the Jats. The Marathas, upon whom Bharatpur had a moral claim for friendship and help, proved no less inimical than her worst enemies. Though Nawal Singh was at peace with the party of Mahadji Sindhia, the other party led by Tukoji Holkar made no secret of their intention to attack Jat territories after subduing Zabita Khan, against whom they were then carrying on war. The Maratha leaders, being virtually independent of the control of the Peshwa, had no unanimity among themselves and followed no common policy. Nawal Singh could, therefore, hardly count upon the help of the Marathas against the Mughals. Misfortunes came thick upon him; the first of the series was the desertion of his faithful French captain M. Madec.

M. Madec leaves the Jat service (1772)

M. Madec, the French free-lance captain, had since 1766 been serving the Bharatpur Raj with rare fidelity and devotion. He had shown steady courage and skill in every action, though it was often his misfortune to be always beaten and to suffer most for the indiscretion and cowardice of others. His corps had been almost annihilated, his horses, camels, arms and artillery captured by the Marathas in the last battle near Govardhan (April, 1770). Raja Nawal Singh had the fairness to compensate the brave captain for his losses. M. Madec set himself to work with all possible quickness in re-organizing his corps. He bought back his fusils from the Marathas who knew not how to handle them. He cast 12 pieces of cannon and one mortar at Agra, and exercised the raw recruits during the rainy season and winter (July, 1770-Feb. 1771). At spring his corps was completely reformed and during the peace that followed he repaired his fortune too. He now thought of returning to France but was prevailed upon to stay by the French Governor of Pondicherry, who represented to him that his departure from India at that critical moment would injure the cause of France. Throughout the year 1771 the enemies of England were watching with intense interest the progress of the Maratha arms in Hindustan and the diplomatic tussle between Warren Hastings and Mahadji Sindhia for securing the control of the shadow of the Great Mughals.

At the beginning of the year 1772 M. Madec was sent by Nawal Singh to raise contribution from the districts in the Doab. He returned eminently successful and was generously rewarded for his services. Soon after this he was employed in the reduction of two fortified places where two of the near relations of the Regent had rebelled against his authority.[1] It took 15 days to reduce one fort, and one

1. M. Madec does not give us the names of these places. He says : "The Regent had confided the defence of two cities to two of his relatives who proud of the confidence had turned rebels and declared themselves masters." [*Le Nabob Rene Madec*, sec. 76]. One

month and a half to capture another. The defenders gained only safety of life and *were conducted outside the frontiers.* But the besiegers lost one thousand men. Raja Nawal Singh paid dearly for his ill-advised clemency. These traitors, as we shall notice hereafter, joined Mirza Najaf Khan, and rendered valuable services to him in enslaving their own kinsmen.

About this time Raja Nawal Singh was virtually at war both with the Emperor and the Marathas. Najaf Quli Khan, lieutenant of Mirza Najaf Khan, was carrying on the conquest of the Jat possessions in Haryana and Niaz Beg Khan in the Doab. The Marathas[2] made no secret of their intention to attack Nawal Singh after the subjugation of Zabita Khan. Fortunately for Nawal Singh, some differences had of late arisen between the Marathas and the Emperor through the intrigue of his faithless minister Hisam-ud-din who became jealous of the ascendancy of Mirza Najaf Khan in the Court. The Jat chief took this opportunity to sound the Emperor's views for a common defensive alliance against the Marathas, as he had despaired of any permanent alliance with them on fair and honourable terms. He sent M. Madec as his envoy to Delhi (beginning of October, 1772) to bring about a peaceful settlement of the territorial dispute and negotiate for the Emperor's help in the emergency of a Maratha invasion of the Jat territories. But M. Madec became a changed man altogether by breathing the atmosphere of the imperial Court, which was now turned into a centre of anti-English activity. He had been receiving repeated letters from M. Chevalier governor of Pondhcherry, who urged him to join the service of the Emperor Shah Alam II. A war was now expected between England and France in Europe and in anticipation, the heated brains of the Frenchmen in India struck out many a brilliant though futile plan of driving the English into the Bay of Bengal. M. Duzarde was visiting every native Court in Hindustan to persuade the Indian

---

of these places was perhaps Ballamgarh which, as we know from other sources, was taken away by Nawal Singh from the grandsons of Ballu Jat, its founder (*Delhi Gaz.*, p. 213).

2. Khair-ud-din says: "In their [Marathas] heart sprang up the design of exterminating [*fiqer dar andokhtan buniad-i-haiyat*] Zabita Khan and Nawal Singh." (*Ibratnama*, MS., p. 214).

princes to assemble under the standard of the Great Mughal, which was to move towards Bengal at an opportune moment. Though M. Madec had no complaints against the Jats who had been his regular and liberal paymaster, he resolved upon leaving their service in obedience to the call of his country. On the 1st Shaban, 1186 H. (28 October, 1772; *Waqa* MS, p. 236), he was granted an interview by the Emperor who gave him a *khilat* of seven pieces, an aigrette, and a sword. Madec immediately returned to Deeg with the design of removing secretly his family, property and troops. This, however, proved no easy affair. The following story of his escape, told by Madec himself, is interesting as well as instructive, showing the helplessness of the Indian armies of the old school before European discipline.

"I returned to Deeg without receiving orders from the regent. This movement made them [the Jats] suspect me of having some understanding with the Emperor, and they began to watch me carefully. On the day of my arrival, I encamped outside the city, beyond the range of the fort-guns. The same evening I departed with 50 horsemen and the same number of infantry, and the conveyances necessary for the transport of my family and property which were at Barpur [Bharatpur]. I arrived at the city six hours from the morning and spent that day in preparing for the transport of my baggage to Deeg. I sent messengers to Agra, and to all my gardens and villages ordering my soldiers, who were guarding them, to come and join me; but they could not arrive on that day. The Regent, ... having learnt that I had departed for Bharatpur with a detachment of troops, inferred rightly that I went there to bring away my family and property. He immediately ordered all troops within his reach to oppose my enterprise; he also sent orders for the villagers on the road from Bharatpur to Deeg, that they should take up arms and arrest me. It could not be done so secretly as not to become known to me. I knew all the dangers to which I was going to be exposed with my family and the difficulties I was to have in rejoining my corps with so few soldiers as I had with me. There was no time to be lost. I hastened the arrangement of my affairs, and four hours from evening (about 10 P.M.), all being ready I set out on my journey with my family and all that I possessed in the world.

At 8 hours from the evening (2 P.M.), having travelled four leagues, I met a force of the Raja. The chief who commanded it asked to speak to me on behalf of the Regent. I made him approach, he told me that he was sent to request me to go to the Regent. I replied that I was going to rejoin my camp, and that it was very late. At the same time I ordered my baggage to march and seize the path in advance. I remained to talk with the chief. After about one hour I thought it was time to join my baggage. I quitted the troops of the Raja. The chief summoned me to follow him to talk with the Regent. Seeing that I was not going to obey him, he began firing upon my detachment. I caused all lights to be put out immediately and returned his fire. The peasants of the neighbourhood, who had been commanded, on hearing the sound of muskets assembled. Other troops arriving, I found myself engaged in a most serious affair against one entire part of the forces of the Raja. Having with myself not even one hundred combatants, my greatest anxiety was on the side of my camp, I felt sure that if it was attacked, on account of my not being present there terror would seize them and they would be routed by the Regent. These thoughts made me hasten my march in order to join them before day-break. To effect this, I was obliged to abandon to the Raja's troops 3 pieces of cannon which I was removing from Bharatpur, and also many carts loaded with my property. The troops of the Raja constantly fought me up to the entrance to my camp, where I arrived three hours after daybreak. The pursuers then quitted me, and my arrival reassured the frightened spirits. I caused the drum to be beaten at once and departed for Kama .... And at the first movement which I made to take the road, I had the whole army of the Raja pursuing me, and all the peasants of the neighbourhood, who are more dangerous on these occasions than regular troops. That army, including the inhabitants, was not less than 100,000 men. I formed a battalion in hollow square in which I put my baggage, and I marched in that manner constantly fighting. The cavalry of the Raja made marvellous efforts to break my battalion in order to carry off my family. But my continual fire of musketry rendered their efforts fruitless. They made all sorts of movements to prevent me from passing a large marsh which I had to cross. I halted in order to make two pieces of my artillery file to that side of the marsh in order to help the passage of my baggage. At that moment the troops of the Raja redoubled their efforts and I received a bullet wound in my arm. I caused to be discharged a terrible fire which made my enemies to turn aside. As soon as my baggage had passed I crossed the marsh. On the other side I was in the territory of the Raja of Jaynagar [Jaipur]. The army of the Jat Raja remained a long time to watch me and they retired in the evening after seeing me encamp under the walls of Kama. I lost in that affair more than 200 men in killed and wounded, and some camels. I saved the rest of the baggage which had escaped in the first attack." [Le Nabob Rene Madec, 84-87.]

It was certainly a remarkable feat of courage and skill. In less than 36 hours, M. Madec had to make a march of 55 miles by the least computation (Deeg to Bharatpur, 21 miles doubled, *plus* 13 miles between Kama and Deeg), and cut his way with a large convoy through the huge host of the enemy. After having rested eight days at Kama, M. Madec reached Delhi in the first week of November, 1772.

Nawal Singh's alliance with the Marathas and Zabita Khan against the Emperor

By the end of September, 1772, the Marathas had reduced Zabita Khan to the same plight in which his father Najib-ud-daula had twice been thrown at Delhi---besieged there once by Raghunath Rao (1757), and the second time by the allied armies of the Jats, Marathas and Sikhs (1764). But they had in their camp Tukoji Holkar the adopted son, to take care of Malhar's *dharma-putras* among whom the father of Zabita Khan was the most illustrious. The Ruhela chief made a successful appeal to Tukoji Holkar, who procured from the other Maratha leaders very favourable terms for his submission (*Ibratnama* MS., 214). They not only gave back all his territories, but also promised to force the hands of the Emperor to restore to him the conquests of the imperial commanders in the Ruhela country if Zabita Khan would join them in an attack upon Delhi.

Having finished the affair of the Ruhelas, the Maratha leaders entered the Jat country immediately after the desertion of M. Madec with his corps. Nawal Singh's army was driven under the shelter of his forts. He held out not with any confidence in his ultimate success but only to secure better terms of submission. The Emperor did not raise a finger to help him except by writing a letter to the Marathas to desist from pillaging the Jat country ! Meanwhile, Mirza Najaf Khan redoubled his efforts in recruiting and equiping the imperial army, which made the Marathas more reasonable in their demands upon the Jats. Nawal Singh could wait, but the Marathas could not; so they readily accepted whatever sum of money they could presently get from him and started for Delhi to attend to the business of another client of theirs, Hisam-ud-din Khan. They held out the same inducement to Nawal Singh for an offensive alliance against the Emperor as that offered to Zabita Khan, *viz.*, restitution to him of all his territories seized by the imperial officers. Nawal Singh could not fail to see that the Emperor was more interested in crushing the Jat power than in freeing himself from the Maratha control. As he was equally interested in the destruction of the army of Najaf Khan, he threw in his lot with the Marathas. Towards the end of November 1772, the allied army of Marathas, Jats and Ruhelas, numbering more than one lakh [?] of troops appeared before Delhi. Against this huge host, Mirza Najaf Khan could hardly bring into the field 38,000 horse and 8,000 infanty.

On the 28th of December (1772) a pitched battle was fought under the walls of Delhi for about 9 hours. The Marathas and their allies displayed determined valour and compelled Mirza Najaf Khan to take shelter behind the lines of M. Madec. While the battle was surging to and fro, the traitor Hisam-ud-din with two regiments of sepoys, 30 guns and His Majesty's own *risala* of Horse, stood idle near the *haveli* of Ghazi-ud-din, watching intently its varying fortunes. As soon as the Marathas threatened to move in his direction, the Khan fled more in joy than in fright into the city. His troops joined hands with the Marathas in plundering the camp of M. Madec (*Le Nabob Rene Madec,* sec. 96).

The Maratha army with Zabita Khan and his Ruhela horse, the Jats and the artillery of Somru, surrounded the city like a complete circle. Hisam-ud-din cleverly represented to the imbecile monarch that Mirza Najaf Khan was the sole cause of all these troubles and quarrel with the Marathas. That faithful general as well as all his Irani and Turani comrades-in-arms were dismissed from service and ordered to leave the city. The Hindustani party rejoiced over the fall of their rivals; the Marathas got 9 lakhs from the royal treasury and 9 lakhs from the private purse of Hisam-ud-din, who further offered one lakh more separately to Tukoji Holkar, if the latter succeeded in removing the Mirza from Delhi. The marathas took Najaf Khan with all his troops into their pay and Marched away with him (March, 1773) to invade the territories of Nawab Shuja-ud-daula and Hafiz Rahamat Khan (*Ibratnama* MS., 219-221). The Jats had the satisfaction of plundering the Mughal territories and regaining many of their lost possessions. Nawal Singh got a short respite to recoup his strength and had reason to feel as much satisfaction and relief as Hisam-ud-din himself at the temporary eclipse of Najaf Khan's fortune.

Mirza Najaf Khan's first campaign against the Jats

Mirza Najaf khan, who had fallen under the momentary displeasure of the Emperor, and been banished from the Court through the intrigue of Hisam-ud-din, returned to Delhi three months after (end of May, 1773), with his reputation and power greatly increased by serving as a *condottiere* general in the Maratha service in their compaign against the Nawab of Oudh and Hafiz Rahamat Khan. About this time Abdul Ahad Khan, a disaffected subordinate and an apt pupil of Hisam-ud-din in the art of intrigue, joined hands with Najaf Khan for the overthrow of his master. Matched in cunning and excelled in warlike fame by these two redoubtable adversaries, poor Hisam-ud-din lost his hold upon the Emperor's mind and with it his place and fortune. The Emperor cast him away with as little compunction as a man feels in making fuel of a broken stick. Abdul Ahmad Khan became *naib-wazir* in his place and was given the title of Majd-ud-daula. Mirza Najaf Khan was created Second Bakhshi and exhalted to the rank of *Amir-ul-umra* (June 5, 1773).[3] Raja Nawal Singh, alarmed at the re-appearance of the Mirza at Delhi, opened negotiations with the Sikhs to secure their help against the Mughals. He planned a campaign against the imperial territories to be fought simultaneously in three important theatres: one division of his army was to act in the region to the west of Delhi from a base at Farrukhnagar[4], another division was to ravage the Doab from Aligarh, while the main army under him was to threaten Delhi from Ballamgarh. The Sikhs were expected to reinforce and act in concert with the Jat army in Haryana and in the Doab Mirza Najaf Khan pitched his camp at Badarpur (?),[5] 14 miles south of Delhi, blocking the great road leading to Delhi from Ballamgarh. About six miles to the west of the Mughal encampment, there was a small Jat fort called Maidangarhi built in the time of Suraj Mal and still held by a Jat garrison. One day the Jats out of sheer bravado drove away some cattle and horses of the Mughals. Mirza Najaf Khan at once ordered an assault upon the garhi, which was captured after several hours of tough fighting. "This victory proved" as Khair-ud-din says "the title page

3. Mirza Najaf Khan returned to Delhi at the beginning of Rabi I. 1187 H. Hisam-ud-din was removed from the office of *naib-wazir* in the first week of that month. On the 14th Rabi 1. (June 5, 1773) Najaf Khan was created second Bakshi, and on that very day Hisam-ud-din was arrested who remained in captivity in the house of Najaf Khan for about five years. His property, worth nine lakhs in cash and goods, was confiscated: one-third of this amount was given to Najaf Khan as a token of the Emperor's favour: the remainder went to the imperial treasury (*Waza,* 270-273).
4. Farrukhnagar (lat. 28°-35'; long. 75°-10') is situated on the Rajputana-Malwa Railway about 10 miles from Garhi Harsaru junction.
5. The *Waqa* names the place of Najaf Khan's encampment as Badarpur or Baranpur which cannot be identified in the map. Khair-ud-din calls it Barahpula (i.e., the bridge of twelve arches near Humayun's tomb); but he is not very accurate. Badarpur is mentioned as one of the stages on the Agra-Delhi road in the *Chahar Gulshan* [Prof. J. N. Sarkar's *India of Aurangzeb,* XCVII]. We take it to be the same place as Madanpur, which lies two miles to the east of Tughlaqabad.

of Mirza Najaf Khan's record of victories and the first rung in the ladder of his fortune" [*Ibratnama,* MS., p. 212]. We may, with as much truth call it the ominoius presage of an era of misfortune for the house of Bharatpur.[6]

Hostilities were thus precipitated before the rainy season was hardly over. It was only the beginning of September and the Sikhs were wholly unprepared to take the field in such an early season. But Nawal Singh's blind fury could brook no delay in retaliating for this defeat. He sent under the command of his brother-in-law Dan Sahi, a strong division to reinforce Durjan Singh Gujar and Chandu [Chandan] Gujar, his own governors at Atrauli and Ramgarh (modern Aligarh). Dan Sahi and other Jat and Gujar chiefs mustered about 20,000 men under their command and began to ravage the Doab. They plundered Sikandrabad[7] and other parganas as far as Ghaziabad,[8] and were literally carrying out the command of Nawal Singh to "hang every Mughal official who would resist his authority" [*Ibratnama* MS., p. 212]. In the western theatre another Jat army under Shankar Jat from its base at Farrukhnagar, overran the greater portion of the open country around it, and laid siege to Garhi Harsaru. The situation became so desperate for the

6. Maidangarhi (*Ibratnama,* MS., p. 212) is situated 2 miles to the south of Tughlaqabad and 6 miles south-west of Madanpur. Khair-ud-din's narrative, though well written, is inaccurate and sometimes deceptive. He says that the capture of Maidangarhi and the defeat of Dan Sahi and Chandu Gujar near Dankaur took place *before the siege of Delhi* by Tukoji Holkar [December, 1772—March 1773]. This is simply absurd, being opposed to every other authority Persian and English. His story of the opening of fire by the Jat garrison upon the cavalcade of Najaf Khan while proceeding from Delhi on a pilgrimage to Qutb-ud-din's shrine, appears to be baseless. We hold, on the authority of the *Chahar Gulzar-i-Shujai,* that the hostilities were precipitated by the carrying off of cattle by the Jats. I have to reject in many places the details of this campaign of Mirza Najaf Khan against Nawal Singh published in my paper in the *Proceedings of the Fifth meeting of Indian Historical Records Commission, because it was based mainly on the narrative of Khair-ud-din.*
7. Sikandrabad lat. 28°-25', long. 77°-45'.
8. Ghaziabad (on E. L. Ry.) about 20 miles east of Delhi.

imperialists that the Emperor wrote to the Governor of Bengal a letter[9] asking for his help. Mirza Najaf Khan refused to move from his encampment at Madanpur. He despatched several Turani and Baloch chiefs such as Niyaz Beg Khan, Taj Muhammad Khan Baloch and others with five thousand horse against Dan Sahi. They were reinforced by the Emperor with one regiment of Lal Paltan and several pieces of artillery under the command of Ramu Kamadan [commandant].[10] At the approach of Mughal commanders, having made a forced march of 10 or 12 *kos*, surprised him at night when he was encamped carelessly near that place. The Jats retreated to Dankaur, 25 miles south-west and in its neighbourhood offered battle to the enemy on 15th September, 1773. Chandu Gujar, who was the commander-in-chief of the Jat army, led the Van and attacked the sepoy regiments and the artillery of the Mughals. With an intrepidity which astonished even the veteran Mughal cavaliers, the valiant Gujar chief charged the enemy's artilery at full gallop, animating his brave followers. But the volleys of musketry and artillery fearfully shattered the attacking column; only a small body of troopers headed by their wounded leader succeeded in penetrating the lines of the sepoys and fell there pierced by bayonets after performing prodigies of valour. The battle raged furiously for two or three hours; it was an awful struggle of the native valour of man against science and discipline. Undaunted by the fate of Chandu Gujar, the son of Rao Durjan Singh Gujar (Governor of Atrauli) led his *risala* of five hundred horse to the attack and lost two hundred men. Two Jat leaders of cavalry, each at the head of three hundred

---

9. It runs as follows : "The Jats have rebelled round the capital, and have sent their army to Sikandrabad. Having committed depredations and outrages upon the inhabitants they have advanced to oppose the royal army and reached close to it. They *have also invited the Sikhs* to join them .... Desires the Governor to sent immediately an English army under the command of brave officers." This is entered under the date September 22, 1773, Calcutta. [Pers. Cor : MS.]

10. *Waqa*, p. 282; *Ibratnama*, p. 212, says "two regiments of sepoys"; *Chahar* mentions Lal Paltan; Ramu Kamadan's name is mentioned in the *Shah Alam-nama* (MS., p. 34) of Ghulam Ali.

men, next delivered determined charges with equally disastrous results; these bands also were slain to a man. Dan Sahi, the second in command on that day, was severely wounded and forced to take shelter in a small mud-fort (where he died two days after). The remnants of the Jat army broke and fled across the Jamuna. Besides heavy losses in the field, the river exacted a further toll of two hundred lives during the passage.[11] Greater disasters awaited the arms of Nawal Singh in other quarters.

The Battle of Barsana

The Mughal victory at Dankaur (15th September, 1773) removed the serious menace caused by the Jat offensive in that quarter. About a fortnight after it news arrived that the Jats were making attacks upon Garhi Harsaru from their stronghold at Farrukhnagar. Mirza Najaf Khan at once sent a strong force under the able command of his lieutenant Najaf Quli to relieve that place, and put an end to the dominion of the Jats in that quarter. In order to fill this gap in the main army; opposed to Nawal Singh, he recalled his troops from the Doab. Nawal Singh who was encamped at *Fatehpur Sikri* [*Baloch*][12] 5 miles south of Ballamgarh became

11. The fullest account of this battle is known from the extract of a paper of news dated 12th October 1773 [Pers. Cor. MS.]

    The news of the Mughal victory reached Delhi on the 29th of Jamada II., 1187 H; allowing two days for the transmission of the message, the battle was perhaps fought on the 27th [15th September, 1773; *Waqa* MS., p. 273]. Khair-ud-din says that this battle was fought after the capture of Maidangarhi which is quite correct; but both these incidents took place after and *not before* the siege of Delhi by Tukoji and Nawal Singh (*i.e.*, before March, 1773). He calls Chandu Gujar, *'Bahadur be-badal'* [unequalled in bravery], and says that he was killed within the ranks of the sepoys pierced by their bayonets [*Ibratnama*, MS., 214] Pers. Cor. MS. says that his head was cut off by Taj Muhammad Khan Baloch. Harcharan gives pretty accurate details of this battle; the date Jamada II, 1187 H. given by him is correct.

12. The MS. of *Chahar Gulzar* as well as a letter written to the Governor of Bengal by Mirza Najaf Khan [Pers. Cor.] mentions Fatehpur Sikri as the place of Nawal Singh's encampment. One *Sikri* is mentioned as a stage between Pirthala and Ballamgarh (3 miles

disheratened by the news of the disastrous defeat of his army in the Doab, and throwing a strong garrison at Ballamgarh retreated to Palwal and thence to Hodal, about 53 miles south of Delhi. Mirza Najaf Khan followed the track of the Jat army and came up with it at the village of Banchari, 3½ miles north of Hodal (middle of October, 1773). Hira Singh and Ajit Singh,[13] the dispossessed heirs of Ballamgarh, had come to offer their services to Mirza Najaf Khan. He appointed Ajit Singh, commandant and governor of Ballamgarh, and left him with a small detachment to besiege that fort. Hira Singh accompanied the Mughal general to play the usual role of a traitor to his country and his people. Both armies encamped at a distance of four miles from each other; several days passed in skirmishes in which the Muslim troopers had generally the better. One day by sheer accident the Jat camp was surprised. Jamadar Ali Quli Khan captured some men from the neighbourhood of the enemy's camp and learned from them that at that time Nawal Singh was eating his meal and that his soldiers were quite busy in cooking theirs. A party at once rode out from Najaf Khan's camp. "A cloud of dust was seen approaching from the west. Some soldiers [in the Jat camp] cried out that the troops of Najaf Khan were coming. The Jats became

---

north of the former and 5 miles south of the latter) on the Agra-Delhi road. [Prof. J.N. Sarkar's *India of Aurangzeb,* xcvii]. No such place is to be found in the modern atlas. A glance at the map would show that *Fatehpur Baloch* is the place meant. This is situated at exactly the same distances from those places. It lies in lat. 28°-0' long. 77°-25'. Curiously enough Harcharan confuses this Fatehpur Sikri with the famous residence of Akbar near Agra. He mentions the next stage of Najaf Khan's halt as Dholpur to be consistent in his error. *Dholpur* may however be a copyist's error for *Hodal* which is the place really meant.

13. Ajit Singh was the son of Rao Kishandas and Hira Singh, son of Bishandas. Ballamgarh was taken away from their fathers by Nawal Singh. Ballamgarh was taken after a long siege in the third week of April, 1774 [Safar, 1188 H; *Waqa* p. 277]. Najaf Khan gave the title of Raja to both the cousins and Hira Singh was honoured with the additional distinction *Salar Jang* [*Delhi Gaz.* p. 213].

panic-struck and fled in all directions. Nawal Singh, quite at his wit's end stood dumb for a while, and then mounting an elephant fled towards Kotman (*Ibratnama*, MS. p. 233).

In the meanwhile Najaf Quli was making steady advance, keeping the hills of Mewat to his right and driving the Jats westward. In his first encounter with the Jat army, he captured four wheeled field-pieces [*rahkala*] from them. Next he reached Bawal[14] (?) and the enemy was reported at a distance of 7 *kos*. On the 19th October, a letter of victory from Mirza Najaf Khan brought to the Emperor the happy news "Nawal Singh has fled and taken shelter in his *garhi* [*i.e.*, Kotman]; Shankar's army has been defeated [Nawal Singh's general at Farrukhnagar] and all his equipages of artillery [*asbab-i-topkhana*] captured by the [imperial] troops; Najaf Quli has gone in pursuit of the enemy" [*Waqa*, p. 270]. Najaf Quli cut off the retreat of this division of the Jat army to Mewat and drove it northwards into Farrukhnagar. He laid siege to this place, but was soon after recalled to Sahar by his chief. Nawab Musavi Khan Baloch, the ex-lord of Farrukhnagar, succeeded him in command there.

After the flight of Nawal Singh, Mirza Najaf Khan summoned at night (17th Oct.) a council of war for discussing the future plan of compaign. All his officers were unanimously of opinion that next morning they should start in pursuit of the fugitives and the camp should be removed from Banchari to the deserted site of the Jat encampment. But Hira Singh Jat submitted to the Nawab that there was yet no certainty about the break-up of the army of Nawal Singh, who might prepare for battle with his rear resting upon the fort of Kotman—men who had been enjoying the bounty of the house of Bharatpur would not so lightly desert the Raja but would surely sacrifice their lives for him on the day of battle. He further pointed out that it would be injudicious to risk an engagement at this stage with such men so strongly posted, because the bulk of the army of the Amir-ul-umra

14. Our MS. of the *Waqa* writes Palwal, which is a place 30 miles due south of Delhi. It is absurd to suppose that Najaf Quli should go to Palwal on his way to Farrukhnagar (!) is certainly a copyist's error for some other place name. Nearest approach to correct reading is perhaps *Bawal* a place 10 miles south of Rewari.

was composed of raw levies of untried valour. "It is advisable" he said "to push rapidly towards Deeg, giving up the project of pursuing the enemy. If Nawal singh comes out of Kotman, knowing this intention of yours, you can offer him battle [with advantage]; if through God's grace he remains inactive in his own place, the capture of Deeg, left without a master, will be easily accomplished. Mirza Najaf Khan approved of this proposal of Hira Singh and at once issued orders for a march upon Deeg. Leaving Kotman at a distance of 4 or 5 miles to the east, the Mughal army moved along the old Delhi-Agra royal road. They plundered Koshi,[15] Chhata,[16] and other parganas on their way and reached Sahar[17] (22nd October) to take the road to Deeg, *via* Govardhan. Nawal Singh guessing the design of Mirza Najaf Khan against his capital, left Kotman with his army, and taking a shorter route *via* Nandgaon[18] arrived at Barsana[19] about the same time. The march of the Muslim army was thus arrested by the sudden appearance of Nawal Singh on their right flank. The surprise of Deeg was no longer feasible, because the Jats were at least one march nearer their objective. Najaf Khan encamped at Sahar, but after a day or two moved his tents to Shahpur [?] half way between Sahar and Barsana, leaving his heavy baggage and the campfollowers behind. Skirmishes went on for more than a week. Owing to the exhaustion of supplies in the neighbourhood, hardship began to be felt by the troops of the Nawab, who was hard-pressed by his officers to attack the enemy.

The key of the situation was in the hands of Nawal Singh. He was encamped with his rear protected by the fortified hill of Barsana; he could safely refuse to fight as long as he wished, because the whole resources of the

15. Koshi, 7 miles south-east of Kotman.
16. Chhata, 10 miles south-east of Koshi and about 11 miles north of Sahar.
17. Sahar, 15 miles n.w. of Mathura and 7 miles west of Barsana.
18. Nandgaon, 8 miles south-west of Koshi and 6 miles north of Barsana.
19. Barsana, 22 miles n.w. of Mathura and 12 miles due north of Deeg.

surrounding tract were at his disposal. He could kill his enemy by playing a waiting game as indeed the officers of Mirza Najaf Khan apprehended. But Fabian tactics were unsuited to his excitable temperament and weak nerve. On the morning of the 31st October [14th Shaban, 1187 H.] Mirza Najaf Khan led out his forces in the array of battle to try the temper of the enemy. Nawal Singh, who had a strange eagerness without ability for a fight, was easily provoked and a general action began after five *gharis* of the day had passed.

Nawal Singh divided his army in three divisions and stationed them at a little distance from each other. Somru with six battalions of musketeers drilled in European fashion, and three battalions carrying flint guns with fuses, and bayonets fixed at the muzzle, commanded by French officers, was stationed on the right wing. Twelve thousand *Naga Bairagis* resembling leopards and tigers [in courage], with about ten thousand horse and foot under the command of the Rajas who had come to Nawal Singh's assistance, formed the left wing. The artillery, tied together with iron chains, was placed in front; trustworthy commanders were stationed in the rear as a reserve; and Nawal Singh himself surrounded by a magnificent retinue stood in the centre. On the other side, Mullah Rahim Dad Khan with his Ruhelas was stationed against the *Naga Bairagis;* Reza Beg Khan and Rahim Beg Khan with their own cavalry and two battalions of His Majesty's infantry were placed opposite Somru's division; and Najaf Quli Khan and Afrasiyab Khan stood in the centre facing the enemy's artillery and Nawal Singh. Mirza Najaf Khan mounted on a fleet horse spurred to and fro encouraging his chiefs, while Masum Ali Khan was made to take his seat upon the elephant of the Amir-ul-umra, a dangerous distinction for which the poor man paid with his life. A furious and stubborn fight began. Nawal Singh's left was broken by the determined charge of the Ruhelas, animated by the example of their brave leader Rahim Dad; while Somru checked and afterwards put to flight the left wing of Najaf Khan. The Jaṭs made a gallant dash at the Amir-ul-umra's elephant, and capturing it despatched Masum Ali with many blows of dagger, taking him to be Mirza

Najaf Khan himself. The day seemed to be almost lost when Mirza Najaf Khan made his way to the centre and ordered Najaf Quli and Afrasiyab to charge the enemy's artillery with drawn sabres. Nawal Singh's centre gave way under the tremendous shock of Najaf Quli's charge: Nawal Singh himself fled on an elephant. The Muslim army fell upon the baggage in the rear and dispersed in search of booty. But Somru, entrenching his position, placed the cannon in front and kept together his sepoy battalions, quite ready to receive the enemy. Jud Raj, diwan of Nawal Singh, with 500 fresh horse-men was seen preparing for fight behind Somru's sepoys. Mirza Najaf Khan thundered and stormed in vain to bring together his scattered troops mad after looting. At last in frantic rage he flung himself upon Jud Raj's horse; followed only by forty troopers, and after an obstinate contest broke their ranks and put them to flight. Somru, considering it fruitless to continue the fight, ordered a retreat and marched away in good order. But one Frenchman, a lieutenant of Somru, refused to turn back and urged his men to fight. They fired volleys with such rapidity and precision as to deprive the Musalmans of their senses. Najaf Khan himself charged them several times, but their ranks stood firm and unshaken. At last matchlockmen and guns were sent for by the Khan to fire upon them. By the grace of God, the very first shell struck the enemy's powder-chest, the second, guided as if by the hand of destiny hit the Frenchman on the head, and the third fell in the very midst of their ranks, carrying to them the message that it was high time to depart. The sepoys slowly marched off dragging their guns behind them. With their departure life seemed to come back to Najaf Khan, and smiles of joy appeared on his face for the first time on that fateful day.[20]

Nawal Singh had fled from Barsana towards Deeg. Abdul Ahad Khan and the Emperor heard the news of the great victory at Barsana with misgiving and apprehension.

---

20. Both the *Waqa-i-shah Alam Sani* [MS. p. 271] and a paper of news in Pers. Cor. MS., dated November 17th, 1773 gives the same date *i.e.*, 14th Shaban 1187 H. The paper of news gives the following details which differ to a certain content from those of the *Ibratnama* "Najaf Quli and Taj Muhammad on the right; Niyar Beg Khan and

They sent letters to Nawal Singh encouraging him to fight the Amir-ul-umra. Some of these letters were captured by Najaf Khan's soldiers. Najaf Khan gave several days rest to his army at Barsana. He sent Rahim Dad to besiege the fort of Kotman,[21] held by Sitaram, the father-in-law of Nawal Singh. After defending his fort for several days [18 days as local tradition says] Sitaram one night escaped with the garrison. About this time news spread that the Nawab Wazir-ul-mulk [Shuja-ud-aula] was coming to the assistance of Nawal Singh; in fact he had sent in advance a detachment for taking charge of the fort of Agra from the Jat garrison. Najaf Khan hearing this gave up his plan of subduing the Jat country around Deeg, and, practically running a race for Agra reached there just in time to prevent the junction of the Jats with the troops of the Wazir-ul-mulk.

Fath Ali Khan Durrani on the left; the English battalion and the artillery were on the front . . . . at about one o'clock in the afternoon an attack was made upon Nawal Singh's army with artillery which kept up a continuous fire till five o'clock. Nawal Singh fled; Somru and Balanand and few others continued the fray. A hot battle followed and in the end Balanand and several others were mortally wounded . . . . about 200 of the enemy [Jats] were killed. Somru lost most of his men; about 2000 Mughals were killed and 300 wounded."

21. Kotman (in the Mathura district) is also known as Kotban. It lies on the Delhi-Agra Trunk Road a furlong or two beyond the boundary line of the Gurgaon district. I have visited this ruined fort in the course of my historical tour. Only the *mahal* (harem), and Kachhari (Court-room) which is now the *Choupad* or village Common-hall, stand intact. These lie within the brick-built inner fort of which only the big gate, about 50 yards away from the Kachhari still remains. There is also a large *pucca* tank outside the gate. The descendants of Sitaram still live there as humble peasants. I met some of them; I was told that the fort had an outer wall of mud 18 cubits high and 16 cubits broad, with a ditch around. One Giribar prasad, a tall, fair and blue-eyed peasant nearing 50 told me the story he had heard from his grandfather, how the Jats were surprised by the troops of Najaf Khan when they were preparing *roti,* how they came to Kotman and next went to Barsana, where they fought a battle for 18 days; in short a tradition exactly coinciding with written history. Harcharan says that Kotman was defended for nineteen days by the Jats.

From the time of Abul Mansur Khan Safdar Jang, the Oudh Nawabs had been the allies of the Jats. Shuja-ud-daula had no mind to see Nawal Singh crushed, and, besides, the ambition and ability of Mirza Najaf Khan had made him uneasy. He reached only as far as Etawah when the news of the victory at Barsana and arrival of Najaf Khan at Agra was heard. Finding his own design upon Agra anticipated, he at once changed front and, with consummate duplicity, sent a letter of congratulation to Najaf Khan, assuring him that he had come to these parts only to assist the Amir-ul-umra! At the same time Major Polier—the commandant of the detachment sent ahead—was thus secretly instructed: "If the *qiladar* of Akbarabad consents to give up the fort according to previous agreement and understanding, then, throwing off the mask at once, you should try to get into the fort by every possible means. If you fail you are to act under the command of Najaf Khan and obey him as your superior." The citadel of Agra was besieged by Najaf Khan aided by Major Polier. The *qiladar* tried without success many tricks to bring in secretly the troops of Shuja-ud-daula. After defending it bravely for some time he gave up the fort on the promise of the safety of life and property of the garrison. He came out and encamped at Naharganj; but apprehending treachery from the Muslims fled towards Bhadawar, leaving his baggage and treasure behind. Najaf Khan appointed Daud Beg Khan Karchi to the command of the Agra fort.[22]

With the capture of Agra from the Jats, the first campaign of Najaf Khan ended. Soon afterwards, he went to Etawa to pay a visit to the Wazir-ul-mulk. His attention was engrossed for a few months by Ruhela affairs and the Court intrigues of Abdul Ahad Khan.

22. Najaf Khan entered the city of Agra on the 26th Ramzan, 1187 H. (Dec. 11, 1773). The fort fell in the month of Ziqada between 7th and 29th of that month *i.e.*, about the beginning of February, 1774 (Harcharan; *Waqa* p. 273). He crossed the Jamuna on the 15th of Zihijja, 1187 H. (Feb. 27, 1774) to meet the Nawab Wazir-ul-mulk (*Waqa* p. 284). He was given valuable presents and made naib-wazir on behalf of Shuja-ud-daula on the 22nd Zihijja (*ibid*, p. 285). Khair-ud-din wrongly calls the Jat commandant of Agra Dan Sahi, who had died about six months before. The news of his death two days after the battle of Dankaur reached Delhi on the 2nd Rajab 1187 H. (19th September, 1773). The Jat defender of the Agra fort was not Dan Sahi but *his brother* as we learn from the *Waqa* (p. 273).

CHAPTER XIV

DECLINE OF THE HOUSE OF BHARATPUR

Nawal Singh provokes fresh hostilities with Mirza Najaf Khan

May 1774 was the most unfortunate month in a year of Nawal Singh's misfortunes. Every week brought the news of some great disaster to him; Ballamgarh surrendered to Hira Singh Jat; Farrukhnagar opened her gates to Musavi Khan and General Somru hitherto the greatest terror to the enemies of the Jats, deserted to the imperial Court. All these heavy strokes of an adverse fate came down upon him in swift succession within the first twenty days of this month.[1] Raja Nawal Singh bore these losses with equanimity. Though he was destitute of the cool courage and strong nerve of a Jat, he had that optimism and that perseverance verging on obstinacy which characterise his tribe.

Mirza Najaf Khan was well satisfied with the results of his late campaign against the Jats. He had no mind to risk his fame and fortune by besieging their impregnable forts which had baffled the energy, skill and resources of many a great conqueror. He considered the task of the subjugation of the Jats as well nigh finished, and now turned his attention to the other rebels against the imperial authority. He started from Delhi to co-operate with the Nawab of Oudh in his contemplated compaign against the Ruhelas. But the battle

1. According to the *Waqa* MS. p. 277) Ballamgarh and Farrukhnagar were surrendered by the Jats between the dates 19th Safar and 8th Rabi I, 1188 H. Somru had an interview with the Emperor on the 9th Rabi I (20th May, 1774), received *khilat* and was appointed *faujdar* of Panipat and other parganas (*ibid*, p. 278).

of Miran Katra (April 17, 1774) had been won by Shuja-ud-daula before he could arrive on the scene. He proceeded to Bisauli where a general treaty[2] for the partition of the territories of the Afghans and of the Mian Doab was concluded with the wazir. He returned to the capital by the end of June with the determination of taking the field against Zabita Khan to enforce the conditions of this treaty and punish him for his late acts of rebellion. But the strange perversity of Nawal Singh drove him to fresh acts of hostility with the Mirza who was compelled to march into the Jat country soon afterwards. The Jat chief imprudently sought a war with a stronger enemy at the moment of his own absolute political isolation. The Sikhs were unwilling to hazard much for a lost cause and Shuja-ud-daula, who had proved a dubious ally, was now an active enemy and in league with Mirza Najaf Khan. The Marathas who would, in their own interests, have given him help against the Mughal general, were still preoccupied with their internal dissensions arising out of the murder of the Peshwa Narayan Rao. Nawal Singh acted like a gambler grown desperate by repeated failure and yet bent upon persisting in a losing game, allured by the hope of gaining all in the last throw.

During the absence of Mirza Najaf Khan, Raja Nawal Singh made an attempt to recover his lost ground. He issued out of Deeg with his army and began to expel the *amils* of Mirza Najaf Khan from the country. Not content with this, he threatened to march upon Delhi. Mirza Najaf Khan decided to postpone the intended campaign against Zabita Khan till he had crushed the Jat Power once for all. While the monsoon was still raging in its full fury, he started on his second campaign against Nawal Singh. The Jat army

2. Two conditions of this treaty were (1) the possessions of Najib-ud-daula and Zabita Khan, lying to the west of the Jamuna, such as Panipat, Sonepat, Maham, Gohana, Hansi, Hisar etc. should pass under the authority of Najaf Khan on behalf of the Emperor. (2) Should Zabita Khan submit to His Majesty the Emperor, and swear friendliness to the Amir-ul-umra and promise not to deviate by a hair's breadth from his authority, the chakla of Saharanpur was to be left to the Ruhela chief. (*Ibratnama*, MS. pp. 260-261).

retreated before the advance of the Mughals and hurriedly sought the shelter of the fort of Sankar[3] [Sunukhar?] when the Mirza arrived at Barsana in pursuit of them. The Khan had no alternative than to besiege the enemy there, as any advance upon Deeg leaving the field army of Jats unbeaten in his rear was extremely dangerous. The heart of the Jat country now presented a formidable chain of strong forts, Sunukhar, Kama (the neutral territory belonging to Jaipur), Deeg, Kumher and Bharatpur.

The task of dislodging Nawal Singh from his fortified retreat, protected in the rear and flank by the neutral territory of Jaipur, proved a task of exceptional difficulty to the Muslim army. No longer proud of his mercenaries, the regent became more considerate to the Jats. They too, thus cornered by the enemy and compelled to fight for their very existence, began to show their wonted courage and stubbornness. They sallied out daily and fought skirmishes with the Muslim troopers, who could no longer claim success in every encounter. The siege dragged on for many days without making the least impression upon the besieged, who were fed by supplies sent secretly from the fort of Kama. The Rajput princes became equally alarmed at the revival of the imperial authority and did not fail to realise that as soon as the Jat resistance would fall to the ground the victorious Mughal would again carry war into the heart of Rajputana and demand tribute from them. The old animosity between the Bharatpur Raj and Jaipur had been buried in oblivion with the bones of the haughty Jawahar and the sensitive Madho Singh. The regency which controlled the affairs of

---

3. The name of the place as written in a MS. of the *Ibratnama* warrants the reading of Sankar, Singar or Sunkar. There is one Singar (lat. 27°25'; long. 77°20') in the Gurgaon district and about 20 miles north of Kaman (Kama). The same authority tells us that the besieged Jat army at this place could so easily draw their supplies from Kama that without first reducing Kama, operations against the former place proved futile. So this cannot be Singar, at such a great distance from Kama. Sunukhar (lat. 27°45', long. 77°18'), about 8 miles north of Kama and 12 miles west of Barsana and situated in a marshy tract answers the description best. About half a mile south of Sunukhar there is a ruined fort called Sabalgarh.

the Jaipur State during the minority of Maharajah Prithvi Singh II decided to help the Jats in their struggle with Najaf Khan. The *amil* of Kama under instructions from his Government continued to supply secretly provisions to the army of Nawal Singh. Mirza Najaf Khan could neither storm the enemy's position defended by numerous guns, nor could he by any means induce his adversary to leave the shelter of the fort and give a pitched battle for the decision of the long drawn out issue. The siege continued for four months when Mirza Najaf Khan was called away to the capital by some intrigues of Abdul Ahad Khan. He left Najaf Quli in supreme command of the army, and after his return to Delhi sent the notorious Somru[4] to reinforce the besieging army at Sunukhar.

Somru, who was well acquainted with the situation of the place, represented to Najaf Quli Khan that as long as grain and fodder would continue to reach the Jat army from Kama it was impossible to bring the siege of Sunukhar to a successful close. Najaf Quli wrote to the *amil* of Kama not to give any assistance to the Jats. This remonstrance having proved ineffectual, that impetuous soldier decided upon attacking Kama without reflecting upon the political consequence of his action. He sent a portion of his army to besiege that fort. Nawal Singh having left a strong garrison at Sunukhar withdrew with his army to Deeg. The Kachhwahas now openly joined hands with the Jats to resist the imperialists. Najaf Quli's guns made very little impression upon the walls of the fort of Kama, which are said to have been so broad that two carts could drive side by side on their top without the least danger. He held out the promise of giving that fort to the brave Ruhela chief Mulla Rahimdad

4. According to Khair-ud-din, Somru deserted to the camp of Najaf Khan during the siege of Sankar, *i.e. at the end of the rainy season* of 1774. He gives a dramatic touch to the whole affair at the sacrifice of accuracy. We have the unassailable testimony of the *Waqa* that on the 20th of May, 1774 (see *ante*) Somru was given leave to depart for his fief of Panipat. It is more likely that Mirza Najaf Khan recalled him from Panipat and sent him against the Jats to aid Najaf Quli with his intimate knowledge of the Jat country and their weaknesses.

if he would succeed in capturing the place by a coup. One day Rahimdad at the head of his dare-devils stormed it by a rush, unmindful of the tremendous cost in the lives of his followers. But Najaf Quli broke his word and appointed Somru to the charge of Kama. Mulla Rahimdad, vowing eternal enmity to both, marched away with his 12,000 Ruhelas, horse and foot, to seek service with Nawal Singh [*Ibratnama*, MS. p. 266].

Nawal Singh gave a warm welcome to the Ruhela chief and his brave followers. He assigned suitable pay for every man and gave them large *jagirs*—in short he showed them every consideration except trusting them within the gates of any of his forts. Prospects became more promising for the Jat at the beginning of the year 1775. Mirza Najaf Khan had not only to fight with the sword the enemies of the empire abroad, but he had also to hold his own at the Court with the subtler weapons of diplomacy against the Emperor and His majesty' well-wishers like Abdul Ahad Khan. Scarcely had the Mirza succeeded in disentangling himself from the meshes of the Court intrigue, when he fell dangerously ill. The news spread abroad that he was dead, and this encouraged the Jaipur *darbar* to make a vigorous effort for the recovery of the pargana Kama. Mirza Najaf Khan recovered from his illness, and on the 4th April, 1775 [Safar 2, 1189 H.] he took leave of the Emperor to march against the Jats and Rajputs (*Waqa*, 287). When the news of the coming of the Mirza became known, Raja Nawal Singh left Deeg with his army and came to Sunukhar which was still holding out. The forces of Jaipur also joined him, and the allied army encamped under the shelter of the fort and strongly entrenched their position. Mulla Rahimdad, now in the Jat service, was posted with his Ruhelas outside the fortifications of Sunukhar. Several petty actions took place in which the Afghans fought against their late comrades with all the vehemence of injured pride. Mirza Najaf Khan tried without success to win them back to his side, promising Kama and in addition several other parganas to Rahimdad as jagir. But Nawal Singh and his shrewd counsellors could not repose in peace on account of their Pathan ally whom they suspected to be in collusion with the imperialists. They feared that Rahimdad was waiting for an opportunity to fall upon them at some unguarded moment. They now hit upon a clever device to avoid a breach with the Ruhela chief and yet relieve themselves of his distrusted presence in their camp. Rahimdad was asked to start on a plundering expedition against Hinduan and Bayana; all property acquired there as booty was promised to him as a free gift, and the districts conquered as *jagirs* to his troops. Rahim, without suspecting the motive of the Jat, readily agreed to this and at once began his march against those places [*Ibratnama,* MS. p. 267].

M. Madec, who held Hinduan and Bayana as *jagirs* from the Emperor, became extremely agitated at the news of Rahimdad's departure in that direction. He left, without Najaf Khan's approval his post at Barsana and reached the neighbourhood of Fatehpur Sikri by rapid marches. At a little distance from this place his troops, while in the act of fording a small stream, were surprised by Rahimdad and Ambaji Maratha. The sepoys of M. Madec formed their ranks with great rapidity, but they missed the first volley owing to their cartridges being spoiled by water. Before they could reload, the Ruhelas fell upon them with drawn sabres and put some to death and others to flight. The rout was complete: M. Madec did not pause to breathe till he reached the fort of Agra. Rahimdad created such an uproar in that quarter that Najaf Khan was compelled to send against him a large detachment of troops under Muhammad Beg Khan Hamadani, who was appointed governor of Agra.

Nawal Singh and his Rajput allies decided to attack the army of Mirza Najaf Khan considerably weakened by the absence of two renowned chiefs like M. Madec and the Hamadani with their divisions. They came out of their entrenched position and offered battle to the Muslim army on the 18th of May, 1775 (17th Rabi 1, 1189 H.; *Waqa,* MS. p. 287). The superior generalship of the Mirza more than made up for the deficiency of the imperialists in number. The Jats and Rajputs sustained a defeat and fled to Deeg.

Death of Raja Nawal Singh

Raja Nawal Singh paid dearly for his folly in rekindling the flames of war which did not subside even after consuming him to death. In spite of many disasters and defeats the Jat chief was as obdurate as ever. The victorious Mughal army was thundering before the gates of Deeg, demanding his submission or a fight to the end. But Nawal Singh coolly refused both. Fond hope whispered in his ear that he need not yet despair of success. Abdul Ahad Khan tried what diplomacy and intrigue could to baffle or divert the arms of Mirza Najaf Khan. He was instigating the Marathas[5] to crush timely the formidable power of the Mirza—the more dangerous to their national safety on account of his alliance with the English who supported the pretensions of Raghoba. In the Deccan the battle of Arras had been fought (18th May, 1775), the issue of which was not very encouraging to the patrons of the usurper. Nawal Singh was heartened by the prospect of a Maratha invasion of Hindustan after the rainy season which would surely compel the Mirza to retire from the Jat country. More hopeful was the *news* of an alliance of Zabita Khan with the Sikhs and their joint attack upon the imperial territories. The son of Najib-ud-daula looked upon the office of Amir-ul-umra and all the territories around Delhi as a part of his heritage from which Mirza Najaf Khan and the Marathas had ousted him under the pretence of restoring the authority of the Emperor. He aspired to play the dictator at the imperial Court like his father; the Ruhela confederacy having disappeared he relied on the Sikhs who were to be pitted against the Marathas. The Sikhs plundered and burnt Paharganj (the western suburb of Delhi between Qadam Sharif and Raisina), and the Ruhela chief himself was ravaging the Doab. The situation was menacing enough to create grave anxiety in the mind of the Emperor, who wrote to Nawab Asaf-ud-daula[6] for help against the rebels. Mirza Najaf Khan refused to move leaving a half-conquered enemy to insult his rear and resolved not to turn his back upon Deeg without capturing it. God spared the Jat chief the mortification of witnessing the inevitable doom of his

5. See Mirza Najaf Khan's letter to the Governor of Bengal, entered under the date 24th January, 1775. (Pers. Cor. MS).
6. See *ibid*, letter of Asaf-ud-daula to the Governor dated 31st May, 1775.

country and people. Raja Nawal Singh, who seemed to have vowed not to die on the battle-field, was happy enough to breathe his last on a sick-bed, two *gharis* after sunset on Thursday, 10th August,[7] 1775. He was sickly in constitution, cowardly in action and rash in speculation. He was obstinate on the wrong side of it and brave in everything except what concerned his personal safety. As a soldier and patriot he was of the type of Demosthenes who could deliver *Philippics* at the forum of Athens, without courage to bear the sight of Philip's phalanx on the field of Charonea. Though he had disappointed his officers and troops at critical moments by his nervous timidity, they never ceased to believe that he would behave better next time. "He did not possess much administrative ability and generalship."[8] Nevertheless, he was loved by his people for his amiable virtues and generosity, and his death was sincerely mourned by all of them.

Rahimdad's treachery and his expulsion from Deeg by Ranjit Singh Jat

Mulla Rahimdad, after his successful raid in the Bayana and Agra districts, had returned to Deeg at the beginning of the rainy season, and pitched his camp under the shelter of the fortguns along with other commanders of the Jat army. He proved faithful to his paymasters while nothing very covetable tempted his fidelity. On the very night of Nawal Singh's death the Ruhela determined to try his luck by a bold piece of treachery. "Having come to learn that the men inside the city had given themselves up to mourning and were neglecting the defence of the place, Rahimdad Khan considered this to be the most opportune moment, and got four or five thousand of his Ruhela soldiers ready for action. At first he himself with a few chosen companions went to the gate of the city which lay opposite to his camp, and secured entrance under the pretence of taking a mere stroll. He seized that gate, and with the assistance of his veteran soldiers, made himself master of the whole city. He posted Ruhelas at every gate to keep watch over it, and

7. 12th Jamda II, 1189 A H.; *Waqa* MS. p. 289.
8. Ghulam Ali's *Shah Alam Nama* MS. p. 4.

going to the door of Jawahar Singh's [palace] got hold of the person of his infant son Kheri Singh by deluding the ladies of his harem with smooth words of deception. He seated Kheri Singh on the *masnad,* and got himself appointed his Deputy" [*Ibratnama,* MS. p. 270]. He established his authority over every department of the State after expelling from Deeg those officers of Nawal Singh who showed hostility to him. Rahimdad took into his pay and confidence a considerable number of Jat soldiers and made preparations to give battle to the Amir-ul-umra. His attitude was a strange one; he determined to hold Deeg in independent authority against the Emperor as well as the sons of Raja Suraj Mal. A counter-revolution was being planned against him in the fort of Kumher, where Ranjit Singh secretly assembled all the loyal chiefs of his tribe and intrigued with those in the city of Deeg for the expulsion of the usurping mercenary leader. One night he started for Deeg with a select body of troops. He himself entered the fort with a few companions and directed Awlia [Inglia?] Maratha, who had 2,000 horse with him, to attack the encampment of the Ruhelas outside the walls of Deeg. They executed their task with skill and bravery, and falling unawares upon the Ruhela camp threw it into utter confusion. Rahimdad on hearing this news hurriedly went out to the rescue of his camp without suspecting the trap laid for him by his clever enemy. In his absence the whole city of Deeg rose against his followers. Reassured by the presence of the prince even those Jats whom Rahimdad had taken into his service joined their brethren in destroying the faithless Ruhelas. Fighting men who had hitherto remained in concealment among the townsfolk issued out simultaneously from every street and lane and within a short time cleared the city of the Afghans killing many and capturing a considerable number of them. Rahimdad,[9] seeing that fortune would no longer befriend

9. Khair-ud-din says that Rahimdad after his expulsion from Deeg again rejected the offer of Mirza Najaf Khan to re-enter his service, that he attached himself to Abdul Ahad Khan and that he attacked Bashir khan, the Lieutenant of Najaf Khan in charge of Hisar and Hansi (*Ibratnama,* pp. 286-289). But one mutilated sentence seems to throw doubt on the above statements of Khair-ud-din.

him in that country, marched away towards Delhi. Ranjit Singh was installed at Deeg as Raja in the place of his infant nephew Kheri Singh, whose claim was set aside in view of the great danger to the Jat nation.

The Siege of Deeg (May, 1775—April, 1776)

Deeg, the deserted capital of the Sinsinwar Jats, is now a sleepy provincial town of sombre look, situated 44 miles w.n.w. of Agra and 22 miles north of Bharatpur. Though humiliated by the neglect of more than a century, and overpowered by enemies, she still keeps erect her Lakwa Burj lifting its head high into the sky like the haughty crest of Jawahar. The town and its neighbourhood have lost their awe-aspiring martial look under British peace. It is situated in a level plain, having nothing noticeable except its beautiful sheets of water which add to the charm as well as strength of the place making it almost inaccessible to the enemy, especially in the rainy season. Whatever human efforts could do to remedy the defects of nature were not spared by the Jat for strengthening this place. The huge mud-wall with bastions encircling the town was so prodigious in height and breadth that it appeared at the first sight "like a long range of hillocks utilised for the purpose of enclosing the city" [*Le Nabob Rene Madec,* sec. 48]. A broad and deep ditch runs all around the city except near the Shah Burj which commanded the main entrance. This Shah Burj was almost a fortress by itself with "an area of fifty yards square on the inside, for the use of the garrison, and presenting four commanding bastions facing the four cardinal points.... About a mile from this place, and nearly in the

---

Under the date 11th Ziqada 1189 A H. (3rd January, 1776) we have the following fragment *"Khabar rashid ke Mullah Rahimdad Khan HAMRAH-I-MIRZA NAJAF KHAN......."* *i.e.,* news reached that Mulla Rahimdad Khan in the company of Mirza Najaf Khan......This perhaps warrants us in inferring that Rahimdad was *with* the Mirza—and certainly as a friend on that date *i.e.,* 3rd January, 1776. So he must have been expelled from Deeg at some date prior to it.

centre of the town, stands the citadel, which is strongly built.....The ramparts are high and thick, furnished with bastions and surrounded by a deep ditch faced with masonry.[10] The approaches to the outer fort were rendered extremely difficult by a number of fortified outworks and small *garhis* strewn all over the surrounding plain. Among these the largest and strongest was Gopalgarh, a small mud-fort which stood at a short distance opposite the Shah Burj. Though the countryman[11] of Vauban could perhaps with justice ridicule the engineering skill of the Jat, Deeg and Bharatpur were then admittedly the strongest and most carefully fortified cities in India.

Withing these formidable fortifications was a flourishing city, the wealth and magnificence of which mocked the decaying grandeur of the proud capitals of the Great Mughal, Delhi and Agra. The honour and wealth of the Hindus were considered nowhere more safe than at Deeg. Merchant princes and "nobles of the robe" of the Mughal Court built there large and handsome mansions for the better security of their treasure and families. Traders of all communities flocked there and turned Deeg into one of the main arteries of commerce by establishing their depots of merchandise within its wall. The beautiful was not altogether neglected by the Jat in his pursuit of the useful. The architect whose skill was no longer in demand at the impoverished Court of Delhi sought the patronage of the wealthy Jat and transformed a robber-chief's retreat into a city of palaces worthy of the capital of a powerful nation. Thakur Badan Singh lavishly spent his great wealth in decorating Deeg with a splendid suite of palaces now known as the *Purana Mahal.* Raja Suraj Mal, though unjust to himself like some pious and charitable Seths, did not grudge any expenditure towards the building of several noble edifices, such as Suraj Bhavan, Kishan Bhavan, and Gopal Bhavan, bearing the impress of a new

---

10. *Memoir of the War in India* by Major William Thorn, p. 414.
11. M. Madec speaking about the fortifications of Bharatpur remarks : "These people are so simple that they well believe that they have found out the true manner of fortifying!" (*Le Nabob Rene Madec,* sec. 47).

style of architecture which experts are disposed to call the Jat style, characterised by a graceful combination of Jat solidarity with Mughal elegance. Maharaja Jawahir Singh, envious of the inimitable grace and symmetry of the Kachhwah capital, sought to turn his own into a veritable paradise of his dreams. Large reservoirs of water for boating and beautiful gardens intersected by canals fed by artificial fountains immeasurably heightened the charm of the royal palaces. Such was the noble city of Deeg, great in beauty and strength, which was now coveted by the conqueror of the Jats to crown his victory.

Mirza Nazaf Khan had withdrawn his main army to Farah (on the bank of the Jamuna, half-way between Mathura and Agra) from the neighbourhood of Deeg during the rainy season, leaving only a small detachment to watch the enemy. At the end of the rains he started to resume the siege and pitched his camp at a distance of one kos and a half from the Kama gate. He passed some days in reconnoitring the defences of the fort; his heart misgave him at the closer view of its strength. So numerous were the guns and matchlockmen manning its walls that Deeg appeared to him a living volcano, every inch of which seemed to emit fire and send forth an inexhaustible flood of molten lead. The fortifications were so extensive that his whole army was considered hardly sufficient to blockade effectively even one side of it. At last his soldier's eye descried the Achilles's heel in this apparently invulnerable monster of war. He assigned the task of erecting batteries against the shah Burj (where the ditch terminated) to half his men, and himself with the other half besieged Gopalgarh[12] to cover their operations [*Ibratnama,* MS. p. 274]. The soldiers in their batteries dug trenches to protect themselves from the galling fire of artillery and musketry from the walls of Deeg. Several thousand Naga foot-soldiers were encamped in the

12. It is interesting to observe that in 1804 Lord Lake also did exactly the same at the siege of Deeg : "On the right of our battery [against Shah Burj] was Gopalgarh an old mudfort . . . . crowded with matchlockmen who by their constant firing annoyed working parties very much and did us considerable damage." [*Memoir of the War in India* – Thorn, p. 408].

intervening ground between Deeg and Gopalgarh. As they knew no fear or anxiety, their leaders would very often with a few of such followers boldly attack the Musalmans in the battery and drive off from the way the bullocks bringing grain to the army of the Mirza. This caused scarcity of foodstuffs in his camp and alarmed his troops. Shortly after Muhammad Beg Khan Hamadani and Najaf Quli who had been sent to reduce the surrounding country to order and obedience, returned to the camp with large convoys of grain and materials of war. The arrival of their victorious troops revived the courage of the besieging army. Mirza Najaf Khan having been thus reinforced, decided to drive away the enemy troops encamped in the open ground between Gopalgarh and Deeg.

One morning the Nawab, with his whole army arrayed for battle and his guns placed in front, marched to his chosen ground. All the Naga Gosains fully equipped for fight and carrying matchlocks in their hands came out to resist the Muslim army. Thousands of Jat soldiers poured in from every direction and rapidly formed ranks of battle. Ranjit Singh himself accompanied by all his brave and renowned chiefs descended from the fort and taking his post in one of the *murhalas* [redoubts] gave an order for attacking the enemy. At the same time the guns of Deeg and Gopalgarh kept on firing incessantly upon the troops of the Nawab, who were also exposed to a heavy fire of *zamburaks, jazail* and muskets from behind the redoubts. From all directions the Jat horse and foot began to press them hard and the furious Gosains dealt out martyrdom to many a Muslim. The troops of the Nawab were losing their ground; many were slain and the knees of others began to shake. The few who had hitherto tenaciously kept the field out of a sense of honour in spite of the deadly fire were at last about to flee. The Nawab, seeing the desperate condition of affairs, dismounted, and his choice companions and guards followed suit. At their head he charged the enemy with great intrepidity. His example spurred the disheartened Muslim troops to one gallant effort to break the enemy's lines. But Raja Ranjit Singh, who had prudently kept himself beyond the danger zone, made no exertion to support his men, and he seems to have left the field at this critical moment. The Jat army, unable to stand the determined charge of the army of the Nawab, were forced to withdraw. The Gosains who had so long scorned the shelter of the fortifications of Deeg, entered the town with their baggage. Muhammad Beg Khan Hamadani pitched his camp on the ground formerly occupied by them.

Mirza Najaf Khan found that the capture of Deeg by force of arms was almost impossible. He ordered Najaf Quli to encamp with his troops, at a convenient place between Deeg and Kumher, and to be vigilant day and night in intercepting the food-supplies sent from Kumher to the besieged and cutting off all communications between these two places. One night two thousand men and women carrying grain from the district of Kumher and escorted by a party of Jat foot-soldiers, fell in with the patrol of Najaf Quli's camp. At the sight of the enemy, they threw down their loads and fled to the jungles; a few were captured and sent to Mirza Najaf Khan. His advisers suggested that these men should be deprived of their noses and ears and sent away to their homes, so that the people of Kumher might know the risk of such an enterprise. But the Mirza refused to punish the helpless and innocent people for the crime of one obstinate rebel. He set them free only with the warning that they should not make any such attempt in future [*Ibratnama* MS. pp. 266-267]. Najaf Khan's kindness proved more effective in disarming the hostility of the Hindu villagers than the usual frightfulness of mediaeval warriors. His exalted character inspired confidence in the hearts of the mass of the Hindu people and his wise and humane policy removed for a while the general feeling of repulsion against Muhammadan rule, a legacy of the age of Aurangzeb augmented by the bloody conquests of the Abdali.

M. Madec who had rejoined the army of Najaf Khan after his defeat by Rahimdad, proposed a night-attack upon one of the towers of the town where the guards were observed to have grown slack in their watch and duty. He offered to lead a party for the surprise, consisting of seven picked companies of grenadiers [*Sipahian-i-garandil*] with two guns; the Nawab was to stand ready in the camp with his army and was to start for the appointed place as soon as he should hear the sound of a volley of muskets which was to be fired as a signal by the storming party. M. Madec and the sepoys concealed themselves in the trench of the battery till midnight. When the guards appeared to have retired to rest, they silently made their way to the foot of the wall and began to ascend it making foot-holds in the wall with their bayonets and daggers. About one hundred men gained the top; M. Madec, owing to his nervousness and perplexity without waiting for others to climb up ordered the sepoys. to fire a volley of their muskets as signal for the Mirza. But it served no less as an alarm to the negligent watch who at once fell upon the sepoys on the wall without giving them time to reload their muskets. Most of them were killed and a few jumped down on the ground below to save themselves from the enemy's sword [*Ibratnama* MS. pp. 269-270]. As soon as the signal firing was heard Mirza Najaf Khan rode with a loose rein and stopped only at the foot of the tower. By this time the day had broken, and the garrison of Deeg throwing open the gates of the fort attacked the troops of the Nawab who found themselves caught at a disadvantage. The army of Najaf Khan was exposed to a terrible fire from the fort-guns and the matchlocks in the smaller *garhis.* Veterans of the Nawab's army fell down at every steps; horses became restive and threw down their riders. "Soldiers and officers who had for years fought valiantly in many a battle were unable to keep their feet firm on that field of Resurrection and fled without a moment's thought, carrying confusion even to their camp-followers. The defenders of the fort became bolder in their attack; it was a strange sight to see one wretched Jat foot-soldier armed only with a spear, rushing upon ten troopers of the Nawab and the latter standing paralysed [with fear] and motionless like pictures and statues, none having the courage to resist the infidels." [*Ibid.*] The cruel-hearted enemy seeing the plight of the army of Islam gradually closed upon them. Out of three or four thousand soldiers only a small number of men held together fighting resolutely around their brave general. When the Nawab found even his companions inclined to turn back, he wavered as to what course he should take. At this critical moment Somru with one battalion of sepoys arrived with great speed to the assistance of the Nawab and interposed his detachment between the two armies. He ordered his guns to be loaded with grape-shot which dealt out death to hundreds at a time in the rank of enemy. The progress of the Jats was arrested and at last they were driven into the fort. Mirza Najaf Khan did not relinquish the ground so bravely won; he ordered a battery to be constructed on that spot [*ibid* p. 281].

Everyday the prospect became more and more gloomy for the besieged. The army of Najaf Khan was being swollen daily by the arrival of fresh troops. Raja Himmat Bahadur joined him with five or six thousand horse and foot, and thirty guns. The Nawab Asaf-ud-daula sent Latafat Ali Khan[13] with three battalions of sepoys to the help of the Mirza. Najaf Quli completely cut off the food-supplies of the besiegers. It was not the task of feeding a small garrison but providing food to every soul in a populous city (of fifty thousand mouths at the lowest computation) that confronted Raja Ranjit Singh. The inevitable came at last, and the Jat was forced to yield but not a day too soon. Famine spread in the city and in its train came epidemic and lawlessness. "Every street and lane was strewn with hundreds of dead bodies of men and beasts. The distressed people made no distinction between clean and unclean food. Anything that came to hand was thrown into the mouth of everybody without hesitation." [*Ibid*, p. 282[14]]. Under the stress of such a calamity Ranjit Singh permitted the citizens to go out, and a stream of wretched humanity passed through the dismal gates of Deeg towards the Muslim camp. The officers of Mirza Najaf-Khan urged him to drive these refugees back into the fort by opening fire upon them so that these people

13. On the 8th of Muharram [1190 H; 28th February, 1776] Latafat Ali Khan with three battalions [*paltan*] sent by Nawab Asaf-ud-daula, presented *nazar* to His Majesty, and receiving *khilat*, went to the *haveli of Safdar Jang* (*Waqa*, 291).

14. Khair-ud-din perhaps transgresses the bounds of credibility when he says *"Hanud az hurmat goshi i-gao igmaz kardah dar zabuh-i-gao ba-Musalmanan ham-dast o iksar dar-manandgan ba-khordan-i-murdah-ba-murdar khawaran ham-kassa shudand."* [*Ibratnama*, MS. p. 282].

might increase the horror of famine within and render the air of the fort pestilential. But the Nawab abhorred this ruthless though clever device of stewing the Jat in his own juice, and said "I do not wish that these poor and destitute people should be caught in adversity along with the rebels and oppressors." He treated them very kindly and provided for their comfort and security. He planted an imperial standard [*alam*] half way between the city and his own encampment and issued a proclamation that those who would take shelter under that standard would in no way be molested. This welcome message brought every day hundreds of refugees to that standard. It so happened that even rich merchants and money-lenders wearing tattered dress and concealing valuable jewels and gold coins in their clothes began to slip out in the company of the poor. The camp-followers and wicked characters of the Muslim army, who used to lie in wait and sometimes rob the refugees before they could reach the standard, discovered this trick. When an accidential search revealed jewels in rags, even the Mirza's soldiers secretly joined them in this business and deprived the poor refugees of every piece of cloth on their bodies. The report having reached the ears of the Mirza, he summoned these soldiers and their officers and severely reprimanded them for their ignoble act of oppressing men in misery. From this time the refugees were ordered to wait under the wall of the fort, and when a large number of them had assembled, the Mirza himself with his guards escorted them to the imperial standard and appointed a strong detachment of troops to protect them. Within a few days almost all the non-combatants left the city.

Insufficient food began to tell upon the spirit and health of the Jat soldiers, who were becoming weaker every day. Still Ranjit Singh would neither evacuate the fort nor offer battle to the enemy. The chiefs of his army and members of his household became disgusted at his indecision and pressed him strongly to make a choice between the two alternatives now open to him: if he cared for honour, he should at once lead them, half dead as they were, against the Musalmans with the resolution either to conquer or to die; or if he wished to wait for any change of fortune by prolonging the struggle he should retire to Bharatpur or Kumher before it was too late. Ranjit Singh descended from the fort one dark night, at a spot near the battery of Raja Himmat Bahadur and eluding the pursuit of the enemy safely reached the fort of Kumher. A considerable number of Jats remained behind guarding the women and children, and being resolved to die in defence of the citadel. Next morning, on the 10th Rabi-ul-awwal, 1190 A.H. (29th April, 1776), Mirza Najaf Khan entered the town. But the garrison, who had retreated with their families into the mansion of Badan Singh and the citadel, did not allow the Muslims to taste the joy of victory, rather "made it more bitter than the wine of death" [*Ibratnama* MS. p. 284]. They kept up an incessant and terrible musketry fire upon the troops of the Nawab, many of whom died in the attempt to dislodge them. The Mirza forbade the plunder of even the deserted houses of the town and posted strong guards everywhere. Impressed by the undaunted spirit of the Jat garrison, he expressed his willingness to grant them pardon and a safe conduct. They rejected his generous offer and persisted in their hostility. At length the Nawab ordered Somru to bombard these places by erecting batteries against them. Towards sunset breaches were made in the walls of the mansion and of the inner fort, rendering them untenable. In the darkness of the night the Jat grimly prepared himself for the last awful journey of life, steeling his heart against all sentiments of love and affection. His near and dear ones were sent ahead by the sword to a region where his own spirit, free from earthly bondage, would seek theirs on the morrow. With the first gleam of dawn the warriors threw open the gates of the citadel and fell upon the battery and the sepoys of Somru. Whoever came in their path instantly fell victims to their sword, sharpened by hatred and despair. Somru's guns loaded with grap-shots opened a destructive fire; but wound had no pain, death no terror, nor life any charm for these heroes, each of whom attacked thirty or forty enemies and piercing the ranks of the sepoys struck the guns with the sword in blind fury. Glutted with the slaughter of their enemies and covered with many wounds they fell gloriously fighting to their last breath. Deeg,[15] dyed crimson with the best blood of her children and her foes alike, awaited her fate at the hands of the conqueror.

15. Khair-ud-din has done full justice to the valour of the Jats in this last phase of their struggle with Mirza Najaf Khan. He says "Not a single man tried to save his life. If they had fought unitedly they would have slain many more and safely made their way [out of the fort]." No *johar* seemed to have been lighted at Deeg; women and children were "put to the sword" according to Khair-ud-din. M. Madec notices that three wives of Nawal Singh prayed to the palace-eunuch to kill them after the capture of the city by Najaf Khan. "They lay on the carpet and he cut off the heads of all the three of them one after another, and ended by killing himself on their corpses [*Le Nabob Rene Madec,* Sec. 48]. There is nothing unusual in the slaughter of females by the Jats at Deeg.

Speaking of the Jats in the reign of Akbar Manucci says "In order to defend themselves these villagers hid in thorny scrub or retired behind the slight walls surrounding their villages. *The women stood behind their husbands* with spears and arrows. When the husband had shot off his matchlock, his wife handed him the lance, while she reloaded the matchlock. Thus did they defend themselves until they were no longer able to continue. When reduced to extremity, they cut their wives and daughter's throats and then in desperation, they threw themselves against the enemy's ranks and several times, they succeeded in gaining the day by mere reckless courage." [*Storia do Mogor,* tr. by Wm. Irvine, i. 134].

CHAPTER XV

REIGN OF RAJA RANJIT SINGH JAT (1775-1805)

Afrasiyab's campaign in the Doab

Raja Suraj Mal had sown well the seeds of liberty and ambition in the heart of every Jat. If the parent-tree of the Jat State was withering in the land of Braj, its off-shoots grew up vigorously on newer soils and kept up the hope and faith of the people in their great political destiny. During the four years of the comparative neglect of the Doab by the Mughal Government since the battle of Dankaur, several Jat leaders, on their individual initiative, had been carrying on war with the object of carving out small principalities for themselves. They had not only created a powerful diversion to draw off a part of the Mughal army, but also found means to "send secret help to the besieged at Deeg" [*Ibratnama*, p. 289]. Mirza Najaf Khan sent Afrasiyab Khan[1] to subdue them and restore order and peace in the Doab. Afrasiyab crossed the Jamuna with an army of fifteen thousand horse and a proportionate number of matchlockmen and guns. After having expelled from that region all the Jat officials who were the ring leaders of disturbance and rebellion, he laid siege to Aligarh. Jawahar Singh had spent a large sum of money in strengthening its fortifications,

---

1. **Khair-ud-din is not definite about the date. He says, "*It is said* that when the seige of Deeg was prolonged the Amir-ul-umra sent Afrasiyab Khan" [MS. p. 289].**

given it the name of Ramgarh[xxx] (it having been known as Sabitgarh before his time), and made it the grand depot of his military stores and treasure. After Afrasiyab Khan had reduced the garrison to great straits by a siege of several months, Raja Bhup Singh of Mudsan and Hathras[2]

XXX. Sabit Khan, Governor of Koil region during the time of Farrukh-Siyar and Muhammad Shah built a fort three miles north of the town Koil and named it Sabitgarh. After the occupation of the Koil, by the Jats the fort was renamed Ramgarh. According to News Letter dated 11th June 1761, Surajmal was staying in Ramgarh. Mirza Najaf Khan with his lieutinent Afrasiyab Khan captured Ramgarh from the Jats in 1775 and named it Aligarh. In 1804, the Britishers named Koil as a separate district called Aligarh. J. M. Siddiqui, *Aligarh District: A Historical Survey*, p. 25-27,112.

Sabitgarh was named Ramgarh by Suraj Mal not by Jawahar Singh. Suraj Mal occupied Koil in Febraury 1753 from its *faujdar* Rao Bahadur Singh Burgujar. (सूदन, सुजान चरित) 98-103; Tarikh-i-Ahmad Shahi, 47a.) But the Jat garrison had to evacuate it (Tarikh-i-Ahmad Shahi, 105a, 106a) about the end of December 1753 because the Maratha and Mughal armies encircled the Jat heartland before the siege of Kumher fort. After Abdali's expedition against Jats in 1757 Malhar Rao Holkar and Imad, the sworn enemies of Raja Suraj Mal, came to terms with him. At this opportune time Suraj Mal not only re-established his out posts, along both the sides of Jamuna but also settled the tracks from Agra to Meerut. It can be inferred that during this period Ramgarh was made stronghold of the Jats. Abdali besieged Ramgarh in his second expedition on 25th March 1760 and after 19 days fort commander Durjan (Sal) Singh surrendered Ramgarh. (G.C. Dwivedi, *The Jats: Their role in the Mughal Empire* p.180, f.n. 46; P.C. Chandawat, *Maharaja Suraj Mal Aur Unka Yug*, p.164, f.n.2.) In the post-Panipat period Suraj Mal captured Agra fort and he himself went to Koil in June 1761, encamped there and recovered his former possessions in that region. (S.P.D., II, 144; Rajwade, I, 285, 295) above News letter cited by Siddiqui also confirms that Suraj Mal was staying in Ramgarh in June 1761. Thus from 1761 to 1775 Ramgarh remained in the possession of the Jats. —Ed.

2. Hathras on E. I. Ry., 25 miles east of Mathura; Mudsan lies 8 miles west of Hathras. Another fort 'Bawal' of the *Ibratnama* cannot be indentified in the map. It may be a mistake for Jowar, a large village 10 miles from Hathras and 4 miles north-west of Mudsan. But this village has no trace of fortification. The first two places are situated between lat. 27°-40' and long. 78°-10'.

commenced hostilities in his rear. At the instigation of the Raja the peasants throughout the Doab refused to pay taxes and resisted the authority of Mughal Government. Afrasiyab, finding himself unequal to the task, summoned his master to his assistance.

Mirza Najaf Khan's departure from Deeg

Mirza Najaf Khan had strained his energy and resources to the utmost in capturing Deeg, in the belief that such a success would bring the Jat down on his knees. The fall of the capital of the Jats sent a thrill of surprise throughout India. Titles and honours were heaped upon the conqueror by the Court of Delhi. But the joy of the Mirza turned into gloom when he found that in parting with Deeg the Jat did not intend to part with his independence. Without suing for terms, Raja Ranjit Singh prepared for a more obstinate defence of his remaining strongholds. The Mirza spent the rainy season in the Jat country and seemed to have contemplated a campaign against Jaipur. But the serious nature of the Jat rising in the Doab and the failure of Afrasiyab Khan against the forts of Raja Bhup Singh Jat made him change his mind. However, before he departed from Deeg he succeeded in planting a thorn to torment both the Jat and the Kachhwah by encouraging the aggressive views of Rao Raja Pratap Singh of Macheri, who gave them no peace for several years from this time.

Mirza Najaf Khan started from Deeg with his 11 chiefs and a numerous army to subdue the Jat rebellion in the Doab. A warweariness seems to have come upon that veteran general, who had no more relish for this never-ending struggle with a people whom no odds could overawe, and no disaster could dishearten. He was inclined to peace, and signified his willingness to confirm Raja Bhup Singh in his possessions as a feudatory of the empire if he would submit and come to his presence. But the Jat who never learns through the experiences of others, was not disposed to yield without a trial of strength with the conqueror of Deeg. He stood a siege at Mudsan and resolutely defended it for some time. Many brave soldiers of the Mirza were killed and wounded by the tremendous fire of guns, matchlocks and *huqqahs* [hand grenades] in their attempt to storm the fort. Raja Himmat Bahadur who was with the Mughal army received a bulletshot and was severely wounded. At last they succeeded in running several mines under the walls of the fort and forced the Raja to evacuate[3] it. Mirza Najaf Khan gave the fort of Mudsan to Afrasiyab and himself undertook the siege of Hathras (eight miles east of Mudsan), whither the Raja had fled. Pressed vigorously by the enemy, Bhup Singh sued for terms and sought an accommodation through Raja Himmat Bahadur. The Nawab gave back to him all his territories on the condition of military service and allowed him to retain those forts which he was holding at that time [*Ibratnama*, MS. p. 291]. He then marched against Ramgarh and having captured it after a siege of twenty-four days, changed its name to Aligarh.[4]

About this time the Emperor summoned Mirza Najaf Khan to Delhi to punish the rebellious Ruhela chief who had slain Abdul Qasim Khan (brother of Abdul Ahad Khan), defeated an imperial army, and forcibly taken possession of many *mahals* of the crownland.

Mirza Najaf Khan's campaign against Zabita Khan

Mirza Najaf Khan reached Delhi and was honourably conducted to the royal presence by Princes Jahandar Shah and Jahan Shah (4th Muharram, 1191 H. = 12th February, 1777). Two months afterwards he accompanied the Emperor in the expedition against Ghausgarh, one of the strongholds of Zabita Khan. The imperial army left Delhi on the 19th April (11th Rabi I., 1171 H.) and arrived in the vicinity of Ghausgarh on the 8th June. Zabita Khan with his main army had already marched out of that fortress to harass the imperialists by acting on their supplies and attacking them

---

3. Mudsan was captured between 9th Ziqada and 7th Zihijja of the year 1190 H. (20th December, 1776-17th January, 1777). (*Waqa*, MS. p. 297).
4. Khair-ud-din says that Aligarh was captured by Afrasiyab Khan before he was confronted with the peasants revolt in the Doab instigated by Bhup Singh. But considering his indifference to the sequence of events we cannot accept this against the testimony of *Imad-us-Saadat*, written at an earlier date.

from the rear. Mirza Najaf Khan laid siege to the fort, but had to suffer great hardships during the rainy season which set in shortly after. He fought a pitched battle with the army of Zabita Khan on the 18th Rajab (22nd August). Though he succeeded in beating off the enemy, the situation, aggravated by the treachery of Abdul Ahad Khan, was one of great peril for him. He summoned Afrasiyab Khan from the Doab, and was joined by that general on the 30th Rajab (3rd September). Another great battle was fought, and a decisive victory won on the 11th Shaban (14th September), mainly through the fortitude and skill of Afrasiyab. On the 22nd Shaban (25th September) the Emperor entered Ghausgarh in triumph, and on the 7th Shawwal (8th November) the families of Zabita Khan and other Afghan chiefs were sent to the fort of Agra under the custody of Daud Beg Khan and Afrasiyab Khan. Having left Najaf Quli as governor of Saharanpur, the Emperor and Mirza Najaf Khan hastily set out for the capital to punish Rao Raja Pratap Singh and Ranjit Singh Jat.

Renewed activity of Ranjit Singh

Ranjit Singh made a good use of the short respite afforded by the embarrassment of Mirza Najaf Khan at Ghausgarh. The Mirza had left his incapable brother-in-law Saadat Ali in charge of Hinduan and Bayana (situated 70 and 50 miles respectively south-west of Agra) with a good deal of wholesome advice to behave himself worthily and watch the movements of the Jats cautiously. This noble, surrounded by a group of carpet-knights, thought of anticipating the Mirza in crushing the Jat, who seemed already to be in his last gasp. He wrested several parganas from Ranjit Singh and laid siege to one of his forts. Ranjit Singh sent a Maratha captain in his service with five or six hundred horsemen to succour the besieged. They made a long night-march, and at early dawn fell upon the Muslim camp, immersed in sleep after midnight gaieties. Saadat Ali and his companions woke up too late; before they could put on their cloths, and get at their arms, the marathas had forced their way into their tents. The Mughals fled and fled for more than 50 miles without turning back till safe within the walls of Agra (*Ibratnama* MS. pp. 292-294).

Ranjit Singh, encouraged by this success, issued out of Kumher and re-occupied the greater part of the territories lost by Nawal Singh. Muhammad Beg Khan Hamadani started from Agra to check the activity of the Jat chief who was driven back into Kumher and forced to stand a siege there. But almost simultaneously the Rao Raja assumed a hostile attitude towards the Mughal Government, and his aggression assumed such serious proportions that Mirza Najaf Khan had to order Muhammad Beg Khan Hamadani to raise the siege of Kumher and march against Macheri. Hamadani inflicted a defeat upon the army of the chief of Macheri in the month of Rajab. 1191H. [August, 1777 : *Waqa,* p. 302]. But this success hardly improved the situation in that quarter. The army of Hamadani was held at bay by the concerted hostility of Ranjit Singh and the Rao Raja. The able and energetic Naruka chief aided by some powerful Maratha captains in his pay threatened to undo the work of Mirza Najaf Khan snatching away the fruits of his long and arduous campaigns against the Jats. The condition of affairs was so desperate that the Mirza had to leave the task of the subjugation of Zabita Khan half completed, and only four days after his arrival at Delhi from Ghausgarh he had to start for Agra to repel the new danger [24 Shawwal = 25th Nov., 1777; *Waqa,* p. 305].

Rao Raja Pratap Singh conquers Mewat from the Jats

Rao Pratap Singh, ascion of the Naruka branch of the Kachhwahs started his career with a patrimony of two villages and a half (Macheri, Rajgarh and half of Rajpura), and closed it as the founder of the Alwar Raj. His opportunity came with the misfortune of the Jats, dating from their disastrous retreat from the field of Maonda. Taking advantage of the pre-occupation of Nawal Singh in the civil war and afterwards in his arduous struggle with the imperialist, Rao Pratap Singh[5] seized with ease all the parganas of Mewat.

5. The *Rajputana Gazetteer* says "Taking advantage of the depressed condition of the Jats, he (Rao P. Singh) between Sambat 1832 and 1839 (1775-1782 A. D.), obtained Bahadurpur, Dehra, Jhindoli, Bansur, Bahror, Barod, Rampur, Harsaura, Hajipur, Hamirpur, Narainpur, Ghadi-Mamur and Thana Ghazi." (1st edition vol. iii, p. 181). The Rao Raja took possession of the fort of Alwar on Mangsar Sudi 3 (Margasirsha), 1832 Sambat (25th November, 1775; see *ibid*).

His crowning success was the capture of Alwar by bribing the Jat garrison, whose pay had long been in arrears. Mirza Naja: Khan, after his decisive victory over the army of Nawal Singh and his Jaipur auxiliaries, summoned the Rao Raja to Deeg and asked him to join the Mughal army in a projected compaign against the Maharaja of Jaipur. The Naruka chief not only refused to bear arms against his suzerain but signified his firm resolve to join the army of Jaipur in repelling such an attack if made. Mirza Najaf Khan would have called him to account had not the rebellion of Raja Bhup Singh Jat demanded his presence in the Doab. He made a virtue of necessity by conniving at the aggressive designs of the Rao Raja as a desirable check upon his neighbours. The Rao Raja fulfilled the expectation of the Mirza even to the extent of making him repent of it.

Siege of Kumher and the submission of Ranjit Singh Jat

Mirza Najaf Khan established his head-quarters at Deeg and ordered Muhammad Beg Khan Hamadani to resume the siege of Kumher. His attention was mainly directed to the destruction of the formidable power of the Rao Raja by taking the help of the Maharaja of Jaipur,[6] Raja Bhagwant Singh of Kanuda and other Rajput chiefs who had equally suffered from the aggression of the Macheri Raja.

Ambaji Rao, Appaji Pandit, Bapuji Holkar and other Maratha allies of the Rao Raja pressed him hard to make peace with Mirza Najaf Khan so that he might be able to prosecute war against his other enemies with greater success. The Rao Raja started with a large and powerful army to meet the Mughal general at Deeg and pitched his camp near Asia [Rasia?] Pahari. On the 9th Ziqada, 1191 (9th Dec. 1777) he was admitted to an interview with the Mirza, who conferred upon him a very rich *khilat* and showed him every mark of esteem and favour. The negotiations for terms of

6. He had already sent, in response to an appeal for help from Maharaja Pratap Singh Kachhwah, a detachment of 1500 horse, two battalions of sepoys and four guns under Mir Muhammad Ali Khan and Zain-ul-Abidin (*Ibratnama* MS., p. 348), possibly to assist at the siege of Rajgarh, a stronghold of the Macheri chief.

settlement were protracted for many days, owing to the unyielding attitude of the Rao Raja. If the agents of the Mirza pressed their demands too hard, he would silence them by directing his glance[7] to his vast encampment, as the most convincing reason of the correctness of his own contention. A plot was set on foot by some officers of the Mirza to make the Rao Raja a prisoner; one day they surrounded his camp while the unsuspecting Rajputs were engaged in their daily ablutions and the Rao in performing his *puja.* The cowards failed to entrap the lion-like Naruka, who with a gallant band broke through their toils of treachery and safely reached the fort of Lachman-garh.[8] The Muslim army besieged him there for four months without much success. One night the camp of Mirza Najaf Khan was surprised and his army badly defeated in a fight by the troops of the Rao Raja. His enemies rejoiced over this reverse as ominous of the declining fortune of their formidable rival, and bestirred themselves to make a concerted attack upon him.

Muhammad Beg Khan Hamadani having been called away to reinforce the army of Najaf Khan before Lachhman-garh, Ranjit Singh issued out of Kumher and again took to plundering and burning the Mughal territories. By a bold night-attack he killed the *Amil* of Farah (situated half way between Mathura and Agra), and ravaged the whole tract up to the walls of Agra so thoroughly that lights ceased to burn in that region.[9] The Emperor, urged by Abdul Ahad Khan, decided to go towards Rajputana and ordered the imperial camp to be pitched at Tal Katora. The Sikh sardars were also won over by the intriguing minister to the side of the Emperor. Threatened by this dangerous league, of his

7. *"Chun karpardazan-i-sarkar dar bab i maamlah chize mi-goftand nazar bar sar kasrat-i-fauj o kanat zahir-i-khud namudah sar garani me-kard."* (*Ibratnama,* p. 340).
8. This is situated 23 miles south-east of Alwar, on the border of the Bharatpur territory. Khair-ud-din says that Lachman-garh was wrested by the Rao Raja from Ranjit Singh Jat. But local tradition, perhaps more authentic, says, it was formerly known as Taur, taken from Swarup Singh Naruka.
9. *Ibratnama,* p. 345.

enemies, Mirza Najaf Khan was constrained to make peace with the Rao Raja, recognizing his title to Alwar and other territories conquered from the Jats [Jamada II. 1192 H. July, 1778]. He sent back Hamdani against Ranjit Singh and himself started for Agra. In order to counteract the designs of his enemies, he released the families of the Afghans and restored Saharanpur to Zabita Khan [Shaban, 1192 H. = September 1778; *Waqa*, p. 310]. Shortly after this, he appeared before Kumher with his whole army to finish the affair of the Jats.

The siege of Kumher was prosecuted with great vigour, but the garrison in the hope of the arrival of the Emperor put up a stiff resistance. Mirza Najaf Khan grew impatient as the siege seemed to be dragging on to an interminable length. The imperial army broke up their camp at Tal Katora in the month of Shawwal and marched in the direction of Rewari. "The Amir-ul-umra out of the consideration of policy and general good sent a letter full of admonitions .... reminding him [Ranjit Singh] that there was yet time to secure pardon through submission and to atone for his past error by loyal service, without dragging several thousand men into destruction. When this letter reached Ranjit Singh his mind became distracted—he found neither strength in himself to offer resistance nor divine grace to guide his footsteps [to the auspicious presence of the Amir-ul-umra]. In the end, this excellent advice failed to find any place in his [obdurate] heart—he remained as haughty and obstinate as before" [*Ibratnama*, p. 346]. The besieging army redoubled their efforts and soon rendered the fort untenable. Despair seized the hearts of the garrison, "who found neither strength to go out nor place to stand upon." In their hour of supreme peril, they remembered the old queen Kishori, who had outlived the glory of the house of Bharatpur, and been pining in neglect and retirement after the death of Jawahar Singh. The wellwishers of Ranjit Singh advised him to send the old queen to the Mughal camp, because she enjoyed the respect and good-will of the high officers of the Amir-ul-umra, and might possibly by her intercession procure pardon for his past offences. But Ranjit Singh hesitated to act upon their advice lest the Mirza should compel him to surrender unconditionally by detaining her in Mughal camp. One night he escaped with a few friends, leaving Kumar to its fate. Next morning the Muslim troops scaled the walls of the fort and overpowered the defenders. Rani Kishori fell a prisoner into their hands and was taken with all honour to the camp of the Nawab. "In obedience to his order, the officers of his Government erected lofty and secluded tents for her residence and expert servants were appointed to wait upon her, so that after a few days her grief might subside" [*Ibid*, MS. p. 347].

It was not with the suspicious and timid steps of a prisoner that she went to meet the conqueror when summoned by him, but rather in the hope and confidence of a mother in distress who goes to see her foster child. "On reaching the presence of the Nawab, she like an affectionate nurse, walked round the person of the Amir-ul-umra, and with a sincere heart took away [on her own shoulders] all his evils.[10] With tearful eyes, she narrated the pitiful tale of her misery. When the Nawab Amir-ul-umra learnt the distress of her heart overflowed with kindness and he very graciously set her up as his own mother. He gave her the fort of Kumher for her residence and the *mahals* around it for her support. To please her, he forgave the guilt of Ranjit Singh and left to him the fort of Bharatpur with territories worth seven *lakhs* of Rupees as jagir." His magnanimity succeeded where the barbarous ferocity of the Abdali had failed.

Death of Mirza Najaf Khan

The Mughal empire now entered on its last phase, illumined by a sudden effulgence of glory, after a gloom of four distressful decades. Rajputana once again bowed before the scetpre of Delhi and a descendant of Timur for the last time performed the impressive ceremony of applying the *Raj-tika* on the proud forehead of a Rajput prince.[11] The sword of

10. *Basan daiya e mihrban girdash gardid o ba-sadaq dil bala gardanash shud* [*Ibratnama* MS. p. 347] *Cf.* Babur's going round the sick-bed of Humayun. This popular superstition has not yet died out.
11. At Narnol, on the 2nd Safar, 1193 (19th February, 1779), Maharaja Sawai Pratap Singh Kachhwah paid a *nazar* of one thousand and one *ashrafis* to the Emperor Shah Alam II, and received *Raj-tika* from His Majesty's auspicious hand [Waqa MS. p. 321].

Mirza Shafi taught the turbulent Sikhs to respect the imperial authority. Majd-ud-daula was at last caught in the meshes of his own intrigue, and visited with well merited disgrace,[12] and the fortune of Mirza Najaf Khan shone resplendent in solitary grandeur. People looked forward to a happy era of strong, just and tolerant rule, but Heaven sent them significant omens of evil days. In the afternoon of the 2nd Jamada II., 1192 H. (29th May, 1778) a meteor was seen trailing its ominous course through the sky for about one-fourth of *ghari,* accompanied by a deafening sound like the boom of a large cannon such as was never heard by the oldest citizen of Delhi. Another[13] came three years after, when a painfully dazzling summer noon became all of a sudden dark like a moonless night, portending, as it were, the eclipse of the glory of the empire and the violent extinction of the light of the Emperor's own eyes. A heavy bereavement had already come upon the royal family by the death of Prince Farkhunda Bakht (Mirza Jahan Shah); a heavier one was yet to befall the whole empire.

Mirza Najaf Khan had been suffering for some time from a disease which baffled the skill of the best physicians. From the Emperor to the meanest of inhabitant of Delhi, Hindus and Musalmans alike became anxious for the life of their beloved hero. When human efforts failed they turned to the heavenly powers and prayed for his recovery. A grand offering (*bhet*) was made at the shrine of the goddess Kalka

---

12. Majd-ud-daula was made a prisoner and brought into the camp of Mirza Najaf Khan by Afrasiyab Khan on the 6th Ziqada, 1193 H. November, 15, 1779. [*Waqa,* p. 313].

13. This occurred on one Monday between the 26th Jamada 1 and 27th Jamada II, 1195 H. (20th May—20th June, 1781). "At noon [*do-pahar*] a strong wind began to blow. It became so dark that nothing could be seen, Then the sky became red and the storm blew more furiously. After a short time the day recovered its usual brightness" [*Waqa,* p. 333]. This may be a duststorm so frequent in summer at Delhi. But there was certainly something unusual so as to deserve notice in the *Waqa.*

Devi (near Oklah) in the night of 7th Rabi II.[14] [?], 1196 H. on behalf of the Mirza, and the blessings of the deity were invoked for his restoration to health. The Nawab distributed sweets to Brahmans and little boys, and released cows meant for slaughter by paying their price in cash to the butchers with a strong injunction to the effect that none should seize or molest these animals. But all was in vain. His great soul passed away on Saturday, 22nd Rabi II., 1196H. (6th April, 1782) and with it the last gleam of the glory of Islam departed from Hindustan.

Here this volume ends. We propose next to follow the fortune of the Jat of Gohad and of Amritsar, and see how the one heroically succumbed under the relentess might of Maharashtra, and the other, drinking *amrit* from the hands of the Guru, triumphed over all the warlike frenzy and resources of the Durrani empire, and saved the whole of Hindustan from a horrible rule of the Pathan Ghazis.

14. The *Waqa* says "About one *pas* and a half on the night still remained when Sheoram Das went to Kalka Dev for offering *bhet* on behalf of Nawab Najaf Khan . . . ." [MS. p. 337]. There is some confusion about the date. The text writes 27th Rabi II. But according to a subsequent entry the Nawab died on 22nd Rabi II; so th first date cannot be true. Therefore either 27th is a mistake for 7th or Rabi-us-Sani is a mistake for Rabi-ul-*awwal*. 7th Rabi II falls on *Friday* (22nd March, 1782) but 27th Rabi I-falls on Tuesday (12th March). So the former is the more likely date because it *agrees with the day of the week.*

APPENDIX A

THE THEORY OF THE INDO-SCYTHIAN ORIGIN OF THE JATS

The Indo-Scythian theory, associated with the names of some of the greatest scholars in the field of Indian History and Ethnology, has so long held the field and stifled doubt by the force of authority. V.A. Smith, the last learned champion of this theory, says "When the numerous Bala, Indo-Scythian, Gujar, and Huna tribes of the 6th *century horde* settled, their princely houses were accepted as Rajput, while those who frankly took to agriculture became Jat."[1] Elsewhere he remarks, "There is reason for believing that the Jats entered India later than the Gujars, rather about the same time."[2]

The following points may, however, be urged against this theory :

(1) Col. Tod's inscriptional evidence of the existence of a Jit ruling dynasty as old as 409 A.D.[3]

(2) The traditional enmity between the Rajput and the Jat[XXXI] makes it extremely doubtful that they had entered

1. *J.R.A.S.* 1899, p. 534.
2. *Ibid*, 1909, p. 63.
3. Crooke's edition of *Rajasthan*, i. 128, foot-note 1. The editor expresses a doubt "whether the Jat Kathida is the Jat or Gaetae of Cathay."

XXXI. **There was no traditional enmity of the Jats with the whole body of the Rajputs. It is the product of later Mughal Period, especially with the Kachhwah rulers of Amber, who were the *mansabdars* of Mughals and were ordered to suppress the rebellious Jat peasants. Secondly, the Jats of Agra province particularly Sinsinwar Jats and Kachhawahs were neighbours and the ambition of expanding their zamindaris became the cause of conflict. So, Kachhwahas cannot be taken for Rathors, Sisodias and other prominent Rajput clans. Zamindars and peasant conflict was natural in other regions also. —Ed.**

India—if they did it at all—at the same time as comrades, but had afterwards become divided into two hostile groups. Everywhere we find the earlier Jat occupant of the soil supplanted by the new Rajput immigrants. The Parmar displaced him in Malwa, and the Tanwar snatched away Delhi from him.[4] The Rathor wrested Bikaner and the Bhatti imposed his rule upon him at Jaisalmir.

(3) The Scythians who were very probably men with broad faces, and high cheek-bones, sturdy and short in stature, are little likely to have been the ancestors of a tall-statured and long-headed people like the Jats.

(4) A great blunder committed by the enthusiastic exponents of the Indo-Scythian theory was to overlook the line of migration of the people who call themselves Jat today. The tradition[5] of almost all the Jat clans of the Punjab (even including an apparently extra-Indian people, the Babbar Jats of Dera Ghazikhan), points to the east or south-east—Oudh, Rajputana and the Central Provinces—as their original home. If popular tradition counts for anything, it points to the view that they are an essentially Indo-Aryan people *who have migrated from the east to the west,* and not Indo-Scythians who poured in from the Oxus Valley. Undoubtedly a certain section of the Jats migrated outside India along with the Bhattis and after several centuries were swept back from the borders of Persia to the east of the Indus. But they cannot be justly called foreign invaders on that account.

---

4. It is not unlikely that this famous city derives its name the Dhillon or Dhillhon Jats, who are still found in large numbers in Delhi district. Folk etymology connects the name Dhillon with *dhila* or lazy.
5. Only the Ghatwal, Kang and Malik Jats remember any connection with *Gajni* or Garh Gajni which, however, they persist in placing *not in Afghanistan, but somewhere in the Deccan.* (Rose's *Punjab Glossary,* ii. 56, 472; iii. 56). But Sir H.M. Elliot goes on saying "Almost all the Jats of N.W. Provinces who do not claim Rajput descent trace their origin from the far north-west, and some of them as the Ganthwaras point to Gajni or *Garh Gajni apparently that in Afghanistan.* Here without any knowledge of the learned discussions about the identity of the Jat and the ancient Gaetae we find traditionary legends of these tribes pointing to the remote *Gajni as their orginal seat*!!! . . . ." [*Memoirs of the N.W. Provinces,* 1. 132].

It is perhaps against the rule of historical evidence to identify the Jats with the Gaete, Yuti, Yetha or other Indo-Scythian people simply for the sake of the resemblance of sound between their names, in defiance of the evidence of philology and ethnology to the contrary. It is of little use to point out the place of the Jatas or Su-jatas in the great genealogical tree of the Yadu race, when doubt hangs upon the very origin of the Yadus themselves. Col. Tod made a rather desperate attempt to prove the common origin of the Tatars, the Chinese and the Aryan Kshtriyas of the Lunar race by a study of the comparative genealogical trees of these three races and the traditions of their origin [Crooke's ed. of *Rajasthan,* i. 71-72]. Wilson, who held the Purans to be not older than 1045A.D., also *suspected* that the Hayas and the Haihayas of the Hindus had some connection with the Hia, ... "who make a figure in the Chinese history .... It is not impossible, however, that we have confirmatory evidence of the Scythian origin of the Haihayas as Col. Tod *supposed*" [Wilson's *Vishnu Puran,* p. 418, foot note 20]. In short, it has been suspected by many European Orientalists that a Central Asian genealogy entered India with the Indo-Scythic races and was cleverly engrafted on the Indo-Aryan genealogical tree by the unscrupulous Hindu ethnologist, who dubbed the descendants of the barbarian invaders as Kshatriyas of the Lunar race.

Fictitious genealogies both of individuals and peoples are among the commonest phenomena in the history of all nations. But what is the *motive* behind this? First, a successful upstart or a little-esteemed tribe rising to importance which had no brilliant past—wants to create one of fanciful grandeur to serve as worthy back-ground of their bright present and brighter future. Secondly, people adapt their genealogy to their newly-adopted religion or to that of their more powerful and more civilized neighbours. Such is the case with the Muhammadan people outside Arabia. Many tribes of Afghanistan, who were idol-worshipping Buddhists as late as the time of Sultan Mahmud Ghaznavi, are found to-day claiming descent from Khalid, a renowned contemporary of the Prophet [Dorn's trans. of the *Makhzan-i-Afaghana]*. The Buddhistic Turks on their conversion to

Islam made similar changes to suit the Arab tradition. It is notorious how Indian converts to Islam set up ludicrous claims to Shaikh or Sayyid origin. What Arabia was to the Muslim people outside it, that India had been before the birth of Christ to the Buddhistic people of the Middle and the Far East. It is a known fact of history that China and Tartary received Buddhism from the Indian missionaries. No Hindu has been ever known to claim a Chinese origin, but the people of China, as Sir William Jones[6] pointed out, claim a Hindu lineage.

The exponents of the Indo-Scythian theory must, in all fairness, admit that if the Central Asian Gaete could somehow become the Aryan Jadu or Jat, by a reverse process the Indian Jadu might as well degenerate into the Gaete in Central Asia. From the time of the conquest of the Indus valley by Darius to the dissolution of the Maurya empire (*cir.* 600 B.C.—200 B.C.), Indian tribes streamed out in continuous flow into other parts of Asia, under various circumstances. Just as the English Government encourage the Gurkha and Sikh mercenaries to found colonies in different parts of the Indian empire, specially in Burma, and as the Russian Government a few centuries back established the hardy and warlike Tatar Cossacks on the Don and other exposed points of their empire, similarly, the Indian mercenaries or forced recruits who served the Persian empire from the day of Marathon and Thermopylae to that of Arbela—were perhaps settled on the coast of the Black Sea where they became known as the *Sindis* and Kerketae.[7] Besides military service, commercial enterprise also possibly took the Indian people to different countries. The greatest impetus to this foreign migration was given by the extension of the Maurya empire to the Hindukush, and the subsequent spread of Buddhism throughout Central Asia and China. The rapid Indianization of Turkistan, attested by Fa-Hian and other Chinese pilgrims who passed through that region to India, could not have been achieved by a handful of

---

6. See *Rajasthan*, i, 69, foot-note 1. W. Crooke remarks "the comparison of Mongol with Hindu tradition is of no value."
7. See Elliot's *History*, i. 518.

missionaries only but also perhaps by the Indian merchant and the Indian mercenary. As with the spread of Islam, the Arab was always a welcome emigrant among Muslim people, so had been the Indian in the newly converted Buddhistic countries. It can be legitimately inferred that those Central Asian Buddhistic kingdoms as well as the Greek principalities of the Middle East encouraged the migration of the Indian people into their own country in pursuit of a policy like that of Peter the Great of Russia, who recruited his official nobility from the Germans and encouraged the migration of artisans from the countries of Western Europe to westernise the Oriental Russia. And the lead in the foreign migration was given by the unorthodox and enterprising Yadus who rapidly multiplied, absorbing no doubt many outlandish elements from the Punjab tribes. That the race of Yadu migrated outside India is supported by the tradition of the Bhattis of Jaisalmir, who ruled Zabulistan till the advent of Islam in that country. In their foreign colonies only the aristocratic section of the Yadus, such as the Bhattis, perhaps kept their blood unadulterated; but the rank and file freely inter-marrying with the alien races of Tartary had produced a people of Turkoman type speaking a Turkish language. Alberuni mentions a Turkish tribe with an unmistakeable Indian name Bhattavaryan.[8] Two other tribes of Central Asia who are supposed to be the ancestors of the Jats are the Dahae and Massagetae (Great Gate), on the eastern coast of the Caspian [*Rajasthan,* i. 55]. The Dahae are said to be the same people as the Dahas of the *Vishnu Puran (Wilson, Vishnu Puran,* p. 192, foot-note 100) and the modern Ḍāhiya Jats. This is a mere suggestion without any historical proof except the similarity of sound. On the same principle one may hold that the Dahae on the Caspian were a section of the Yadus,

---

8. "Leaving the ravine by which you enter Kashmir, and entering the plateau, then you have to march for two more days on your left the mountains of Bolor and Shamilan, Turkish tribes who are called *Bhattavaryan. Their King has the title of Bhatta-Shah.* Their towns are Gilgit, Aswira and Shiltas, and *their language is Turkish."* (Eng. trans. Sachau, p. 207).

who bore in the time of Mahabharat the tribal name of *Dashai*, easily reducible to *Dahai.*[9]

We are told that the Jats were called *Sus, Abars,* and by many other names. The fact is not that the Jats adopted the name of Su-Sakas or Abhirs but that these latter people took the tribal designation of the former, their more esteemed superiors. Further we find "The Yuchi, established in Bactria and along the Jihoon, *eventually* bore the name of Jeta or Yetan, *i.e.*, the Gaetes." [*Histoire des Huns*, i. 42]. What on earth could induce all these conquering tribes, the Saka, the Yuchi, the Hun, and other Turkish people to assume such designations as Yeta, Gaete, and Bhattavaryan? This leads one naturally to suspect that there must be some fascination, some great tradition of nobler blood and higher civilization associated with this name, having as much attraction for these Central Asian tribes as the proud name "Rajput" has for all the martial Hindu tribes of India. These descendants of the ancient Indo-Aryan colonists settled on the banks of the Oxus and the coast of the Black Sea stood in the same relation to Aryandom as the descendants of the present generation of th Indian emigrants in the far off Fiji and in the wilderness of Africa will stand to ours after a century or two when their Indian nationality will hardly be recognisable owing to admixture of blood, and religious and linguistic differences from their parent stock.

---

9. Dahiyas : In the *Mahabharat* Shri Krishna is often addressed as दाशार्ह *i.e.*, descendant of Dasharha. Sisupal angrily designates him *Dasharha, unworthy of the title of King* (Sabha, chap. 39). In the list of people दाशार्ण (*Dasharna*) comes before कुकुर (*Kukura*) : but this seems to be a mistake for Dasharha (Bhishma, chap. 8: also Bana Parva, chap. 183). *Brihat Samhita* of Baraha-mihira mentions दाशार्ण (Dasharna) as people inhabiting the south eastern (आग्नेय) quarter (S. Divedi's Sans text vol. x. p. 288), but in a following chapter this tribe is mentioned in the north west along with the Kakayas and Gandharas (*ibid*, p. 314). Though repetition is by no means unusual, the latter is perhaps a mistake for दाशार्ह।

APPENDIX B

THE LEGEND ABOUT THE YADU TRIBE

In the Rig Vedic age the Yadus lived in the land of Sapta-Sindhu and were characterized by adventurous habits and heterodox beliefs. Indra[1] is said to have crossed the ocean and brought back to the shores of Sapta-Sindhu, Yadu and Turvasu who used to live on the farther shores of the ocean as unanointed kings, probably in a new colony of their own. After their return, they performed many sacrifices on the banks of the Saraswati. But they relapsed to heresy again; owing to their heterodoxy and indifference to the worship of Indra, they are denounced in a hymn of the Rig Veda [*Rig.* x. 62, 10] as unbelieving Kshatriyas in the same way as the orthodox Pandit of to-day would condemn a non-conforming Hindu as a Mlechha. Yadu, the legendary progenitor of the tribe, was the eldest son of King Yayati[2]

1. Rig. VI. 120, 12 and IV, 30, 17.
2. Mr. R.P. Chanda notices the two conflicting legends in the *Harivamsa* about the origin of the Yadus, *viz,* one from Yadu the son of Yayati, and the other from another Yadu, son of Haryasva of Solar Iksvakn race. (*The Indo-Aryan Races,* pp. 28-30). His preference of the second legend tracting the descent of the Yadus from the son of Haryasva has not been perhaps very judicious and scientific, because it militates against the whole tradition of the Lunar Race recorded in the *Mahabharat* and all the *Purans.* Besides *the second one is not the main version* of the *Harivamsa* but an incidental narration of a legend by Bikadru to Shri Krishna. This appears to be an extempore fabrication of the genealogy of Shri Krishna like that of the Sayyid origin of Tipu Sultan by his ambassadors at Constantinople. If the legend has any truth it shows that a branch

who disinherited him and cursed his line for disobedience, saying "Wicked and without dominion shall be thy progeny." Yayati made his youngest son Puru his successor on the throne of Aryandom proper, and gave Yadu an appanage in the far south—some say south-west, where the race of Yadu multiplied and prospered, and carried on a sort of hereditary feud with the descendants of Puru for recovering the birth-right of their eponymous ancestor. They seemed to have formed republican military aristocracies, often very tyrannical. We perhaps catch a glimpse of it in the *Mahabharat*[3] where a rebellion *en masse* of Vaishyas and Shudras, headed by the Brahmans against the powerful Haihaya Yadavas—of whom the Jats or Su-jats were a branch—is alluded to. The Brahmans, displaying *kusha* grass on their standard marched with a motley host of Vaishyas and Shudras against the Kshatriyas.

A great avenger arose among the Brahmans in the person of Parashuram who exterminated the Kshatriya race twenty-one times. The few who escaped his battle-axe took shelter in mountains and among the lower classes; some were protected by kind-hearted Brahmans. Without instruction and without ceremonial they grew up like Shuddras. *Rishi Kashyapa reclaimed them* and restored them to the rank of Kshatriyas again. This was perhaps the first creation of a class of Neo-Kshatriyas of adulterated blood claiming descent from the Lunar race.

Another important feature of the history of the Yadus was their hereditary feud with the kings of the Solar race.

---

of the Solar Race became engrafted upon the Lunar Race descended from Yadu, son of Yayati. It is strange that Mr. Chanda has overlooked the words of Madhu to his son-in-law Haryasva, "My darling! in the course of time your race shall mingle with the Yadu Race, descended from Yayati: and, though you are of Solar Race, your clan would become subordinate to the Lunar Race" (*Harivamsa*, chap. 93). Mr. Chanda evidently prefers this self-contradictory Solar origin of the Yadus because it conveniently makes the Kathiawar peninsula the original home, of the Yadus whom he is eager to prove *Aryan emigrants from Mesopotamia with a good deal of Semitic beood. (The Indo Aryan Races*, p. 33).

3. See *Udyoga Parva*, chap. 154, and *Shanti parva*, chap. 49.

The sons of Yadu made a great attempt to overthrow their more cultured and orthodox rivals by forming a confederacy with the Saka, Palhava, Parada, Yavana, Kamboja and Barbara tribes against the father of the famous king Sagara. This king Sagara annihilated nearly the whole of the Haihayas, and would have destroyed their Mlechha alies also but for the intercession of Rishi Vashista.[4] From this time the decline of the political power and social ascendancy of the Yadus began.

The Yadus never recovered completely from the shock of their disastrous defeat and degradation at the hands of king Sagara. They seem to have since been fast sinking into something like the present Jat status, considered socially inferior and not entitled to regal honour by their erstwhile compeers.[5] About the time of the *Mahabharat,* they occupied the Surasena or modern Mathura country. Eighteen clans

---

4. "Sagara in compliance with the injunction of his spiritual guide, contented himself therefore with imposing upon the vanquished nations some humiliating conditions. He made the Yavanas shave their heads entirely; the Sakas he compelled to shave the upper part of their heads; the Paradas wore their hair long; and the Palhavas let their beards grow, in obedience to his commands . . . . Them also, and *other Kshatriya races,* he deprived of the established usages of oblations to fire and the study of the Vedas." – Wilson's translation of the *Vishun Puran,* p. 376.
5. The following passage in the *Vishnu Puran* perhaps faithfully reflects the attitude of monarchical tribes like the Kurus to the Yadavas. The Kuru chiefs who looked upon the Yadu Race as not entitled to regal dignity angrilly retorted against the imperious tone of Balaram – who came to demand the release of Shri Krishna's son captured in an attempt to carry off the daughter of Duryodhan – "What shall the Yadava give orders to the chiefs of the family of Kuru? If Ugrasena issued his mandates to the Kauravas, then we must *take away the white umbrella that he has usurped* and which is only fit for the kings . . . . The *homage that is due to us, their superiors,* by the Kukkura and Andhaka tribes, may not be paid by them, but whoever heard of a command issued by a servant to his master?" The Yadava envoy with his instinctive republican contempt for princes and thrones cried out furiously, "Fie upon the pride that boasts of a throne, the leaving of a hundred mortals." (*Vishnu Puran,* p. 603).

lived together, obeying the command of Ugrasena, the head of the leading clan of the Bhojas (who being descended from the Haihayas represented the eldest line of Yadu). Ugrasena was called King only by courtesy. He was the Grand Patriarch of the whole tribe by sufferance, without any pretension to despotic authority; real power was vested in a Council of Elders, consisting of the most influential persons of the different *gotras*. His position was, so to say, like that of the recognized head of a Jat *bäräh* or *chaurasiä*, *i.e.*, a group of twelve or eighty-four villages inhabited mainly by the same people. But an Aurangzeb was born to Ugrasena—the cruel and resolute Kansa, who imprisoned his father and usurped despotic authority over the Yadus with the help of some powerful mercenary fighters. The upstart, having married two daughters of the powerful Magadha Emperor Jarasandha, swelled up with pride and was half ashamed to call himself a Yadava. He reduced the junior clans of the Yadavas to the position of subjects and his tyranny drove many of them to cattle-rearing[6] as a means of livelihood, which could no longer be earned by the sword and as members of the ruling aristocracy. Shri Krishna killed the wicked Kansa and restored Ugrasena to his authority. Eighteen times did the haughty prince of Magadha renew his attack upon the Yadavas to avenge the death of his son-in-law; as often was he forced to retire discomfited. At last worn out in an unequal conflict, the Yadava chiefs decided upon the evacuation of the Mathura region, where their powerful enemy gave them no peace.

The Yadus were indifferent in their allegiance to the Vedic gods and the Brahmans, nay more positively hostile, if we are to believe the Pauranic traditions. They insulted their *purohit* [family-priest] Gargya, who vowed vengeance upon them and did penance to *Rudra* in order to get a son[7] "capable of humbling the pride of the Andhaka and Brishni clans" [*Harivamsa*, chap. 114]. They owed their final

6. Vasudeva, father of Shri Krishna is described as "living as a tributary (*karada*) of Kansa at the hill of Govardhana, *attached to the cows*" (*Harivamsa*, Chap. 55).
7. The son was the Black Yavana prince whose enmity drove the Yadavas to seek refuge on the western sea-coast.

destruction at Prabhas to the curse of Rishi Durvasa, upon whom their wicked young sons played an indecent prank. Shri Krishna himself abolished Indra-worship in the land of Braj, even when he was a mere boy, and after his accession to power he humiliated the pride of the king of gods by forcibly taking away the heavenly flower tree [*Parijat*] from the Garden of Paradise. The ancient Haihayas worshipped Dattatreya, while their descendants in the time of the *Mahabharat* are found worshipping Shiva. The most striking feature of the Yadava people was their great republican confederacy upheld by extreme clannish spirit. Though divided into numerous branches, and often so remote from one another as to permit intermarriage, they continued to hold together as sons of the same father, presenting a united front to the common enemy, sharing the common weal and woe, and living and moving as one body. While left to themselves, petty jealousies and family feuds marked their lives. Drinking, gambling, and gay festivities enlivened their society. The *Harivamsa* gives a very animating picture of their social life. They go out for excursion; men and women young and old, all joining in the mirthful sports either in the pleasant shady woodland or on the smiling beach. Balaram, always in a state of intoxication, begins singing aloud, with his wife keeping tune with the clapping of his hands. His younger brother Shri Krishna, with his wife, his sister, *and his friend,* follows him and sings in chorus. The younger people, quite unabashed, catch the contagion and sing tumultuously. Next a water-sport (sprinkling water at one another while bathing) is proposed by Shri Krishna. They divide into two parties; one under Balaram consisting of one half of the Yadavas and the sons of Shri Krishna with their wives; the other half under Shri Krishna with Balaram's sons and their wives. Heavily drunk, they plunge into the water, taking off their clothes and begin throwing water at one another. So excited do they become that the playful emulation assumes the turn of a serious fight regardless of the presence of the ladies. The coolheaded Shri Krishna sees the danger, and puts a timely stop to the sport. They come out of the water, dress themselves, and sit at their meals Pomegranates and other fruits, different preparations of meat and a roasted buffalo-calf are severed. After their meals they drink various kinds of wine in the company of their wives. There were, however, some vegetarians and teetotallers among them, such as, Uddhava and Bhoja, who content themselves with rice-pudding, curds and sweetmeats. Such sporting and feasting of the young and old, men and women together, so repugnant to the more refined section of Aryans, prevailed perhaps among the Yadavas only, though we hear of such tribal festivities in the country of Magadha in the earlier years of the great Emperor Ashoka. The author of the *Harivamsa* tells us explicitly that "placing love above everything else, the Brishnis, Andhakas, and Dasharhas *used to behave to their sons as friends*[8] (*i.e.,* without the reserve usually due to age and parental relation).

In the twenty-sixth year of the reign of Yudhisthira (*i.e.,* after the battle of Kurukshetra), a terrible catastrophe came upon the race of Yadu and destroyed it almost root and branch. They had become wicked, arrogant, cruel, and disrespectful to their elders and to the venerable Brahmans. The most influential heads of the tribe, Balaram, Shri Krishna, Babhru, and Ahuka met in a council to devise means for the reformation of the morals of the Yadavas. They issued a proclamation in the city that any person drinking wine even alone and in privacy should be put to death with his whole family. But such Puritan severity could hardly succeed in a city of Epicureans. Shortly afterwards, they made a grand pilgrimage with their wives to the sea-coast of Prabhas. Putting aside all restraints, they held drinking parties, enlivened by the songs and dances of courtesans and the performances of expert actors. The younger folk, in a state of intoxication, gave to the monkeys food prepared for

8. See *Harivamsa,* ch. 145, 146. It is interesting to notice that this सखाभाव between father and son still seems to prevail among almost all sections of the rural population of western India. A father generally addresses his son not as *Bawa* or *Beta* but as *Bhai*. When sons grow up in age they follow literally the moral injunction of Chanakya "प्राप्तेतु षोड़शेवर्षे पुत्रांमित्रा वदाचरेत्" *i.e.,* a son should be treated as a friend when he attains his sixteenth year. It is not unusual to hear little daughters and sons of educated Sindhi gentlemen addressing their father as Dada (elder brother).

feeding the Brahmans in order to see how the animals fought! Kritavarma, Satyaki, and even the sons of Shri Krishna emptied their wine-cups in his very presence. A quarrel broke out between Satyaki and Kritavarma, who had fought on opposite sides at the battle of Kurukshetra. Satyaki suddently rushed upon Kritavarma and cut off his head. Their friends, and members of the different *gotras* soon ranged themselves into two parties and a deadly conflict ensued. Mad with wine and the spirit of revenge the warlike Yadavas fought to their last breath. When weapons became useless they plucked up sea-reeds and attacked one another desperately; none thought of saving himself by turning back or by standing aloof.

Several days afterwards Arjun came to Dwaraka and led back towards Hastinapur the woeful remnant of a mighty tribe, consisting mostly of widows, orphans and old men. One day he halted near the Panjnad river, at a place *rich in cattle and agricultural produce,* and inhabited by Abhira Dasyus (pastoral robber tribes). A large convoy of females with a slender escort was too great a temptation for them; with no other weapon than their quarter-staves they fell upon the rear of Arjun's line of march. The victor of Kurukshetra lost a part of his convoy and found it extremely difficult to conduct the rest through the land of the sturdy robbers. He left the Bhojas under the son of Kritavarma in a colony in the city of *Martikavati*[9] in the western Punjab. A second colony of the Yadus was founded by him on the banks of the Saraswati where he established the son of Satyaki with the old men and the boys of his family. He crowned Vajra, the grandson of Shri Krishna, as king in the old Pandava capital of Indraprastha. Thus the seeds of the race of Yadu became scattered over the land of the Five Rivers and the valley of the Jamuna.

---

9. The city is mentioned both in the *Mahabharata* and the *Harivamsa*. *Brihat Samhita* (ed. S. Divedi, Sans. text. vol. x. p. 294) mentions it along with Takshashila, Gandhara and Pushkalavati, *i.e.,* cities of the north-west. Col. Tod evidently identifies it with the hill of Jud of Yadu-ka-tila.

APPENDIX C

THE JAT RISING DURING AURANGZEB'S REIGN

Professor Jadunath Sarkar has recently secured from the Jaipur State archives copies of many hundreds of official letters and news sheets (*akhbarat-i-darbar-i-muala*) sent to Rajas Bishan Singh and Sawai Jai Singh by their agents at the imperial Court. These came to hand after my History had been printed, and hence I can give here only a brief summary of the new facts thus brought to light about the activity of the Jat rebels during the last two decades of the reign of Aurangzeb.

In these letters, the audacious Jats are invariably designated *Jat-i-badzat* (the Jat of evil breed). This clearly indicates the impotent fury of the Mughal Government, which knew not how to suppress them. The sphere of the marauding activity of the Jats, as these letters illustrate, extended from Mathura to the border of Jaipur, and from the hills of Mewat to the bank of the Chambal. Peace and order fled from this region. The roads became so unsafe that Rs. 200 used to be demanded as escort-hire for accompanying a caravan only from Agra to Dholpur. Merchants and wayfarers could travel only under passes bought for a heavy price from the freebooting Jat leaders. Among the strongholds of the Jats in that period Sinsini, Sogar, Sonkh, and Wair are often mentioned.

The Mughal administration, we find again and again, was hopelessly corrupt; local officials and soldiers alike connived at the rebellious activity of the Jats and even entered into collusion with them for sharing the plunder of their own master's subjects. One example may be given here from a news-letter: Fazil Khan, an officer posted at Agra, was ordered to escort some imperial treasure to the Chambal. He gave secret notice of his journey to the Jats, who replied that their ammunition had run short. Fazil Khan then secretly sent them a supply of it, and the pre-arranged highway robbery of the treasure was carried out as per plan.

On 28th March 1688, Mir Ahmad, the custodian of the tomb of Akbar, reported to the Emperor that at night a party of Rajaram's men had fallen upon the tomb and carried off its carpets, vessels, lamps and other decorations. Another report was to the effect that Rajaram had sacked eight villages assigned for the support of Shah Jahan's tomb near Agra.

The extant news-letters do not mention the burning of Akbar's bones by the Jat rebels, for which the only authority hitherto known is Manucci. But Aurangzeb's inexorable wrath towards the Jats and his repeated orders for the *general* massacre of the Jat people, which these letters mention again and again, lend support to the belief that the current rumour about the burning of Akbar's bones was probably based on truth.

Several letters to Bishan Singh (Raja of Jaipur) from his Court agent Kesho Rai tell us of the Emperor's constant anxiety at the growing menace of the Jat rising and his impatience at the delay of Bishan Singh in taking the field against them. The Raja was repeatedly told that he would be most highly rewarded if he could subdue the Jats and capture Sinsini before the arrival of Prince Bidar Bakht for the same purpose. But he delayed. At last he joined his forces with those of the prince and laid siege to Sinsini. Bidar Bakht having been soon afterwards recalled,[XXXII] Bishan Singh was left in supreme command of the Jat expedition. The Jaipur general Hari Singh conducted the siege of Sinsini and carried on punitive operations. In one encounter with the rebels, Hari Singh was severely wounded, and a rumour even spread that he had been killed. The Jats, probably under pressure of scarcity within the walls, secretly evacuated Sinsini and the Jaipur troops occupied it after a show of

---

XXXII. Bedar Bakht left for Deccan in March 1690 after the fall of Sinsini (Jan. 1690). K.R. Qanungo, *History of the house of Diggi*, 64,77. —Ed.

assault! This was the version of the affair that reached Aurangzeb, and naturally he refused to give any reward to Bishan Singh. The Jaipur agent at the imperial Court tried hard to contradict this news as a malicious fabrication of his master's enemies, and at the same time wrote to Bishan Singh to placate the local *waqianavis* with rich bribes and induce him to magnify the heroic services of the Jaipur troops!

APPENDIX D

DETAILS OF THE DEATH OF SURAJ MAL

Documents and tradition by no means agree as to the manner of Suraj Mal's death. Father Wendel, writing within five years of this incident, says, "One day Suraj Mal getting news that a large body of the enemy was coming to pounce upon Nahar Singh (his son and destined successor), who was in that expedition, marched in haste with a few thousand horsemen, to succour him. Unfortunately, in passing through a ditch (*mullah*) which the river Hindan had left there, he was surprised on both sides by a party of Ruhela infantry—who had been placed in ambush there. By a furious discharge of their muskets .... on the Jats still in disorder, they brought down Suraj Mal with all his retinue who lay there on the plain either slain or wounded" (French MS., 50). Suraj Mal died on Sunday 25th Dec. 1763 A.D. and the event was recorded in the *Waqa* only two days after its occurrence, i.e., Tuesday. Besides those quoted in the text it contains the following details: "Sayyid Muhammad Khan Baloch cut off the *head* and a hand from the body of the Jat, and brought and *kept them with himself for two days.* After that these were taken to the presence of Nawab Najib-ud-daula. Then only could he believe that Suraj Mal was dead." [Ibid]. The *Siyar* narrates the event as follows; "He was galloping up and down, to examine the field of battle, and to make his choice, after which he stopped awhile to make his considerations. Whilst he was thus standing, there passed by him some of Afzal Khan's troops who having been beaten by Mansaram Jat—who Commanded Suraj Mal's vanguard, were flying by troops one after another. The few people that were with Suraj Mal, represented the impropriety of his remaining so near the enemy with only a few friends about his person; and Kalimulla, with Mirza Saifulla respectfully insisted on his returning. He paid no attention to what they said and seemed intent only on considering the enemy's motions. They both renewed their instances and he gave no answer; but sending for another horse, he mounted and stood in the same place. Whilst he was mounting, it happened that Sayyid Muhammad Khan Baloch, better known under the name of Seydo, was just flying close by him with about 40 or 50 troopers; when one of these turning about recollected Suraj Mal's features, and advancing to Seydo, he cried out that "the Thakur Sahib [Suraj Mal] was standing there . . . . Seydo hearing these words turned about and fell upon Suraj Mal; and one of his men singling the Jat prince smote him with his sabre, and cut off one of his arms, which bye the bye was maimed and actually entangled. Whilst the arm was falling off, two other men rushed together upon him and dispatched him, as well as Mirza Saifulla and Raja Amar Singh and two or three more. The few remaining fled towards their own people. But one of Seydo's troopers taking up the severed arm, fixed it on the spear of a standard and carried it to Najib-ud-daula. The latter could not believe it to be Suraj Mal's and continued doubting it for *two whole days* together. But it was past doubt in the Jat army, which had retreated with still a formidable countenance. The second [?] day Najib-ud-daula, having received a visit from Yaqub Khan, showed him the arm, and the latter at once affirmed it to be Suraj Mal's not only from the maimed appearance but also from the sleeve which was on it, and which happened to be that very calico of Multan which Suraj Mal had put on in his presence. After this the death was ascertained and it became public" [p. 32]. The tradition as recorded by Col. Tod (*Rajasthan,* 1223), and improved upon by Growse that Suraj Mal was ambushed by a party of Najib Khan's troops, *while hunting defiantly in the royal preserve near Shāhdara,* is better suited to a heroic ballad of the Middle Ages, like *Chevy Chase* than true history.

It is proper to examine critically the above statements for getting an approximation to truth. Nothing can be more contemporary than the entry in the *Waqa,* yet some of its details cannot bear common sense criticism. Sayyid Muhammad Baloch, who must have known the value of his trophy *i.e.,* the head and hand of Suraj Mal, cannot be believed to have kept them uselessly *with himself for two days.* He did not cut off the head which could have at once settled all doubt; but only one hand, which was identified perhaps two days after by Yaqub Ali Khan.

Did Suraj Mal fall into an ambush as father Wendel says? It is quite likely that the surprise of the reconnoitring party under Suraj Mal by Najib Khan's retreating troopers was taken as an ambuscade. But the versions of the Father and the author of the *Siyar* do not tally with that of the *Bayan* and the *Waqa-i-Shah Alam Sani.* The *Bayan* says that Suraj mal led six thousand troops to the attack; and according to the *Waqa* 1,000 men died on both sides and Suraj Mal met his death in a rash charge upon the enemy's centre. This is much more credible than the version of the *Siyar,* and therefore cannot be justly rejected. The narrative in the text appears to be the nearest approach to truth.

BIBLIOGRAPHY (A)

The Jats have no written history of their own. Their political history is interwoven with the general histories of the empire of Delhi, and these have necessarily been laid under contribution in the present work. I shall confine myself to the discussion of the merits of only the most important works frequently referred to in the text.

Persian

1. The *Waqa-i-Shah Alam Sani* [M.S.] Professor Jadunath Sarkar who possesses the only copy of this work, rescued it from deplorable neglect in the house of a Kayeth family at Patna. It is a skeleton diary of Delhi occurrences and news, the leaves still surviving run with many gaps from 1739 to 1799. Prof. Sarkar who styles in the *Delhi Chronicle during the Anarchy,* thus remarks of it, "It is of priceless importance and constitutes a record of supreme value to the critical historian of this period. Here we have an absolutely contemporary chronicle of the events and rumours of Delhi, written down immediately afterwards by an inhabitant of the city, without any embellishment, garbling or artificial arrangement of a later date.... While studying it, I have often been tempted to liken it to the old *Anglo-Saxon Chronicle* during Danish incursions. The artless truthfulness, the exclusion of emotion or comment, and accuracy of record are the same in both works." [See pp. 5-6 of the proceedings of the third meeting of the Indian Historical Records Commission at Bombay]. I subjected this *Chronicle* to a strict comparison with the Persian as well as Maratha and French sources which can also claim contemporary value. Now I have been so far convinced of its accuracy that in cases of conflicting dates and statements in other histories of this particular period, I accept its testimony in preference to

theirs. The *Waqa-i-Shah Alam Sani* has been the touchstone for judging the value of all Persian histories of the latter half of eighteenth century.

2. The *Ibratnama* [MS.] of Khair-ud-din Muhammad Allahabadi [1751-1827].[1] He was an influential official in the employ of Prince Jahandar Shah, son of Shah Alam II, and an eye-witness to many of the occurrences described in the latter part of the work. The author in the opening pages of the *Ibratnama* tells us that he was impelled to write this "Book of Warning" by the shocking atrocities of Ghulam Qadir whom he curses with honest indignation, as *nimak-haram* (false to his master's salt). He mentions with gratitude and respect the name of Sir George Henry Barlow, Governor-General who encouraged his historical studies.

As regards the value of this work Dr. E.D. Ross quotes with approval the opinion of Dr. Charles Rieu "*Ibratnama is the fullest and most accurate* account we possess of the chequered career and troubled times of Shah Alam, and *it has all the value of contemporary record,* penned by one who had taken an active share in some of the principal transactions of the period and was personally acquainted with some of the most prominent actors on the scene." Those who may have an occasion to study this history in the light of the more authentic records of the period would possibly dissent

1. For an account of the life and works of Khair-ud-din, see Dr. E.D. Ross's article in *J.R.A.S.* 1902, pp. 136-138. Though it is fuller than that of Prof. Dowson, some errors have crept into it: e.g. "He (Khair-ud-din) then attached himself to the fortunes of the Shahzada Jahandar Shah, the eldest son of Shah Jahan [?] whom he assisted in his attempt to seize upon the throne [?] of Delhi." Shah Jahan in the text is evidently a mistake for Shah Alam II. Khair-ud-din assisted the prince not "in seizing upon the throne of Delhi" as Dr. E.D. Ross would make us believe, but in trying to secure possession of the citadel and imperial treasure lest they should fall into the hands of Ghulam Qadir and Ismail Beg Khan. He was made the prince's supreme agent [*ibid,* 60] and in this capacity visited Begam Samru at her camp near Delhi. He procured for the prince her powerful support against Ghulam Qadir and Ismail Beg [MS., p. 63; for fuller details, see Brajendranath Banerji's *Begam Samru*]. The prince praised the author for his eminent services and wise counsels.

from this view. Though it is undoubtedly the fullest history of the reign of Shah Alam and is indispensable to students of this period of Indian history, it is by no means the most accurate one. Up to the 12th regnal year to Shah Alam II, this work does not throw more light on Delhi history than what is supplied by the *Siyar-ul-Mutakhkharin.* Khair-ud-din no doubt gives us useful details for the period between the 12th and 20th regnal years, but almost all his dates are wrong and inaccurate. From the 20th year onwards, however; *Ibratnama* has certainly great value.

His graphic details often produce the effect of a melodrama, and this very fact often leads us to suspect his accuracy. My admiration for this history decreased with the progress of my studies in and around this period. However, we have no option but to accept as true all his statements which have not been definitely contradicted by more reliable authorities.

3. *Chahar Gulzar-i-Shujai* of Harcharan Das[2] (Prof. Sarkar's MS.) The author was in the employment of Nawab Qasim Ali Khan, a nobleman of Delhi. He migrated to Oudh with his master's family in the first year of the reign of Alamgir II. and began the study and writing of history to enliven the dreary days of his exile and penury. He says that he reached his 80th year in 1194 A.H. *i.e.,* 1780 A.D. He writes in a simple style and his facts and dates are generally accurrate. But the memory of the old man seems to have failed him sometimes. We need not be surprised if he commits mistakes here and there and confuses names and dates. The following will serve as a typical example. "Jawahar Singh Jat, after the death of his father Suraj Mal, laid siege to the citadel of Agra. But having despaired of taking it by force of arms owing to the bravery and faithfulness of the imperial commandant Fazil Khan, he had recourse to intrigue. He secured entrance into the fort by bribing Muyyid Beg who was in charge of the gates—with three *lakhs* of Rupees. When the fort was captured after its evacuation by the Muslim garrison in 1174 H. (1761 A.D.) Jawahar Singh threw the traitor Muyyid Beg into prison, and as a reward for the

2. For an account of his life, see Elliot, viii, 204-260.

fidelity of Fazil Khan granted him a monthly pension of three hundred rupees." The real facts are diferent, *viz.*—The fort of Agra was captured in 1761 by Suraj Mal and not by Jawahar Singh. Father Wendel tells us nothing about such an incident in his valuable sketch of Jawahar Singh's reign. It is, on the other hand, not likely that the whole story is altogether false. The details may be true of the capture of Agra by Suraj Mal.

4. *Tarikh-i-Muzaffari* (MS.) of Muhammad Ali Khan. The author Muhammad Ali belonged to a distinguished family of Panipat. His grandfather Lutfullah Khan held the rank of a *hafthazari* [7,000 horses], and during the reign of Muhammad Shah served as governor of Kabul and Multan. One of his uncles Shakir Khan was the author of a history called *Tarikh-i-Shakir Khani* (prof. Sarkar's MS.) The author left Panipat for Bihar in search of employment and became the darogha of the Faujdari Adalat of Tirhut and Hajipur through the patronage of Muhammad Reza Khan Muzaffar Jang, the *Naib Nazim* of Bengal. The *Tarikh-i-Muzaffari* was composed about 1800 A.D., and named after the patron of the author. Prof. Dowson says, "This is one of the most accurate general histories I know.....The history of the later empire is particularly full." (Elliot, viii. 316). There was a learned discussion over the historical value of this work in the second meeting of the Indian Historical Records Commission, held at Lahor (1920). Prof. Jadunath Sarkar remarked, "We possess three nearly contemporary and fairly long histories of the Delhi empire during the second half of the 18th century, viz., the *Siyar-ul-Mutakhkharin,* the *Ibratnama* of Fakir Khair-ud-din Allahabadi, and the *Tarikh-i-Muzaffari.* Of these the second is the longest, most accurate, and (in his opinion) the best, as the author lived at or near the Court of Delhi, while writers of the other two works lived in Bengal and Bihar and had no access to the imperial Court records and other original sources of information. For the period before 1760 (covering the years 1760-1809) was composed later than the *Ibratnama* and is much inferior to the latter. In short, the *Tarikh-i-Muzaffari,* in most parts, is neither an eye-witness's report nor a summary of State-papers." Chaudhuri Abdul Hamid maintained that the author of *Tarikh-i-Mazaffari*

belonged to a "family of historians and high officers of the Mughal Court, and as such he presumably had access to State-papers" [Proceedings, Indian Historical Records Commission, 1920, p. 23].

But the fact is that none of the three histories bears any trace of the use of State-papers. All the three authors relied mainly upon what they had heard from others. Even Khair-ud-din often cites as authorities little known persons such as Mir Muhammad Yaqub who found the date of the battle of Barsana in the chronogram *"larza bar ek o sang az in fathe haidari"* which is found wrong [vide text]. It is perhaps unjust to pronounce a verdict against an author merely on theoretical grounds, without patiently examining the contents of his work. A test-study of the period between the accession of Ahmad Shah and the battle of Panipat as dealt with in all these three histories in the light of independent sources convinces me of the originality and trust-worthiness of *Tarikh-i-Muzaffari.* The civil war between Safdar Jang and Ahmad Shah, and the diplomatic activity of the Abdali before Panipat have been described with greater accuracy and fuller wealth of details in this book than in the other two more popular histories.[3] Some minute details given by the *Tarikh-i-Muzaffari* warrant us in inferring that the author derived his information from reliable eye-witnesses, perhaps some members of his family who lived so near the capital. The following instance bears out the truth. The *Waqa-i-Shah Alam Sani* which is the diary of events kept by an inhabitant of the capital says, "On the 21st Jamada I., 1165 H., Nawab Safdar Jang, having taken leave, started [from the city] *while it was raining* . . . . and pitched his camp at the garden of Ismail Khan" [*Waqa,* p. 76]. The *Tarikh-i-Muzaffari* also says, "The Nawab started from his palace and proceeded by the road running along the bank of the river [Jamuna]. When he was passing opposite the imperial citadel, he alighted from his horse, and made the customary salute towards it. At that time *a shower was falling* from the sky and drops of tears too appeared in the eyes of the Nawab" [MS. p. 69]. The *Ibratnama* and *Siyar-ul-Mutakhkharin* do not take notice of

3. Khair-ud-din gives us only a brief summary of these two episodes, devoting not more than 15 lines to each.

these minute details. The only history from which *Tarikh-i-Muzaffari* may have borrowed this is *Chahar-Gulzar-i-Shujai*, which says: "At the time of his departure, *it was raining heavily*. While he reached near the Auspicious Residence [the citadel], he alighted from his elephant and did obeisance towards." The *Tarikh-i-Muzaffari* gives some valuable information which we miss altogether in every other regular history of the 18th century. The following passage gives us the only recorded indication of the fact that the Mughal Government also had some Jat mercenaries who fought against Suraj Mal. "Ghazi-ud-din Imad-ul-mulk . . . . with his own troops and *His Majesty's Jats* [*firqa-i-Jat Badshahi*] exerted himself in the defence of the city [against Nawab Safdar Jang and Suraj Mal]."[4] This is indirectly supported by the unassailable testimony of the *Waqa*: "On the 22nd Ziqada, 1165 H. [20 September, 1753] . . . . *men of the Jat contingent went inside the citadel* and created disturbance for their pay. They obstructed the audience chamber of the Emperor and the *deohris* [out-apartments] of the Begams. His Majesty came to the Diwan-i-Am" [MS., p. 70].[5]

5. *The Siyar-ul-Mutakhkharin*, the most popular and widely known history of the period, hardly requires any comment. The English translation of this book by Mustafa is generally accurate; but he seems to have taken a liberty like that of Briggs in his translation of Ferishta to add here and there a phrase or two of his own unwarranted by the text. Though the author, Ghulam Hussain lived in Bengal, his father and uncles served at Delhi and as history is based on information supplied by them, the chapters dealing with the history of the Delhi and Oudh Courts have been found useful and trustworthy. He does not give us anything of value about Jat history after the death of Suraj Mal.

---

4. *Tarikh-i-Muzaffari*, MS., p. 69.
5. The *Waqa* contains another passage telling us about the unruly character of the Emperor's Jat mercenaries: "On the 19th Rabi II., 1166 H. (13th February, 1754), the soldiers of the Ali Shahi, Walah Shahi, and the Jat regiments assembled in the mosque of Quddus-ul-Ahad for their pay, raised a tumult and prevented men from going inside the fort . . . . took away the turbans and clothes of the passers-by and blocked the *Shah Rah* [Royal road]" (MS., p. 85).

6. *Imad-us Saadat* by Mir Ghulam Ali (Persian text, Nawal Kishore Press, Lucknow). This work was composed about 1808 at Lucknow whither the author was forced to flee from Delhi, when that city was in agony from the atrocities of the accursed Ghulam Qadir. Though this work is mainly a history of the Oudh Nawabs, it throws interesting and useful side-lights upon the affairs of Delhi. The book reads like a string of entertaining stories which are the typical product of Lucknow. But a careful study reveals the inquisitiveness of the author and his habit of taking pains to know the truth. Sometimes he contradicts popular stories and enters into a critical examination of them. He almost always gives us the names of his informants. Though his history is neither full nor methodical, it amply repays, perusal.

7. *Bayan-i-Waqa* [MS.] by Abdul Karim Kashmiri. The account of the reign of Ahmad Shah and incidental notices about the Bharatpur Jats down to the murder of Ratan Singh are very valuable and accurate.

8. *Calendars of Persian Correspondence,* published by the Imperial Records Department, Calcutta. We have three volumes of these valuable Calendars covering the period between 1767-1772. These contain English translations of the Persian letters issued by the Government of Bengal to their officials, agents, and foreign notables along with the answers and news-letters, received from them about occurrences in Upper India. These may be regarded as *primary sources* of the history of this period. They stand next to the *Waqa-i-Shah Alam Sani* in importance and very often prove valuable supplements to the latter. Their destruction would have been an irreparable loss to the students of Indian history.

Marathi

Though the Marathi *bakhars* or chronicles were generally composed at a much later date than the events they relate and hence are not considered by scholars to be sound material, yet the *Bhao Sahibchi Bakhar* (in the scholarly edition of Kashinath Narayan Sane) is an exception. I have found it most useful and reliable for my period. The writer, Krishnaji Shyam Rao, resided at Indraprastha near Delhi. He seems to have been well versed in Hindi and acquainted with the affairs of Jats, Rajputs and Ruhelas. The speeches put by him into the mouths of different historic personages may not have been true word for word, but they undoubtedly represent the spirit of the actors.

Minor mistakes are not infrequent, e.g., he says that during the Mathura expedition of Ahmad Shah Abdali, "8000 Bairagis took up arms at Brindaban and died fighting . . . . The Ghilzai [=Abdali] butchered several pious Bairagis who resided at Gokhri [=Gokul], (p. 32). We know from the Persian sources (cited in my text) that it was at Brindaban that the *Vaishnav* Bairagies were massacred. G.S. Sardesai (*Panipat Prakaran.* p. 77) quotes a letter from Krishna Joshi of Delhi, which tells us that Gokul was saved from Abdali by the *Naga* monks, two or three thousand of whom died in its defence.

2. *Delli-yethil Rajkaranen* or letters of the Maratha envoy at Delhi, published by D.B. Parasnis, in two volumes. Of first-rate importance as regards dates and events (except hearsay reports of distant occurrences).

3. Marathi historical documents, mostly published by the Bharat Itihas Samsodhak Mandal of Poona,—esp. in its annual reports, Sammelan reports, and recently started quarterly journal. No student of the history of the Delhi empire during the second half of the 18th century can afford to neglect the ever-increasing mass of contemporary Marathi records and letters brought to light by a band of devoted Maratha workers. But the sifting of sound historical material out of them requires as much skill and labour as are demanded in collecting particles of gold from sand.

A letter from Antaji Mankeshwar—(published in the Mandal's *Journal, vol.* III. Nos. 2-4, 1924 A.D.) throws interesting side-light upon the civil war between the imperial Paymaster and Safdar Jang. This is perhaps the only evidence to show that Maratha auxiliaries took part in the first stage of the struggle and that the success of Ghazi-ud-din was partly due to their valour. Antaji would naturally exaggerate the services of the Marathas, but be it said to his credit, he does not ignore the heroism of the Jat chief Suraj Mal on the enemy's side. This letter adds flesh and skin to the dry bones of the narrative of the battle of Faridabad given in the *Waqa,* and therefore we translate both of them here.

Waqa-i-Shah Alam Sani: "Sunday, Zihijja 1165 A.H. (=June 1752 A.D.) News arrived (at Delhi of a battle having taken place near the tank of Faridabad between the Bakshi-ul-mulk and the troops of Nawab Safdar Jang. The latter was defeated and put to flight" (p. 81 of MS.)

Letter from Antajai Mankeshwar to Babu Rao Baba, from Indraprastha, Bhadra Badi Ekadashi: "Mansur Ali and Suraj Mal were at Faridabad and the imperial army encamped at Kalikaji (near Okhla) .... Daily skirmishes, marching and counter-marching took place. After that, on Shravan Badi II, Friday, Mansur Ali with the Jat advanced in readiness for battle. A fight took place at Faridabad. The Jats fought obstinately, but were defeated. Suraj Mal displayed great valour, and a personal encounter took place between him and ourselves, in which he received a spear-thurst. The Jats have retreated beyond Ballamgarh, to which the Mir Bakshi has laid siege. We are plundering the Jat territory in the neighbourhood."

4. *Marathi Riyasat,* by G.S. Sardesai Vol. II. (1707-1740), Vol. III. (1740-1760), Vol. IV. (Panipat Prakaran).

Every student of the history of India in the 18th century owes a heavy debt of gratitude to Mr. Sardesai, who has nearly completed the stupendous task of sifting the vast mass of printed materials available in Marathi, critically testing their value, and presenting a synthesis of them in an attractive garb. What we admire in this great historian is his fearless love of truth and freedom from bias, even more than his unsurpassed industry and critical power. So far as Marathi sources are concerned we can confidently rely on his valuable works. But it should be remembered that his failure to use the Persian sources has left his narrative one sided and defective at some places, just as the Persian chroniclers on their part have missed out many facts concerning Maratha affairs. For example, Sardesai makes no mention of Suraj Mal's participation in the war between Madho Singh and Ishwari Singh. (Vol. II. 65-70).

French

1. *Geographie de 'l' Indoustan,* by Joseph Tieffenthaler. This celebrated Jesuit missionary came to India in December 1743 and visited Deeg, "the residence of the prince of the Jats" next year. He has left brief descriptive notices of Deeg, Kumher, and Bharatpur as they then were.

2. *Le Nabob Rene Madec,* par Emile Barbe. An extremely valuable documented history of this celebrated French mercenary general's career in India. The long extracts from his memoirs and those of certain other Frenchmen who came into direct contact with Jat and Delhi affairs, printed by M. Barbe, have been fully utilised by me as the evidence of "eye-witnesses".

3. *Memoires de l' origine, acroissement, et etat present de puissance des Jats dans l' Indostan.* (Orme MSS. O.V., 216 No. 2, pp. 86 + 86; a second copy in *India* XV. No. 11, pp. 150).

Mr. S.C. Hill ascribes its authorship to Father Francois Xavier Wendel, who lived in India from 1751 till his death in 1803, and resided for several years at Agra. He is frequently referred to in the *Calendar of Persian Correspondence (of the English E.I.Co.)* He was in high favour with the Bengal Government and sincerely devoted to the English interests.[6] We find him acting as the agent of the English at Lucknow after the flight of Mir Qasim from Bengal.

We do not know what made the Reverend Father repair to the Jat country, accept service under Jawahar Singh as his political adviser, and stay at Deeg till the death of that Raja. The fact that he went there shortly after the flight of Samru to the Court of Jawahar Singh leads us to suspect that he was in the pay of the English and that his real object was to keep the Bengal Government informed of any hostile designs of the powerful and ambitious Jat Raja who held the balance of power in Northern India between the Abdali and the Maratha.

The Father set about collecting information about Jat history, administration and manners at Deeg, and wrote this long account, which is of priceless value as regards the fulness and authenticity of its information on most points. My

6. See esp. his letter from Lucknow, 12 Nov. 1763 in *Pers. Corr.* i. 263.

chapters on Suraj Mal and Jawahar Singh owe their detail and freshness to this French manuscript.

The most astonishing assertion which he makes,—apparently on hearsay,—is that Suraj Mal was not at all the son of Badan Singh. He has also cast some doubt on the birth of Jawahar Singh, which was probably based on a mischievous rumour started by the malicious Jat nobles who wanted to set the eldest prince aside from the throne of Bharatpur.

4 and 5. *Memoire sur l' Empire Mogol* by Jean Law and Gentil. These have yielded very little new information.

BIBLIOGRAPHY (B)

In the first 1925 edition the author has mentioned only important works in the Bibliography. In this 2002 edition other works have also been given below used by the author.

Brihat Samhita	Sudhakar Dwivedi, Ed., Sans. Text, Vol X, part I.
Harivamsa, Mahabharat	-------------
Vishnu Puran	Wilson, (Ed.).
Chach	Mirza Kalich Beg (Trans).
Makhzan-i-Afghan	Dorn (Trans.).
Ghulam Ali	Shah Alam Nama (M.S.)
--------	Gulsitan-i-Rahamat
Shakir Khan	Tarikh-i-Shakir Khani
Perso, Cro.	Persian Cronicals
	Contemporary Maratha Letters.
Manucci, Niccolao	Storia Do Mogor, Irvine (Trans.).
Ishwardas	Futuhat-i-Alamgiri
Krishna Shyam Rao (Ed.)	Bhao Bakhar (Bhao & Sahibchi Bakhar)
Surajmal (Bard of Bundi)	Vansh Bhaskar
A.H. Keene	Asia, Sir Richard Temple (Ed.)
A.S. Beveridge	Memoirs of Babur
Elliot, H.M.	Memoirs of the Races of North-Western provinces of India.
	History of India.

Irvine William	Later Mughals.
Jawala Sahai	History of Bharatpur.
K.R. Qanungo	Shershah
Macdonell	History of Sanskrit Literature
Major William Thorn	Memoir of War in India
Risley	People of India
R.P. Chanda	Indo-Aryan Races
Sarkar, J.N.	History of Aurangzeb, I, II , III
Thakur Narender Singh Verma	Life of Maharaja Sawai Ishwari Singh (Hindi).
	Bombay, Gazetteer, Vol. IX, Part I.
	Delhi Gazetteer
Growse	Mathura Gazetteer
	Gazetteer of North-West Provinces, Old Series, Vol . VIII
	Hoshiarpur Distt. Gazetteer, 1883.
Ibbetson	Census Report, 1881
	Marwar Census Report (Vernacular) 1892, Vol. III
	Rajputana Gazetteer
	Modern Review, October, 1923
Rose	Punjab Glossary
	Rennell's Atlas

INDEX